6-STEP PRISMS METHOD TO BUILD A
BUSINESS, MAKE MONEY, AND GET RICH

RISK FREE STARTUP SUCCESS

BY MORNING LEE

Risk Free Startup Success 6-Step PRISMs Method Build a Business, Make Money, and Get Rich with Zero Risk Copyright by Morning Lee. All rights reserved.

Published by WealthDao Investing and Consulting, PO Box 83008 Kingsway Burnaby BC Canada V5H 0A4

Please find the following contact information for more information about the book and related topics

Book Website: www.RiskFreeStartup.com

Publsiher Website: www.WealthDaoinc.com

Youtube & Tiktok: @RiskFreeStartup

Facebook & Instagram: RiskFreeStartup

Version:20250126

Dare to dream

Dare to act

Dare to move forward

Anything is possible

Help more people

For you who is reading this book - The Real Entrepreneur

Table of Content

PROLOGUE

The path to Risk-Free startup success

Starting a business is one of the most exhilarating and challenging endeavours a person can undertake. It's a journey filled with dreams of financial freedom, creativity, and leaving a mark on the world. But for many, the prospect of failure looms large. The idea of taking risks—financial, emotional, time, and professional—can paralyze even the most ambitious entrepreneurs. This book is about rewriting that narrative. It's about showing you that success isn't about gambling everything on a single idea; it's about planning, validating, and executing in a way that minimizes risk and maximizes potential.

When I started my entrepreneurial journey, it wasn't with a grand plan or a safety net. I dove headfirst into various businesses— computers, moving services, furniture store, cleaning, shipping, trading, real estate, and even jade mining. Some ventures showed promise, but most didn't survive the harsh realities of the market. The failures were painful but invaluable. They taught me resilience and, more importantly, the critical need for strategy and preparation.

Those experiences, both the wins and the losses, led me to develop the 6-step PRISMs method for Risk Free Startup Success. It's a framework born not from theory, but from the trenches of real-world entrepreneurship. It's a method that allows you to build a business intelligently, using calculated steps that protect your resources, preserve your sanity, and give you the best chance to succeed.

What Exactly Is the 6-Step PRISMs Method?

The 6-Step PRISMs Method is a carefully crafted framework designed to help entrepreneurs build, scale, and sustain successful businesses with minimal risk. Each step represents a critical phase in the journey, ensuring that your actions are deliberate, calculated, and effective.

1. **P: Plan**
   Every business starts with a solid plan. This step focuses on defining your idea, identifying your audience, and evaluating your resources. Planning smartly sets a strong foundation for long-term success.

2. **R: Reconfirm**
   Before moving forward, it's essential to reconfirm your concept and strategy. This step involves validating your business idea through real-world feedback, testing, and adjustments to ensure it aligns with market needs.

3. **I: Ignite**
   With a reconfirmed plan, it's time to ignite your business. This step includes setting up operations, building your team, and officially launching with confidence and clarity.

4. **S: Scale**
   Once your business is running, scaling smartly becomes the priority. This involves expanding operations, retaining customers, and optimizing processes to handle growth sustainably and profitably.

5. **M: Multiply**
   To achieve exponential success, this step focuses on replicating your business model, creating passive income streams, or

exploring franchising and partnerships to multiply your efforts and impact.

6. **S**: **Success**
The ultimate goal is to build a self-sustaining business that thrives without depending on your constant presence. This final step emphasizes creating lasting wealth, freedom, and a legacy.

The **6-Step PRISMs Method** isn't just a theoretical framework— it's a proven roadmap developed from real-world entrepreneurial experiences. By following these steps, you'll avoid unnecessary risks and unlock your potential for sustainable, long-term success.

This book is a reflection of those lessons—a guide to help you avoid the pitfalls I encountered and leverage the strategies that worked. It's about creating a pathway to success without gambling everything. Whether you're starting your first business or looking to refine an existing one, the PRISMs method will show you how to plan, validate, ignite, scale, multiply, and ultimately success, the real success.

This isn't a book about avoiding challenges altogether—that would be impossible. Instead, it's about controlling the factors you can and preparing for the ones you can't. Think of it as building a ship that's strong enough to weather the storms of entrepreneurship while staying agile enough to navigate toward your goals.

What Does Risk-Free Mean?

Risks are everywhere—they always have been, and they always will be. While we can't eliminate risks entirely, we can control how we respond to them. The key lies in identifying potential risks early and preparing to avoid or mitigate them. When we've taken the necessary precautions and minimized the chance of failure, those risks no longer hold power over us. At that point, for us, it's as close to "risk-free" as it gets.

Risk-Free doesn't mean a perfect, obstacle-free journey; it means being proactive, adaptable, and ready to face challenges without letting them derail your success. By taking calculated steps and preparing for what lies ahead, you turn risks into manageable hurdles rather than insurmountable barriers.

The term "Risk-Free" might sound like an oxymoron. After all, doesn't every business inherently involve risk? Yes and no. While there's no such thing as a completely risk-free venture, the Risk-Free Startup approach focuses on reducing unnecessary risks through preparation, strategy, and smart decision-making.

Consider Amazon's early days. Jeff Bezos didn't start with a global empire—he started with books. He chose a product category with predictable demand, low inventory costs, and a scalable online model. By starting small and refining the business before expanding, Amazon minimized its initial risk while paving the way for exponential growth.

For you, Risk-Free might mean starting your business as a side hustle while keeping your full-time job. It could mean testing your idea with a small group of trusted customers before scaling up. Whatever your approach, the goal is to avoid betting everything at once and instead build a strong foundation.

What This Book Will Teach You

The path to Risk-Free startup success isn't just a roadmap—it's a mindset. You'll learn how to think like a strategic entrepreneur, balancing ambition with caution. Each step of this book is designed to guide you through the process of building a business that's not only profitable but sustainable. You'll discover how to:

1. Plan effectively, using resources you already have.

2. Validate your ideas to ensure demand before committing.

3. Scale and multiply your success without unnecessary risks.

4. Develop systems that allow your business to thrive without depending solely on you.

Every chapter is packed with actionable insights, real-world examples, and practical tools to help you navigate the challenges of entrepreneurship. Whether you're launching your first startup or your fifth, this framework will give you the clarity and confidence to move forward.

Why This Journey Matters

Success isn't just about making money—it's about creating something meaningful. It's about solving real problems, building relationships, and leaving a legacy. The Risk-Free Startup framework isn't just a strategy; it's a way to align your business with your values and vision.

Remember, success isn't reserved for the lucky or the fearless. It's for those who plan, learn, and take calculated steps. As you embark on this journey, know that every decision you make brings you closer to your goals. The path may not always be easy, but with the right approach, it can be transformative.

Success is the goal, not risk-free

The ultimate aim of starting a business isn't to avoid every risk—it's to succeed. Success, whether measured in financial freedom, personal fulfillment, or creating a lasting impact, is what truly matters. Risk is simply a part of the journey, not the destination. When we focus solely on avoiding risk, we often limit our potential. Instead, the goal should be to manage risk intelligently while keeping our sights firmly set on success.

The Reality of Risk in Business

Risk is inevitable in any entrepreneurial venture. Markets shift, competitors emerge, and unforeseen challenges arise. Yet, some of the most successful businesses in history have thrived not by avoiding risks entirely, but by understanding and preparing for them.

Take Apple, for example. When Steve Jobs introduced the iPhone, it was a bold gamble. The smartphone market barely existed, and the company risked alienating its loyal iPod customers. But Apple's team anticipated these risks and mitigated them by focusing on innovation and user experience. The result? A product that revolutionized technology and established Apple as a global leader.

For smaller startups, the stakes may not seem as high, but the principles remain the same. Success comes from balancing ambition with preparation, not from attempting to sidestep every challenge.

Why Success Matters More

Success is the culmination of planning, execution, and persistence. It's not about whether you faced risks but how you overcame them. A business that avoids risks altogether often sacrifices growth opportunities. For instance, launching a new product or expanding into a new market carries inherent risks, but the rewards of doing so can far outweigh the potential downsides.

In my own ventures, I learned this firsthand. Starting a moving company wasn't without its risks—competition was fierce. But instead of fixating on avoiding every misstep, I simply went forward, prepared to resolve any potential problems, take any risks, and focused on delivering unparalleled reliability and customer service. By embracing calculated risks and staying committed to the end goal, that business became one of my successes.

Reframing Your Mindset

It's essential to view risks not as barriers but as opportunities for growth. When you encounter a risk, ask yourself: How can I prepare for this? What's the worst-case scenario, and how would I recover from it? By asking these questions, you shift your mindset from fear to empowerment.

Remember, success isn't achieved by standing still. It's about moving forward with confidence, even in the face of uncertainty. The PRISMs method is designed to help you identify and minimize risks so they don't overshadow your journey toward success. The focus is always on progress—one step closer to the goals you've set for yourself.

Success Over Avoiding Risk

You can take risks, take the right risks at the right time. Success, on the other hand, is what defines your entrepreneurial journey. It's about reaching the milestones that matter most to you, whether that's financial independence, building a legacy, or making a difference in the world. Keep your eyes on the prize, and let risk be a guide, not a deterrent.

What's Success?

Success means different things to different people. For some, it's financial freedom—a life where money is no longer a constraint. For others, it's about impact—changing the world through innovation, service, or creating something truly meaningful. Whatever your definition, one thing is universal: success is deeply personal. It's not about following someone else's blueprint; it's about crafting your own.

When I first ventured into entrepreneurship, I thought success was measured solely in money. My first business—a computer company, you can not call it a real company really, made money, but it didn't fulfill me. Over time, I realized that success isn't just about numbers; it's about creating something that aligns with your goals, values, and vision for the future.

Defining Success for Yourself

The first step to achieving success is defining what it means to you. This clarity will guide your decisions, keep you focused, and help you measure progress. Ask yourself:

1. Do you want to build a legacy that outlives you?

2. Is your goal to provide for your family and achieve financial stability?

3. Are you driven by the desire to solve a problem or improve lives?

For instance, Elon Musk's definition of success includes pushing humanity forward—whether through electric vehicles, space exploration, or sustainable energy. His vision guides every decision, helping him whether failures and setbacks because the goal remains clear.

Your success might look different. It could be as simple as creating a business that allows you to spend more time with loved ones or as ambitious as disrupting an industry. There's no right or wrong definition—only what feels authentic to you.

The Dimensions of Success

Success often has multiple dimensions. These include:

1. **Financial**: Generating enough income to sustain and grow your business while providing for your personal needs.

2. **Personal Fulfillment**: Enjoying the work you do and feeling proud of your achievements.

3. **Impact**: Making a difference, whether for your customers, community, or the world.

For example, when I shifted focus to the shipping and moving industries, my definition of success included not only financial stability but also delivering exceptional service that eased the stress of my customers' lives. That sense of impact made the work more rewarding.

Why Success Is a Journey, Not a Destination

It's important to remember that success isn't a static endpoint. It evolves as you grow, learn, and achieve. What felt like success when you started may no longer satisfy you years later, and that's okay.

Consider Jeff Bezos's transition from running an online bookstore to building Amazon into a global powerhouse. Each stage of growth brought new challenges and opportunities, expanding his definition of success. Similarly, your journey will present chances to redefine what success looks like as you reach new heights.

For some people, success might be opening a neighbourhood coffee shop that not only supports their family but also provides a cozy gathering place for the community.

Success is both personal and evolving. By defining it clearly and staying true to your vision, you set the foundation for a fulfilling entrepreneurial journey. Remember, success isn't about avoiding failure—it's about what you build, who you become, and the legacy you leave behind.

What's your success?

Are you ready to embrace your own success? Let's start with the first step of risk-free entrepreneurship!

STEP 1: PLAN - FIRST CREATION

Every great business begins with a plan. Step 1 is about laying the foundation—the first creation of your vision. Before you dive into execution, you must define what success looks like, understand your resources, and chart a path forward. Planning isn't just about writing a business plan; it's about creating clarity, direction, and a sense of purpose.

Think of this step as building the blueprint for a house. Without a solid design, the structure will be weak, no matter how much effort you put into construction. In the same way, a business without a strong plan is vulnerable to collapse, no matter how passionate or skilled you are.

Planning saved me from repeating many mistakes I made in my early ventures. When I started my shipping and freight-forwarding company, I took the time to assess the market, understand my strengths, and outline how I could provide value better than my competitors. That planning made all the difference—it turned an idea into a sustainable, thriving business.

Why Planning Matters

Planning allows you to:

1. **Clarify Your Vision**: Understand what you're building and why.

2. **Identify Resources**: Take stock of what you have and what you need to move forward.

3. **Minimize Risks**: Spot potential challenges early and develop strategies to overcome them.

Without a plan, you're not just taking risks—you're gambling. With a plan, you're making calculated moves that increase your odds of success.

The First Creation

This step is called the "first creation" because everything starts in your mind. Before you can create a product, service, or business, you must first create the idea of it. Stephen Covey, in his book *The 7 Habits of Highly Effective People,* explains that everything is created twice: first mentally and then physically. This step is about that mental creation.

In this section, we'll explore the foundational questions every entrepreneur must answer:

1. Why do you want to start your business?

2. What are you going to sell?

3. Who are your customers and why will they pay you?

4. How are you going to price?

5. Who do you need in your team?

6. How and how much will you fund your business?

7. What resources do you have?

Through these chapters, you'll develop the mindset, strategy, and clarity to move from dreaming to doing.

A Foundation for the Future

Planning is more than a one-time activity—it's a continuous process. As you progress through the PRISMs method, your plan will evolve. But the groundwork you lay here will support every future step. By the end of Step 1, you'll have a clear, actionable roadmap to guide your journey and the confidence to take your first steps toward success.

CHAPTER 1: THE MINDSET - THE FOUNDATION OF YOUR SUCCESS

Your mindset is the cornerstone of your entrepreneurial journey. It's not just about what you do—it's about how you think. The right mindset will guide you through challenges, help you make better decisions, and keep you focused on your ultimate goals. Without the proper foundation in your mind, even the best plans and resources can falter.

When I look back at the businesses I started—some successful, others not—it's clear that mindset made all the difference. Early on, I approached ventures with a mix of ambition and fear. In my first few failures, I realized that fear clouded my judgment and led to rushed decisions. But when I shifted to a mindset of learning, resilience, and confidence, the trajectory of my successes—like my shipping business, moving business, and my real estate business — changed completely.

Why Mindset Matters

Success in business isn't a straight road. There will be setbacks, doubts, and unexpected challenges. What separates successful entrepreneurs from those who give up isn't luck or talent—it's the way they think.

Mindset shapes how you respond to failure. Some see failure as the end, while others see it as a stepping stone. It affects how you approach risks—whether you avoid them out of fear or face them with preparation and confidence. And most importantly, it determines how you stay motivated and persistent when the road gets tough.

Think of Elon Musk's journey with SpaceX. His first three rocket launches failed, nearly bankrupting the company. But his mindset— one of relentless innovation and belief in his vision—pushed him to keep going. That same mindset turned SpaceX into a global leader in space exploration.

Building the Right Mindset

This chapter will guide you through the mental shifts you need to make as you start your business. You'll learn:

1. Why your reasons for starting a business matter more than you think.

2. How to think big but act smart and start small.

3. Why perfection isn't the goal, but progress is.

4. How to align your values, principles, and mission with your actions.

5. The importance of staying mentally engaged until your business becomes self-sustaining.

These principles will help you build a mindset that doesn't just react to challenges but anticipates and thrives through them.

The Mindset Journey

A successful mindset isn't developed overnight. It's a journey of learning, adapting, and growing. As you progress through this book, your mindset will continue to evolve. This chapter sets the stage for that growth, providing you with the tools and perspectives needed to approach entrepreneurship with clarity, confidence, and resilience.

The businesses that succeeded for me weren't the ones with perfect conditions—they were the ones where my mindset allowed me to adapt, innovate, and persevere. With the right mindset, your business can succeed too, no matter the obstacles.

Why do you want to start your business?

Every entrepreneur begins their journey with a reason—a spark of inspiration, a deep desire, or a pressing problem they want to solve. Understanding your "why" is one of the most critical steps in starting a business. It's the fuel that will keep you going when challenges arise and the compass that will guide your decisions. But knowing why you want to start isn't always as simple as it sounds.

When I started my moving company, my initial motivation was just to make some money instead of looking for a job. Also I saw an opportunity to provide a service that was reliable, professional, and customer-focused in an industry that often lacked those qualities. But as the business grew, I realized my "why" ran deeper. It wasn't just about making money—it was about building a reputation, solving real problems for people, and creating a business I could be proud of. That realization gave me a sense of purpose and direction that kept me going through the toughest days.

Finding Your True Motivation

Many people start businesses for reasons like financial freedom, independence, or following a passion. These are valid and powerful motivations, but it's important to dig deeper. Ask yourself:

1. Are you trying to solve a specific problem?

2. Do you want to create something that aligns with your values and vision?

3. Is that your only reason to start your business? Be honest to yourself.

4. Are you motivated by a desire to leave a legacy?

Your "why" is unique to you. For example, Howard Schultz, the former CEO of Starbucks, wasn't just interested in selling coffee. He wanted to create a space where people could connect—a "third place" between home and work. That deeper motivation shaped Starbucks into the global brand it is today.

Similarly, when I ventured into the shipping and freight-forwarding industry, my "why" wasn't just about logistics. It was about connecting businesses and individuals to opportunities across borders, solving complex challenges in a way that added real value. That clarity kept me focused even when the market presented obstacles.

Aligning Your "Why" with Your Goals

Once you've identified your motivation, ensure it aligns with your business goals. A strong "why" not only inspires you but also informs your strategy. If your goal is to help others, how does your business model support that? If it's to achieve financial independence, have you planned for profitability and sustainability?

Take Sara Blakely, the founder of Spanx, as an example. Her "why" was to create a product that made women feel more confident. This purpose guided every decision she made, from product design to branding, and turned Spanx into a billion-dollar company.

For your business, start by writing down your "why." Revisit it regularly, especially when faced with tough decisions or moments of doubt. It will serve as a reminder of what you're working toward and why it matters.

The Foundation of Your Success

Your "why" isn't just a motivational poster—it's the foundation of your business. When times get tough, as they inevitably will, your reason for starting will keep you grounded. It will inspire your team, attract customers, and set you apart from competitors. More than anything, it will give your business a soul, turning it into something more than just a money-making machine.

So, take the time to reflect on why you want to start your business. Be honest with yourself and think deeply about what drives you. Your "why" is the beginning of your journey—and it will be the force that carries you to success.

What's your Why?

Is it a good business to start up?

Not every business idea is a good one to pursue, and knowing which opportunities to embrace is a critical skill for any entrepreneur. Over time, I've developed a personal standard to decide whether a business is worth starting. For me, the business must have the potential to grow big enough to make me proud, and the risks involved must be ones I can afford. If it doesn't meet these criteria, it's not the right fit for me. But I didn't always have this clarity.

When I started my first ventures—selling computer parts in college or launching my moving company—I didn't give much thought to long-term potential or calculated risks. As a result, I quickly hit a ceiling and found myself considering new business ideas soon after. At that time, my primary focus was simply making money and finding a way to get started. While those ventures provided invaluable lessons, they also highlighted the importance of establishing a clear standard for choosing opportunities.

Setting the Standard

A good business idea isn't just one you can do—it's one that aligns with your goals, resources, and capacity for risk. This doesn't mean the idea needs to be perfect or risk-free, but it should meet a few key criteria:

1. **Growth Potential**: Can this business grow big enough to make you proud? A business that can scale, expand, or create meaningful impact is more likely to sustain your interest and provide long-term rewards.

2. **Manageable Risks**: Are the risks involved ones you can afford? Starting a business is never risk-free, but taking risks beyond your financial or emotional limits can lead to unnecessary stress and failure.

For example, when I entered the shipping and freight-forwarding industry, I knew the market was large enough to support significant growth. At the same time, I assessed the risks and determined they were manageable given my resources and experience. That combination of potential and feasibility made it a good business for me.

What Makes a Business "Not Good"?

On the flip side, a business that doesn't meet your personal criteria can become a drain on your time, energy, and resources. Early in my journey, I didn't have a clear standard, so I took on whatever opportunities I could find. Selling computer parts in college was a great starting point—it helped me learn the basics of buying, selling, negotiating, marketing, and customer service. But it wasn't a scalable business or something I could turn into a career.

Similarly, my moving company began as a way to make good money rather than as a carefully chosen opportunity. I reached the ceiling quickly; not long after I launched the business in 2006, it was recognized as the largest moving company within the Vancouver Chinese community. However, scaling it further—to a size I could truly take pride in—proved challenging. While the business was a success, it lacked the strategic thought and planning that now guide every decision I make. If I had relied solely on that approach, I might have found myself stuck in businesses that didn't align with my long-term vision.

On the positive side, the moving company was an incredible learning experience. It was an extremely tough business, filled with challenging situations that forced me to grow and adapt. Over time, these difficulties significantly enhanced my problem-solving skills and overall business acumen, preparing me for future ventures.

Aligning Business with Vision

To decide if a business is good to start, ask yourself:

1. **Does this business excite me?** If you're not passionate or at least deeply interested, it's hard to sustain the effort required to succeed.

2. **Can I see this business growing?** A business should have room to evolve, whether by scaling operations, expanding markets, or diversifying products.

3. **Am I willing to take the risks?** No business is without challenges, but you should feel confident that the risks won't overwhelm you.

As you gain more experience, your standards will become clearer, just as mine did. But even if you're at the beginning of your journey, thinking through these questions can help you avoid costly mistakes.

Conclusion

A good business to start isn't just one that makes money—it's one that fits your goals, resources, and capacity for growth. Early on, you may need to start with whatever opportunities come your way, as I did. But as you grow as an entrepreneur, developing a standard for evaluating opportunities will save you time, effort, and frustration. Remember, the best business is one that aligns with your vision and has the potential to become something you're truly proud of

What Resources Do You Have?

Starting a business isn't just about ideas—it's about execution. And execution requires resources. Whether you're launching a tech startup, a coffee shop, Real Estate Agent service, or a marketing company, understanding what you already have and what you need is a critical step in the planning process. Often, entrepreneurs focus too much on what they lack and overlook the resources they already possess. Recognizing and maximizing your available resources can be the difference between success and failure.

When I launched my moving company, I didn't have much. My experience in the industry was minimal—just one week as a mover in one company and three days in another. I didn't have any money either, but I had a willingness to work hard. To get started, I borrowed $10,000 from the bank and relied on three of my credit cards to buy a truck. What I lacked in experience and funds, I made up for with determination, energy, and a quick ability to learn. By focusing on what I had—good credit and a drive to succeed—instead of dwelling on what I didn't, I built a successful business that served countless clients

Assessing Your Resources

Every entrepreneur has resources, even if they don't realize it. Take stock of what you have in the following areas:

1. **Physical Resources**: Do you have equipment, inventory, or access to a workspace? For example, when I started selling computer parts in college, my dorm room became my makeshift warehouse. If you're resourceful, even the smallest physical assets can be put to good use.

2. **Financial Resources**: How much money can you invest without jeopardizing your personal stability? Consider savings, credit, or support from family and friends. When I began my shipping business, I approached it strategically to minimize costs. I didn't need a huge budget or substantial investments. By starting smartly and leveraging existing resources, I was able to launch the shipping business successfully with almost no upfront investment.

3. **Skills and Knowledge**: Your expertise is often your most valuable resource. What skills do you bring to the table? Perhaps you're great at networking, marketing, or managing logistics. When I started as a Real Estate Agent, my knowledge of the local market and ability to connect with people were instrumental in closing deals.

4. **Relationships**: Never underestimate the power of your network. Who do you know that can support, advise, or collaborate with you? Early in my career, I relied on mentors, advisors, and friends to guide me through difficult decisions.

5. **Time**: Time is a resource that many entrepreneurs overlook. If you're starting while working a full-time job, evenings and weekends can be dedicated to building your business. For me, those extra hours were crucial in growing my ventures without overextending my finances.

Maximizing What You Have

Once you've assessed your resources, the next step is to leverage them effectively. Don't let a lack of money or experience stop you from moving forward. Instead, ask yourself:

1. How can I stretch my budget to cover the essentials?

2. Are there ways to trade or barter for what I need?

3. Can I learn new skills instead of outsourcing tasks?

For example, when I needed to market my moving company but couldn't afford expensive advertising, I leaned heavily on word-of-mouth referrals. By focusing on delivering exceptional service, I turned every satisfied customer into a promoter of my business. It didn't cost me much, but it paid off significantly.

Filling the Gaps

After identifying and maximizing your existing resources, take note of what's missing. This isn't a reason to panic—it's a chance to get creative. Look for ways to acquire what you need, whether through partnerships, loans, or innovative solutions.

For instance, when I started my furniture store, I partnered with a supplier who offered flexible payment terms. This arrangement allowed me to stock my store without overextending my budget. Identifying gaps and finding smart ways to fill them is a hallmark of successful entrepreneurs.

Conclusion

Your resources are the building blocks of your business. By taking the time to assess what you have, maximize its potential, and address gaps strategically, you set yourself up for success. Remember, it's not about having everything—it's about making the most of what you have and finding creative ways to fill in the rest. Every great business starts with resourcefulness, and the more you focus on what you can do with what you have, the closer you'll get to your goals.

Think Big, Start Smart and Small

Dreaming big is an essential part of entrepreneurship. It's what inspires us to build something meaningful, solve significant problems, and create lasting impact. However, while thinking big gives you direction, starting small and smart ensures you stay grounded and realistic. A grand vision without a practical first step often leads to frustration, burnout, or failure.

When I began my journey as an entrepreneur, I had big aspirations but limited resources. I learned quickly that chasing a massive idea without a foundation was a recipe for disaster. Instead, I started small, testing the waters and learning from each step before scaling up. This balance between ambition and practicality became a cornerstone of my success.

Why Thinking Big Matters

Thinking big gives you purpose and clarity. It's about visualizing the future you want to create and setting a bold goal to guide your actions. Big dreams are what pushed Elon Musk to envision a world where electric cars are the norm or space travel is accessible to everyone. Without that expansive vision, businesses often plateau, unable to inspire their founders or customers.

For me, thinking big meant imagining a shipping company that could connect people across borders or a real estate business that wasn't just about transactions but about helping families find their dream homes. These visions gave me motivation and a clear sense of where I wanted to go.

Why Starting Smart and Small is Crucial

While thinking big sets the destination, starting small ensures you don't stumble at the first step. Many entrepreneurs fail because they try to do too much too quickly—launching on a grand scale without validating their ideas or building a stable foundation.

When I launched my moving company, I didn't try to compete with established giants right away. I started with one truck and focused on delivering exceptional service to local clients. That small start allowed me to learn the industry, build a reputation, and grow steadily without overextending myself. Similarly, in my shipping business, I strategically minimized costs, proving the model before expanding.

Starting smart means:

1. Testing your ideas on a small scale.

2. Managing risks by controlling costs.

3. Learning and adapting without significant consequences.

Building a Bridge Between the Two

Thinking big and starting small aren't opposites—they're complementary strategies. Start by visualizing your end goal, then reverse-engineer the steps to get there. Focus on what you can do today to bring you closer to your big vision.

Consider Amazon's beginnings. Jeff Bezos didn't launch a marketplace selling everything under the sun. He started small—selling books online—while keeping the bigger vision of "the everything store" in mind. That initial focus allowed him to refine operations, build trust, and expand strategically.

For your business, start with what you have and what you know. If you dream of opening a nationwide chain of coffee shops, begin with one location, perfect the model, and then expand. Starting small doesn't limit your vision—it ensures you're prepared for sustainable growth.

Conclusion

Think big to inspire yourself and set a course for the future. Start small and smart to ground your efforts in reality and learn as you go. By combining ambition with practicality, you create a powerful balance that leads to success. Remember, every big business started small, but what set them apart was their ability to think big and take measured, strategic steps toward their vision.

Patience: Hold On vs Let Go

Success in business rarely happens overnight. Even with the perfect setup, the right product, and a clear strategy, results take time. Patience is not just a virtue in entrepreneurship—it's a necessity. However, there's a fine line between being patient and wasting time on something that isn't working. Knowing when to persist and when to pivot is one of the toughest challenges entrepreneurs face.

The Importance of Patience

When I started my moving company, I worked tirelessly to build my reputation and attract clients. Even with all the pieces in place, it took months before I began seeing consistent results. This isn't unusual—businesses need time to build momentum. Customers need to hear about you, try your product or service, and trust that you'll deliver. That process doesn't happen in days or even weeks; it often takes months or years.

Take Airbnb, for example. In its early days, the company struggled to attract users and faced repeated rejections from investors. But the founders were patient, refining their platform, adjusting their strategy, and slowly building a loyal customer base. Today, Airbnb is a household name, but it wouldn't exist if its founders hadn't been willing to wait and adapt.

The Danger of Blind Patience

While patience is critical, it's not a license to ignore reality. Some businesses or models simply won't work, whether due to market conditions, flawed assumptions, or unforeseen challenges. The difficulty is that you can't always predict this in advance, especially with limited knowledge or experience.

When I started my furniture store in 2010, I quickly realized it wasn't the right business for me. At that time, I was already juggling too much—running a moving company, launching a shipping company, and welcoming my son into the world that same year. On top of that, I was using a flawed strategy, attempting to sell both new furniture and antique furniture in the same space. The result was exhausting: thin margins and effort that far outweighed the returns. In hindsight, it wasn't a viable long-term business for me. Within a year, I decided to close the furniture store and focus on my shipping and moving companies. This experience reinforced the importance of setting clear terms for evaluation and knowing when to let go.

Finding the Balance

The key to balancing patience and decisiveness is creating a framework for evaluation. Instead of endlessly waiting for things to improve, set specific milestones, timelines, or conditions. For example:

1. **Timeframe**: Decide how long you're willing to stick with the current approach—six months, a year, or longer if it's not successful.

2. **Metrics**: Identify measurable indicators of progress, such as customer growth, revenue, or market traction.

3. **Review Points**: Schedule regular check-ins to assess whether the business is meeting your expectations.

This approach allows you to stay patient without becoming complacent. It also removes emotion from the decision-making process, helping you make objective choices about whether to persist or pivot.

Learning to Let Go

Letting go of a business or idea isn't a failure—it's a learning experience. Even the best entrepreneurs have walked away from ventures that didn't work. The key is to take the lessons you've learned and apply them to your next endeavour.

For example, when I realized that my furniture store wasn't meeting my growth expectations, I made the tough decision to close it. While it was painful at the time, that decision freed up resources and energy that I used to grow my shipping business, which became one of my successful ventures.

Conclusion

Patience and decisiveness aren't opposing forces—they're complementary tools. Success takes time, but waiting indefinitely for results isn't the answer either. By setting clear terms for evaluation, you can strike the right balance between persistence and pragmatism. Remember, the goal isn't to avoid failure altogether—it's to learn, adapt, and move forward with purpose

You aren't the "boss" until you're

Titles like "Boss" or "CEO" often carry a sense of authority and prestige, but the reality of being a business owner is much more complex. Until you've reached a point where your business operates independently of your daily involvement—where it thrives on its own systems and leadership—you're not truly the boss. In those early and growth stages, the real "bosses" are your employees, customers, suppliers, subcontractors, and anyone else who plays a role in keeping the business alive.

For me, I don't rush to call myself the boss of any business unless absolutely necessary. It's not because I don't value my position—it's because I recognize that being a boss is about responsibility and outcomes, not a title. Whether I'm considered the boss or not is irrelevant to me. What matters is that the business runs smoothly, serves its purpose, and achieves success.

Who Is Really the Boss?

In the day-to-day reality of running a business, the authority isn't always yours. Employees make decisions on the ground, customers dictate demand, and subcontractors or suppliers can influence how well you deliver. These stakeholders hold significant power over the success or failure of your business. Until you've built a company that can function without being tethered to your direct involvement, your role as "boss" is limited.

When I was running my moving company, I often felt like I was at the mercy of external forces. Employees determined the quality of service customers received. Subcontractors controlled critical aspects like equipment availability, and customers' satisfaction dictated the company's reputation. While I was technically the owner, I wasn't the true "boss" because I didn't have the systems and independence in place to remove myself from daily operations.

The True Boss: Systems and Sustainability

A business truly becomes yours when it can operate independently of you. This happens when:

1. Systems and processes are strong enough to manage daily operations.

2. Leadership teams can make decisions without relying on you.

3. Customers trust your brand, not just you, to deliver value.

When you transitioned your company into a well-oiled machine, you finally felt like the business truly belonged to you. It no longer relied on your constant presence to operate successfully. That moment highlighted the difference between being an owner and being a boss.

Titles Don't Matter

For many people, being called "boss" is a validation of their hard work. But for me, it's just a name. Whether someone acknowledges me as the boss or not doesn't change my focus. What matters is the success of the business, the satisfaction of my team and customers, and the ability to build something meaningful.

This mindset helps me avoid distractions and ego-driven decisions. It reminds me that leadership is about outcomes, not appearances. A title won't make your business succeed—actions and strategy will.

The Boss Mindset

To truly become the boss of your business, you must:

1. Build systems that allow the business to run without your constant oversight.

2. Empower employees and leaders to take ownership of their roles.

3. Focus on long-term sustainability rather than short-term control.

Until then—what we call Step 6: The Success, The Real Success—embrace the reality that your role is to serve the needs of the business, not simply to hold a title. Acknowledge and value the contributions of everyone who helps bring your vision to life—your team, your customers, your subcontractors, and even your competitors, who challenge you to improve

Conclusion

You're not the boss until your business no longer depends on you. And even then, being the boss is just a title. What truly matters is creating a company that operates effectively, serves its customers, and grows sustainably. Leadership isn't about claiming authority — it's about earning it through results. Let the success of your business speak for itself, and the title of "boss" will naturally follow

Risk-Free Startup Mindset

The right mindset can be the difference between a thriving business and one that falters under pressure. The Risk-Free Startup Mindset is about approaching entrepreneurship with both ambition and caution. It's not about eliminating every challenge but about preparing for them intelligently, reducing unnecessary risks, and maximizing your chances of success.

When I started my first few businesses, I didn't have a defined mindset. I was eager and willing to work hard, but I often underestimated risks or jumped into opportunities without sufficient preparation. Over time, I realized that success wasn't just about effort — it was about strategy, resilience, and calculated decisions. The Risk-Free Startup Mindset is the culmination of those lessons.

What Does a Risk-Free Mindset Look Like?

1. **Focus on Preparation**: Entrepreneurs with a Risk-Free Mindset understand that success begins with preparation. They take the time to analyze markets, understand their audience, and assess their resources before making big decisions.
   For instance, when I launched my shipping company, I strategically minimized costs by starting small and building relationships with reliable subcontractors. This preparation

allowed me to test the waters without taking on overwhelming financial risks.

2. **Adaptability**: Business is unpredictable. A Risk-Free Mindset embraces change and adapts to new circumstances. Instead of fearing obstacles, you learn to see them as opportunities to pivot and grow.
When COVID-19 disrupted traditional logistics, businesses with adaptable mindsets shifted to digital solutions or diversified their offerings. Those who resisted change struggled to survive.

3. **Balancing Optimism and Realism**: This mindset isn't about being overly cautious or pessimistic. It's about dreaming big while staying grounded in reality. Entrepreneurs with this mindset believe in their vision but don't ignore red flags or risks.

Lessons from Failure

The Risk-Free Mindset also involves learning from failure. Not every venture succeeds, and that's okay. What matters is what you take away from the experience. When I started my furniture store, I underestimated the sheer workload involved—managing inventory, ordering new products, buying old ones, arranging advertisements, hiring sales staff, coordinating deliveries, handling customer service and warranties, and maintaining a consistent image for the store. Combining two vastly different product types—new and antique furniture—also created confusion for customers. While the business didn't last, it taught me the importance of having a clear, focused, and scalable strategy.

Failures aren't the end of the road—they're stepping stones to future success. With the right mindset, you can use these lessons to refine your approach and build better businesses in the future.

Why Mindset Matters More Than Money

Having financial resources is essential, but mindset drives how those resources are used. Entrepreneurs who focus solely on money often overlook other critical elements like planning, innovation, and customer relationships. On the other hand, those with the right mindset can achieve remarkable results even with limited funds.

Take Airbnb's founders, who famously sold cereal to fund their startup in its early days. Their resourcefulness and belief in their idea carried them through tough times and eventually transformed their vision into a global business.

Developing Your Risk-Free Mindset

To cultivate this mindset, start by asking yourself these questions:

1. Am I prepared for the challenges this business might face?

2. How can I minimize risks while pursuing my goals?

3. What lessons can I learn from my past failures or experiences?

The Risk-Free Mindset isn't about avoiding risks altogether—it's about approaching them strategically, learning from setbacks, and building a resilient foundation for your business.

Conclusion

The Risk-Free Startup Mindset is a blend of preparation, adaptability, and resilience. It's about dreaming big while staying grounded, embracing challenges as opportunities, and learning from every step of the journey. With this mindset, you don't just minimize risks—you maximize your potential for success. Remember, the right mindset is the foundation of any great business.

3-Time Creation

Every successful business is created three times. This principle reflects the journey from idea to reality through three essential stages: the mental creation, the validating phase, and the physical execution. Each step is distinct but interconnected, forming the foundation of a sustainable and impactful business.

This concept applies universally, whether you're a first-time entrepreneur or a seasoned business owner. I've seen it in my ventures, and it's echoed in the success stories of iconic businesses worldwide. Skipping any stage risks undermining your entire effort, while respecting and refining each step increases your chances of long-term success.

First Creation: The Mental Vision

The first creation begins in your mind. This is where your ideas take shape and your vision for the business emerges. It's about imagining what you want to build and the problem you aim to solve. The mental creation is your dream and your purpose.

For example, Sarah Blakely, the founder of Spanx, had a mental vision of a product that would empower women to feel confident in their clothes. Her idea was clear: comfortable, practical shapewear that didn't compromise on style. This vision became the guiding star for her journey.

When I launched my shipping company, my mental creation was rooted in simplifying logistics for customers. I visualized how the business would operate, what kind of clients it would serve, and the gaps it would fill in the market. This clarity gave me direction as I moved forward.

Key Question: What does your ideal business look like, and what value will it bring to the world?

Second Creation: Validating

The second creation is about validation—testing your idea in the real world to ensure it works. It's where you move beyond theory and start gathering evidence that your concept is viable. Validation minimizes risks by helping you refine your offering before making significant investments.

Take Dropbox as an example. Before launching, founder Drew Houston created a simple explainer video showcasing how the product would work. The video generated overwhelming interest, proving that there was demand for a cloud-based storage solution. This validation phase allowed Houston to refine Dropbox and attract early adopters.

For my shipping company, validation involved a low-cost, low-risk strategy. I started by modifying my moving ads to include phrases like "shipping from Vancouver to Canada, USA, Asia, and Europe." This change required no extra expense but allowed me to test the market. When inquiries came in, I selected a few customers to run actual shipments. These tests confirmed that I could execute the process efficiently and helped me calculate real costs and refine my pricing. Only after this successful validation did I expand into a full-scale operation.

Key Question: How can you test your idea with minimal resources and risk?

Third Creation: Physical Execution

For some people, the first and second creation may be simple and short, but it must be there. Some people may merge the first two creation into the third one and keep planing, adjusting, and executing. It's only about the differences of definition and name.

The third creation is the physical realization of your business. This is where you put your validated idea into action, launch your product or service, and adapt to real-world challenges. Execution is where all the planning and testing come together.

Apple's execution of the iPhone illustrates this stage perfectly. The mental creation was a revolutionary device, and validation came through years of development and prototyping. When the iPhone launched, it wasn't perfect, but it was good enough to disrupt the market and establish Apple as a leader in mobile technology.

In my moving company, the physical execution involved delivering exceptional service to customers and learning from their feedback.

Every interaction was an opportunity to refine operations, improve efficiency, and build trust. The success of this phase depended on the alignment of the previous two creations.

Key Question: How will you bring your validated idea to life and adapt to new challenges?

Why All Three Matter

The 3-Time Creation principle ensures that each step of your journey builds on the previous one. A vision without validation leads to wasted effort. Validation without execution results in missed opportunities. And execution without a clear vision often ends in chaos.

Jeff Bezos's journey with Amazon demonstrates the importance of aligning all three creations. His mental creation envisioned an online marketplace selling everything. Validation came by starting with books, a manageable product category. Execution involved launching and iterating on the platform, eventually scaling into the global giant Amazon is today.

Conclusion

The 3-Time Creation principle is a framework for turning ideas into reality. Start with a bold vision, test it through validation, and bring it to life with purposeful execution. By respecting each stage and ensuring they work together, you set the foundation for a business that doesn't just survive—it thrives. Every great business is created three times—make each creation count.

Don't Wait to Be Perfect to Start

Perfection is often seen as the ultimate goal, but in entrepreneurship, waiting for perfection can become your greatest obstacle. The truth is, no business idea, product, or plan is flawless from the outset.

Success comes from starting, learning, and improving along the way. If you delay launching until everything feels "perfect," you might never start at all.

I've learned this firsthand in my journey. When I launched my moving company, the operation was far from perfect. I had limited experience, borrowed money, and a single truck. Yet, by starting small and focusing on delivering good service, I was able to grow the business, gain experience, and refine my processes. If I had waited for the perfect setup, I might still be waiting.

Why Perfection is a Myth

Perfection is an illusion. Markets change, customer needs evolve, and unforeseen challenges arise. What seems perfect today may be irrelevant tomorrow. Instead of chasing an unattainable standard, focus on creating a version of your business that's functional and adaptable.

Consider Facebook's early days. Mark Zuckerberg didn't wait to create the perfect social network before launching. The first version of Facebook was simple—designed specifically for college students. Over time, user feedback and market trends helped shape it into the global platform we know today. If Zuckerberg had waited for perfection, someone else might have seized the opportunity.

Start Now, Improve Later

Starting doesn't mean you launch recklessly—it means you launch strategically. Focus on delivering value with what you have, and let experience and feedback guide your improvements.

For example, when I started my shipping business, I didn't invest heavily in infrastructure or marketing right away. I tested the waters by modifying my existing ads and offering shipping services alongside moving. I even didn't change my any of own trucks' body ads at the beginning, cause that change would cost something not very cheap. I finally changed all my trucks ads after the shipping service was stable and predictable.

This allowed me to validate the idea and refine my operations without risking significant resources. Once the foundation was solid, I scaled the business with confidence.

Key Principle: The perfect time to start is now, with what you have.

Learning by Doing

Starting before you're ready forces you to learn quickly and adapt. Real-world experience is often the best teacher. You'll discover what works, what doesn't, and where improvements are needed far faster than if you waited to perfect everything on paper.

Take the example of Reid Hoffman, the founder of LinkedIn, who famously said, "If you are not embarrassed by the first version of your product, you've launched too late." His point is clear: what matters is getting your product out there and iterating based on real feedback. LinkedIn's early platform was basic, but launching early allowed the team to refine it based on user needs.

The Cost of Waiting

The longer you wait to start, the more opportunities you miss. Markets move quickly, and timing can be critical. Waiting for perfection often leads to procrastination, missed chances, and increased pressure to perform when you finally launch.

When I started my furniture store, I initially hesitated, trying to perfect the inventory mix and store layout. By the time I launched, I realized that those details mattered less than simply meeting customer needs. In hindsight, starting earlier and learning from customer behavior might have given the business a better chance.

Conclusion

You don't need perfection to begin—you need action. Starting now allows you to build momentum, learn from experience, and grow your business step by step. Remember, every successful entrepreneur began with an imperfect version of their idea and improved it over time. Perfection isn't the starting point; it's the result of persistence and progress

100 - 1 = 0

The Critical Role of Details

In business, success is often attributed to grand visions, innovative ideas, and bold strategies. But the truth is, no matter how strong your overall plan, even a single overlooked detail can derail everything. The formula "100 - 1 = 0" highlights this reality: all your effort, no matter how substantial, can be nullified by one critical error.

This principle has guided me throughout my entrepreneurial journey. I've learned that while it's essential to think big and act strategically, attention to detail is what separates success from failure. Whether it's a minor oversight in customer service or a small error in logistics, the smallest mistakes can have outsized consequences.

Why Details Matter

Details may seem insignificant in the moment, but they often form the foundation of trust, efficiency, and reputation. Customers and clients notice when small things go wrong, and those details can shape their perception of your entire business.

Take Toyota, for example. The company built its reputation on quality and reliability, but a series of recalls due to small manufacturing defects in the 2000s damaged its image. While Toyota's cars were still among the best in the world, those small errors highlighted how missing details could impact even the most successful companies.

In my shipping business, I learned this lesson the hard way. Early on, I overlooked a minor discrepancy in shipment labeling, which caused a delay in delivery. While the issue seemed trivial, it led to a frustrated client and additional costs and of cause a big loss for reputation and money. That experience taught me the importance of double-checking every step, no matter how minor it seemed.

Balancing the Big Picture with Small Details

Entrepreneurs often get caught up in the big picture, focusing on scaling their business or launching the next product. While this ambition is critical, it must be balanced with meticulous attention to execution. Small details are what make big ideas work.

Consider Apple's legendary focus on detail. From the intuitive design of its user interface to the packaging of its products, every element is carefully considered. Steve Jobs famously obsessed over even the unseen parts of a product, believing that excellence in details reflected the company's values. That attention to detail didn't just enhance Apple's products—it built customer loyalty and a reputation for innovation.

Avoiding "The One" That Brings It All Down

To avoid the "1" in the formula "100 - 1 = 0," you need systems that catch potential issues before they escalate. This includes:

1. **Checklists and Processes**: Standardizing workflows ensures consistency and reduces the likelihood of mistakes.

2. **Feedback Loops**: Regularly gathering input from customers and employees can help you identify small problems before they grow.

3. **Prioritization**: Not all details are equal. Focus on the ones that have the greatest impact on your customers, operations, and reputation.

In my shipping company, I implemented detailed checklists for every job, from quotation, packing, pickup, and delivery. This ensured that no step was missed, creating a smoother experience for clients and fewer complaints for my team.

The Cost of Ignoring Details

Overlooking details can lead to:

1. Lost customers: A single negative experience can erode trust and drive clients to competitors.

2. Increased costs: Fixing mistakes often costs more than preventing them.

3. Damaged reputation: In a world where reviews and word-of-mouth carry significant weight, even small errors can have big consequences.

One of my ventures involved a courier service. During a busy holiday season, a small scheduling error led to late deliveries for several customers. While we apologized and resolved the issue, the damage to our reputation lingered. That incident reinforced my commitment to detail-oriented processes.

Conclusion

The formula "100 - 1 = 0" is a powerful reminder that the success of your business depends on more than just vision and strategy—it hinges on execution. By paying close attention to details, you ensure that all the effort you put into your business isn't undermined by preventable mistakes. Remember, in entrepreneurship, there's no such thing as a "small" detail. Every detail matters, and it's your job to ensure they align with your larger goals

Align with Nature and Trends

In business, as in life, success often comes to those who align their actions with the natural flow of things. Just as nature follows predictable patterns—like the seasons changing or water flowing downhill—markets and industries evolve according to their own trends and dynamics. Entrepreneurs who understand and adapt to these forces are far more likely to succeed than those who resist or ignore them.

This principle has shaped many of my decisions. Whether it was transitioning from personal to commercial shipping in response to market demand or capitalizing on emerging trends in real estate, aligning my businesses with the natural laws of the market and global trends often made the difference between struggling and thriving.

The Laws of Nature in Business

Nature teaches us that going against the current requires immense energy and often leads to failure. Similarly, in business, trying to create demand where none exists or forcing outdated strategies into evolving markets can be futile or very difficult.

Consider Kodak's resistance to the digital photography trend. Despite inventing the digital camera, the company clung to its film business, going against the natural flow of technological advancement. The result was a dramatic decline in relevance and profitability. Had Kodak embraced the trend, it might have become a leader in digital imaging instead of a cautionary tale.

When I started my moving company, I noticed a growing demand for professional, customer-focused services in Vancouver. By aligning my business with this trend, I was able to grow rapidly and build a solid reputation. It wasn't about creating demand—it was about recognizing and meeting an existing one.

Why Trends Matter

Trends are powerful indicators of where markets and industries are heading. Ignoring them is like planting crops in the wrong season—your efforts won't yield results or a little. Following trends doesn't mean blindly copying others; it means understanding the direction the world is moving and positioning yourself to thrive within it.

For example, Tesla's rise is a testament to the power of trends. Elon Musk recognized the growing global interest in sustainable energy and electric vehicles long before they became mainstream. By aligning Tesla's mission with this trend, the company not only gained a competitive edge but also helped shape the future of the industry.

In my shipping business, I saw a shift from personal effects shipping to commercial logistics. Recognizing this trend early allowed me to pivot, focus on high-demand services, and reduce the operational headaches of dealing with individual customers. It wasn't about abandoning my initial model—it was about evolving with the market.

Aligning with Trends

To align your business with trends:

1. **Stay Informed**: Pay attention to market data, customer behavior, and industry innovations.

2. **Adapt Quickly**: Be willing to pivot your strategies as trends emerge or evolve.

3. **Think Long-Term**: Not all trends are worth following. Focus on those with lasting impact rather than fleeting fads.

For instance, when I noticed the growing importance of digital marketing, I shifted from relying solely on traditional methods to incorporating online advertising and social media strategies. This adaptation not only helped me reach more customers but also positioned my businesses for future growth.

The Danger of Fighting the Current

Trying to force a business against prevailing trends is not only exhausting but often unsustainable. Blockbuster's refusal to embrace the streaming trend, for example, allowed Netflix to dominate the market. Blockbuster's attempt to maintain its outdated model ultimately led to its downfall.

On a smaller scale, I experienced this lesson with my furniture store. By trying to sell both new and antique furniture, I confused customers and struggled to compete with businesses that specialized in one or the other. Had I aligned with the growing trend toward minimalism or focused exclusively on a niche, the outcome might have been different.

Conclusion

Following the laws of nature and going with the trend is about working smarter, not harder. It's about recognizing the flow of the market and positioning your business to thrive within it. By aligning your efforts with larger forces—whether they're customer demands, technological advancements, or cultural shifts—you set yourself up for success. Remember, it's not about resisting change—it's about embracing it and evolving with it

You are not done yet until Step 6 is

Finished

Starting a business is an achievement, but ensuring its sustained success requires ongoing attention and effort. Many entrepreneurs, after building a functional and profitable company, shift their focus too early, assuming the foundation they've laid is strong enough to carry the business forward. However, until your business is truly self-sustaining—with robust systems, leadership, and a clear growth trajectory—you're not done.

This lesson came to me firsthand with my moving company. After years of hard work, I brought on a manager to oversee daily operations, making him a shareholder while I retained the majority shares. Feeling confident in his capabilities, I shifted my focus to other ventures. However, the business began to struggle for various reasons. Challenges compounded, and the moving company entered a difficult period. This experience was a stark reminder that a business isn't truly finished until it can operate and thrive independently of your constant input.

The Dangers of Stepping Away Too Soon

Entrepreneurs often underestimate the time and effort required to transition a business from "owner-reliant" to "self-sustaining." Without proper systems and leadership in place, stepping away too soon can lead to instability.

Consider Howard Schultz's first departure from Starbucks in 2000. Although Schultz had built Starbucks into a coffee empire, the company lost its way in his absence, focusing too heavily on expansion at the expense of quality and customer experience. Schultz returned as CEO in 2008 to lead a turnaround, proving that even the most established businesses require ongoing oversight until their systems and leadership are strong enough to uphold the founder's vision.

Building a Business That Doesn't Need You

The ultimate goal of entrepreneurship is to create a business that doesn't rely on you for its survival. This means developing strong systems, empowering capable leaders, and ensuring the company's mission and values are deeply ingrained in its culture.

For my moving company, I realized too late that I hadn't invested enough in building these elements. While my manager was capable, the company lacked the operational robustness needed to adapt to challenges. I had assumed my presence was no longer necessary, but the business wasn't ready to stand on its own. Moreover, I failed to monitor it closely or implement necessary adjustments in a timely manner.

Lessons from Other Entrepreneurs

Famous entrepreneurs often emphasize the importance of staying engaged until their businesses are truly self-sustaining:

1. **Steve Jobs**: After being ousted from Apple in 1985, Jobs watched as the company he co-founded lost its innovative edge and struggled financially. When he returned in 1997, he rebuilt Apple's culture and systems, ensuring its long-term success. Apple's resilience today is a testament to the systems Jobs put in place during his second tenure.

2. **Reed Hastings**: The Netflix founder remained actively involved as the company transitioned from DVD rentals to streaming. Hastings didn't step back until Netflix had firmly established itself as a leader in the streaming industry, with a robust infrastructure and a clear path forward.

Signs That You're Not Done Yet

To determine whether your business is ready for you to step away, consider these questions:

1. Are there systems in place to handle daily operations without your input?

2. Is leadership strong and aligned with the company's mission and goals?

3. Can the business adapt to challenges and changes without your direct involvement?

If the answer to any of these questions is "no," your work isn't done yet. Stepping back prematurely can undo years of hard work and put your business at risk.

Conclusion

"You are not done until it's done" is a reminder that building a business doesn't stop at profitability or hiring a capable team. It stops when the business can sustain itself, grow, and thrive independently. By staying engaged until your business reaches that stage, you ensure that your hard work isn't undone by avoidable challenges. As entrepreneurs, our job is to finish what we start—not just for ourselves, but for our employees, customers, and stakeholders who rely on the vision we set in motion

Your North Star: Mission, Values, and Principles

Every successful business needs a clear direction. Mission, values, and principles serve as your North Star, guiding your decisions, actions, and growth. They provide clarity, inspire your team, and communicate your purpose to customers. Without these foundational elements, even the best business plans can lose focus and momentum.

When I started my shipping business, I didn't fully understand the importance of these guiding concepts. But as the company grew, I realized that having a clear mission and values wasn't just a formality—it was essential for building trust with customers and consistency in operations. These elements became the bedrock of my business.

Mission: Why Does Your Business Exist?

Your mission is your purpose. It's the reason your business exists beyond just making money. A strong mission statement captures your goals, the problem you're solving, and the value you bring to the world.

Take Tesla, for example. Its mission, "to accelerate the world's transition to sustainable energy," goes beyond selling cars. It defines the company's broader impact and motivates employees, investors, and customers to rally behind its vision.

Key Question: Why does your business exist, and what impact do you want to make?

Values: How Do You Operate?

Your values define how your business operates. They reflect what you stand for and guide your behavior, both internally and externally. Values shape your company culture and ensure consistency across every interaction.

Apple's commitment to innovation is a cornerstone of its values. This focus drives product development, marketing, and customer experience. It's why Apple products are associated with creativity and quality across the globe.

Key Question: What values will shape the way your business operates?

Principles: What Do You Believe In?

Your principles are the non-negotiable beliefs that guide your business decisions. They're the ethical and operational standards that define your approach and set the tone for your team.

Jeff Bezos famously built Amazon around principles like customer obsession and long-term thinking. These guiding beliefs have driven Amazon's success, from its relentless focus on improving customer experience to its willingness to invest in innovations like AWS and Prime.

Key Question: What principles will you never compromise on, no matter the circumstances?

Aligning Mission, Values, and Principles

Mission, values, and principles aren't standalone elements—they work together to guide your business. Your mission provides direction, your values define how you'll get there, and your principles ensure integrity along the way. Together, they form the foundation of a resilient, purpose-driven business.

Conclusion

Your North Star—your mission, values, and principles—is more than just a statement on your website. It's the heart of your business, shaping every decision and action. By defining these elements clearly and living by them, you not only build a strong, consistent company but also inspire trust and loyalty among your team and customers

Why Are Most Startup Businesses Failed?

Starting a business is one of the most exciting and challenging endeavours an entrepreneur can undertake. Yet, the harsh reality is that most startups fail. According to research from the U.S. Bureau of Labor Statistics, a fifth of startups fail within their first year, and up to 65% of startups will fail within 10 years of opening for businesses. (Data source: https://www.forbes.com/advisor/business/software/startups-failure-rate/)

These statistics might seem discouraging, but they also offer valuable lessons. Understanding why startups fail is the first step toward avoiding common pitfalls and setting your business up for success.

The Top Reasons for Startup Failure

1. **Lack of Market Need (35%)**

   One of the most cited reasons for startup failure is launching a product or service that doesn't address a real problem. According to a study by CB Insights, 35% of startups fail because there's no market demand for their offering. Entrepreneurs often fall in love with their ideas without validating whether customers actually need them.
   A famous example is Juicero, a high-tech juicer that raised over $100 million in funding but failed because consumers didn't see the value in an expensive juicing machine when

they could achieve the same results with their hands. The lack of market need was its undoing.

If you follow the 3 times creation method, you won't be easily one of the 35% of the failed starters.

2. Running Out of Cash (38%)

Another major cause of failure is financial mismanagement. CB Insights also notes that 38% of startups run out of funding before they achieve profitability. Poor budgeting, overestimating revenues, or underestimating expenses can quickly drain resources.
When I started my furniture store, I faced this challenge firsthand. Thin profit margins combined with high operational costs made it difficult to sustain the business. Learning to manage finances strategically is crucial for survival.

3. Poor Team and Leadership (23%)

About 23% of startups fail due to team-related issues, including lack of experience, poor management, or internal conflicts. Building the right team and fostering effective leadership are essential for overcoming challenges and maintaining focus.
Consider the example of Theranos. While the company initially garnered attention for its bold claims, internal mismanagement and a lack of technical expertise eventually led to its collapse. A capable, transparent team might have steered the business differently.

4. Failure to Adapt (19%)

Startups that cannot pivot in response to changing market conditions often find themselves irrelevant. About 19% fail because they stick rigidly to their original plan, even when it's clear adjustments are needed.

Blockbuster is a prime example. Despite having the opportunity to partner with Netflix, it clung to its outdated rental model, unable to adapt to the emerging trend of streaming. This inflexibility ultimately led to its demise.

What These Numbers Mean for Entrepreneurs

The statistics aren't just numbers—they're warnings and opportunities. They highlight areas where entrepreneurs can focus their attention:

1. Validate your idea before launching. Is there a genuine need for your product or service?

2. Manage your finances carefully. Do you have a budget and a plan to sustain cash flow during tough times?

3. Build a strong, adaptable team. Are you surrounding yourself with the right people who share your vision and bring complementary skills?

4. Stay flexible. Are you willing to pivot if the market demands it?

Learning from Failure

While failure rates are high, they don't mean you shouldn't try. Many successful entrepreneurs have experienced failure before achieving their breakthroughs. For example, Elon Musk's first ventures, including an early online directory, didn't succeed. However, those experiences laid the groundwork for his later successes with PayPal, Tesla, and SpaceX.

In my own journey, early failures taught me invaluable lessons about focus, strategy, and perseverance. My first businesses, like selling computer parts in college, didn't scale. But each setback helped refine my approach and align my efforts with long-term success.

Conclusion

Most startups fail because they overlook fundamentals: market demand, financial management, team building, and adaptability. By understanding these challenges and preparing for them, you can significantly improve your odds of success. Remember, failure is not the end—it's an opportunity to learn, adapt, and come back stronger.

Marketing Any Time Any Where

Marketing is the lifeblood of any business. It's not just about promoting products or services—it's about building relationships, creating awareness, and delivering value to your audience. In today's fast-paced, interconnected world, marketing isn't confined to a specific time or place. Successful entrepreneurs know that opportunities to market exist everywhere, and leveraging those opportunities effectively can make all the difference.

When I started my moving company, my marketing efforts were simple yet consistent. I made sure to talk about my business in every relevant conversation, placed ads in local newspapers, and ensured that my truck, with its branding, was always visible in high-traffic areas. These small, everyday actions created a steady stream of awareness that built my customer base.

Why Marketing is Everywhere

Marketing doesn't always look like a billboard or a social media ad. It happens in every interaction you have with potential customers, partners, or even competitors. It's about how you present your business, communicate your value, and leave an impression.

Take Starbucks as an example. Their stores are not just places to buy coffee—they're immersive marketing tools. The atmosphere, product presentation, and even the way your name is written on the cup all contribute to reinforcing the brand. Every customer interaction becomes a marketing moment.

Similarly, when I launched my shipping business, my marketing started long before I invested in formal campaigns. I added a simple line to my moving company ads: "Shipping from Vancouver to Canada, USA, Asia, and Europe." That minor change cost nothing but served as a powerful tool to attract new customers.

Marketing Doesn't Wait

Entrepreneurs often make the mistake of postponing marketing efforts until they feel "ready." They wait for a perfect website, a polished product, or a bigger budget. But the truth is, marketing doesn't wait—and neither should you. Starting small and being consistent are far more effective than waiting for the perfect moment.

Reid Hoffman, the founder of LinkedIn, famously said, "If you are not embarrassed by the first version of your product, you've launched too late." The same applies to marketing. Begin where you are and let real-world feedback refine your approach. Marketing doesn't have to be grand; it just has to be effective.

Leveraging Every Moment

To make marketing a constant part of your business, consider these strategies:

1. **Be Present**: Whether online or offline, ensure your business is visible. Engage on social media, attend events, and participate in community activities.

2. **Think Beyond Ads**: Marketing happens through customer service, word of mouth, emails, t-shirts, your own car, and even the way you package your product.

3. **Capitalize on Everyday Interactions**: Talk about your business when the opportunity arises. Every conversation is a chance to market.

When I ran my moving company, my truck wasn't just a means of transportation—it was a moving billboard. By strategically parking it in high-visibility locations, I generated inquiries and reinforced my brand without incurring additional costs. Later, when I started my real estate agent business, I added my name and headshot to the sides and back doors of all my trucks. This approach made my real estate business stand out immediately, attracting attention and boosting recognition.

The Digital Advantage

Today, digital platforms have revolutionized marketing, allowing businesses to reach audiences anytime, anywhere. Social media, email campaigns, and online marketplaces have made it easier than ever to connect with customers.

Take the example of Gary Vaynerchuk, who turned his family's liquor store into a multi-million-dollar business by leveraging YouTube to host wine-tasting videos. His innovative use of digital platforms not only grew his customer base but also positioned him as a thought leader in the industry.

Even with limited budgets, tools like social media ads, content marketing, and SEO can make your business visible to a global audience. The key is to start and adapt as you grow.

Conclusion

Marketing isn't confined to a time or place—it's a constant, dynamic process that thrives on authenticity and consistency. Every interaction, online or offline, is an opportunity to showcase your business and build connections. By embracing marketing as an everyday practice, you set your business on a path to growth and recognition. Remember, the best time to market is now, and the best place to market is wherever you are

The Most Important Person: Yourself

In the whirlwind of starting and running a business, it's easy to forget one crucial fact: you are the most important person in your company. Your vision, decisions, and energy drive the business forward, and if you're not at your best, everything else suffers. Taking care of yourself isn't just a personal responsibility—it's a business strategy.

When I was deep in the trenches of managing multiple ventures, I often neglected my health, working long hours and pushing myself to the limit. Over time, I realized that no matter how ambitious my goals were, I couldn't achieve them if I wasn't mentally and physically fit. That's when I started treating myself as the most valuable asset in my business.

Physical Health: Your Foundation

Running a business demands energy, focus, and stamina—all of which come from maintaining your physical health. Prioritize regular exercise, a balanced diet, and sufficient sleep.

1. **Exercise**: Regular physical activity doesn't just keep you fit; it also boosts your mood and sharpens your mind. Even a short daily workout can help you manage stress and increase productivity.
   Richard Branson, the founder of Virgin Group, credits his success in part to staying active. He's a strong advocate for exercise, saying it gives him four extra hours of productive work each day.

2. **Healthy Eating**: Fueling your body with nutritious food ensures you have the energy to tackle challenges. Avoid relying on junk food or excessive caffeine, which can lead to energy crashes.

3. **Rest and Sleep**: A tired mind makes poor decisions. Prioritize getting enough sleep to recharge and maintain clarity. Elon Musk, despite his busy schedule, has spoken about the importance of getting at least six hours of sleep to function effectively.

Mental Health: Your Stability

Your mental health is just as important as your physical well-being. Building a business is stressful, and without proper care, it's easy to feel overwhelmed or burnt out. Make mental wellness a priority:

1. **Practice mindfulness**: Techniques like meditation or journaling can help you stay focused and reduce stress.

2. **Set boundaries**: Learn to say no when necessary and carve out time for yourself and your loved ones.

3. **Seek support**: Don't hesitate to talk to a mentor, coach, or therapist when you need guidance or reassurance.

When I felt overwhelmed with managing businesses, taking a step back and reflecting on my goals helped me regain perspective. A clear mind is essential for making sound decisions and sustaining long-term success.

Continuously Invest in Yourself

You are your company's most valuable asset, so treat yourself as such by investing in personal growth:

1. **Learn new skills**: Stay updated with industry trends and tools to maintain your competitive edge.

2. **Expand your network**: Surround yourself with people who inspire and challenge you.

3. **Take breaks**: Stepping away from work can often lead to breakthroughs. Many entrepreneurs find their best ideas come when they're not actively working.

Conclusion

As an entrepreneur, you are the heart of your business. Prioritizing your health and well-being isn't a luxury—it's a necessity. By staying physically active, mentally balanced, and continuously growing, you ensure that you're in the best possible position to lead your business to success. Remember, the most important person in your company is you. Take care of yourself, because your success—and the success of your business—depends on it.

Anything Is Possible vs Make a Real Action

The phrase "Anything is possible" is a powerful mindset that inspires innovation, fuels ambition, and sparks the courage to explore uncharted territories. It encourages us to see opportunities where others see obstacles and to believe in the potential to achieve the extraordinary. However, while this mindset is essential for entrepreneurship and growth, it's not a call to reckless action. Instead, it's a foundation for problem-solving, finding solutions, and expanding the boundaries of what we believe can be achieved.

The Power of Believing That Anything Is Possible

Believing that anything is possible opens your mind to opportunities you might otherwise dismiss. It helps you approach challenges with curiosity rather than defeat and pushes you to find creative solutions to problems. When I first considered entering the shipping and freight-forwarding business, many would have called it impossible for someone with no prior experience in logistics. However, adopting the mindset that "anything is possible" gave me the confidence to learn, adapt, and eventually succeed in an industry where I initially had no footing.

Similarly, great innovators like Elon Musk have demonstrated how this mindset can lead to transformative achievements. From reimagining space travel with SpaceX to accelerating the shift to sustainable energy with Tesla, Musk's ability to believe in the impossible has driven breakthroughs that seemed unthinkable just a decade ago.

The Caveat: Possibility Doesn't Equal Immediate Action

While embracing the belief that anything is possible is critical, it's equally important to recognize that this mindset alone isn't enough. Possibility must be paired with planning, strategy, and incremental steps to transform vision into reality. Taking action without preparation often leads to wasted resources, unnecessary risks, and even failure.

Let's consider an audacious question: Is it possible to create a company that can beat Google? The answer is yes—anything is possible. But does that mean you should immediately start building a tech company with the goal of toppling one of the largest corporations in the world? Certainly not. Success requires more than ambition; it requires a process.

Aligning the "Anything Is Possible" Mindset with the Three Creations

To turn the "anything is possible" mindset into tangible results, you must follow a structured approach, such as the Three Creations:

1. **Plan: Mental Creation**: Begin by envisioning your idea clearly. What is the problem you want to solve? What does success look like? For instance, before challenging Google, you might identify a niche where its services are lacking or imagine a new way to improve search engines.

2. **Reconfirm: Validation:** Test your idea before making significant commitments. Validate whether your concept resonates with potential customers or solves a genuine problem. Maybe you start by developing a prototype of a search tool that excels in a specific area, like privacy or personalization, and gather feedback.

3. **Ignite: Physical Execution**: Only after validating your idea and refining it based on real-world insights should you take larger steps to build and scale your vision. At this stage, you're not just chasing an impossible dream—you're executing a well-thought-out plan.

A Balanced Mindset

The "anything is possible" mindset is a starting point, not a destination. It motivates you to dream big and think beyond conventional limits. But true success lies in pairing this mindset with disciplined action, deliberate planning, and a willingness to follow the process.

Possibility isn't about diving in headfirst—it's about taking that first step in the right direction, building momentum, and creating a foundation for sustainable growth. By following the three creations, you ensure that your actions are as powerful as your vision, turning the impossible into achievable reality.

CHAPTER 2: WHAT ARE YOU REALLY GOING TO SELL?

The essence of any business lies in what it offers to the world. Whether it's a product, service, or solution, your business's success depends on its ability to provide value. Chapter 2 delves into the heart of this concept: identifying and refining what you're going to sell. This chapter isn't just about the "what" but also the "why" and "how" behind your offering.

Every entrepreneur faces this fundamental question early in their journey. For me, it was a learning process across various businesses —from selling computer parts in college to managing a moving company and eventually transitioning into shipping. Each venture taught me that what you sell must resonate with your market, align with your capabilities, and be scalable.

This chapter is about more than just picking a product or service— it's about understanding its role in your business model, identifying the problem it solves, and ensuring it's something people genuinely want and need. It's also about balancing ambition with practicality. You can dream big, but your offering must be realistic and executable within your resources.

Why This Chapter Matters

Defining what you're going to sell is the cornerstone of your business strategy. It sets the direction for everything else, from marketing and operations to pricing and scaling. A clear and compelling offering builds confidence—not just for you, but for your customers, team, and stakeholders.

Take Airbnb, for example. Its founders didn't start with the goal of creating a global platform for short-term rentals. Instead, they focused on solving a specific problem—helping attendees of a conference find affordable accommodations. By starting with a clear and focused offering, they were able to test their idea, refine it, and eventually scale it into a multi-billion-dollar business.

What This Chapter Covers

This chapter will help you:

1. Understand the problem you're solving and how your offering addresses it.

2. Define the core of your business—whether it's a product, service, or a combination of both.

3. Explore the potential of your offering, including profit sources, scalability, and market fit.

4. Navigate practical considerations like licenses, permits, and industry-specific requirements.

Throughout this chapter, I'll share lessons from my own journey as well as insights from famous companies and entrepreneurs. Whether you're selling a physical product, a digital service, or something entirely unique, this chapter will provide the tools to clarify and refine your offering.

Conclusion

Knowing what you're going to sell is more than just deciding on a product or service—it's about creating something that aligns with your vision, solves a genuine problem, and adds value to your market. By the end of this chapter, you'll have a clear understanding of how to define and position your offering as the foundation of your business's success.

What's the Problem and What's Your Solution?

At the heart of every successful business is a simple equation: problem and solution. Customers buy products and services not because they're flashy or exciting, but because they solve real problems. As the saying goes,

"NO ONE WANTS A DRILL. WHAT THEY WANT IS THE HOLE."

Identifying the problem your business aims to solve and designing a solution that resonates with your audience is the foundation for achieving long-term success. Perhaps your product or service doesn't solve any practical issues but instead caters to customers' desire to show off or feel cool. Even in such cases, it fulfills a genuine need for status or vanity.

This concept is more complex than it appears. If you can grasp this deeper meaning, you'll rethink the true value of all businesses. For example, what do luxury handbags sell? What do ordinary restaurants sell? What do high-end restaurants sell? And what do taxis sell? What did Kodak film sell?

Taxis sell a convenient travel solution for customers. That's precisely why they were quickly replaced by ride-hailing services. Kodak film sold people their cherished memories, but it was soon overtaken by digital cameras and even smartphones. Luxury handbags sell a sense of superiority to the wealthy. That's why certain brands would rather destroy excess inventory than offer discounts.

Many entrepreneurs, myself included, start with an idea we're passionate about. But passion alone isn't enough. The real question is: does your idea solve a meaningful problem for your target market? When I launched my shipping company, it wasn't just about moving goods from point A to point B—it was about providing a cost-effective, reliable service that filled a gap in the logistics market. Recognizing that gap was the key to our growth.

Start with the Problem

Before you develop your product or service, you need to clearly understand the problem it solves. Start by asking:

1. Who are your customers?

2. What challenges or pain points do they face?

3. Why hasn't this problem been solved effectively before?

Consider Uber. The problem was clear: traditional taxis were inconvenient, often unreliable, and limited in availability. Customers wanted an easier, faster way to get around. By addressing these pain points, Uber revolutionized transportation and created a solution that was simple and scalable.

For my moving company, the problem was similar: customers were frustrated with unreliable movers who damaged their belongings or failed to show up on time. By focusing on professionalism and customer care, I positioned my business as a trustworthy alternative, solving a common frustration in the market.

Define Your Solution

Once you've identified the problem, the next step is crafting a solution that stands out. Your solution should be:

1. **Practical**: Can it realistically solve the problem within your available resources?

2. **Scalable**: Will it continue to work effectively as your business grows?

3. **Affordable**: Is it priced in a way that is accessible to your target customers while still ensuring profitability?

4. **Unique**: What differentiates your solution from competitors, making it the preferred choice?

Let's look at Spanx, founded by Sara Blakely. The problem was simple: women wanted comfortable shapewear that didn't roll down or feel restrictive. Her solution—innovative, seamless undergarments—was practical, unique, and designed to scale. Spanx didn't just fill a gap; it created a whole new market.

In my shipping business, I refined the solution through testing. I started with small shipments to ensure my processes were efficient and reliable. As I gained experience, I scaled the solution to serve larger, commercial clients. This iterative approach allowed me to address problems effectively while staying within my resources.

Aligning Problem and Solution

The alignment between the problem and your solution is crucial. A mismatch—like creating a complex product for a simple issue or an over-engineered solution for a niche problem—can lead to failure. Always validate your solution with your target market to ensure it resonates.

Dropbox, for instance, solved a universal problem: people needed a simple way to access their files from anywhere. Their initial offering was straightforward—cloud storage with easy syncing. The simplicity of their solution was its strength, aligning perfectly with the problem users faced.

Conclusion

Understanding the problem you're solving and crafting the right solution isn't just the starting point—it's the cornerstone of your business. Focus on deeply understanding your customers' pain points and building a solution that is practical, scalable, and unique. When your business becomes the answer to a pressing problem, success will follow

What Are You Selling, Product or Service?

Every business begins with a core offering—something you sell to create value for your customers. But in today's entrepreneurial landscape, the line between products and services is increasingly blurred. A product can be packaged as a service, and a service can be transformed into a product. Understanding this flexibility not only broadens your business opportunities but also opens the door to innovative ways of reaching and serving your market.

Blurring the Lines: Products as Services

One way to innovate is to package products as ongoing services. This approach can create consistent revenue streams and foster deeper customer loyalty.

For instance, coffee shops often sell coffee by the cup, but what if they sold memberships instead? A membership model could provide customers with unlimited coffee for a monthly fee, turning a product-based business into a service-based one. Not only does this model encourage repeat visits, but it also guarantees predictable income.

Another example is subscription boxes. Companies like Dollar Shave Club and Blue Apron have taken traditional products—razors and meal ingredients—and turned them into subscription-based services. Customers receive curated, regular deliveries, enhancing convenience and creating a unique value proposition.

Transforming Services into Products

Services can also be repackaged into tangible products, expanding their accessibility and scalability. For example, a consulting firm might traditionally offer one-on-one advice. By writing a book, creating a training video, or offering an online course, they can transform their expertise into a product that reaches a broader audience with minimal additional effort.

Consider Tony Robbins, the renowned motivational speaker. While he offers live events and coaching sessions, much of his knowledge is also accessible through books, video courses, and audio programs. By transforming his services into products, Robbins extends his reach to millions of people who may never attend an event in person.

Subscription Models: A Hybrid Approach

Another innovative approach is combining products and services through subscription models. This allows businesses to offer both tangible goods and value-added services under a recurring payment structure. For example:

1. A beauty company might provide skincare products along with personalized advice from a dermatologist.

2. A fitness brand could offer workout equipment paired with an app that provides daily exercise routines.

These models not only diversify income streams but also create long-term relationships with customers.

What's Right for Your Business?

The choice between product and service—or a blend of both—depends on your market, resources, and business goals. As you consider your options, think about:

1. **Customer Needs**: Do your customers prioritize convenience, expertise, or physical ownership?

2. **Scalability**: Can your offering grow with your business?

3. **Revenue Potential**: What pricing structure makes sense for your target audience?

Looking Ahead

This discussion of products and services is just the beginning. Later, we'll explore more business models that illustrate how to structure and monetize your offering effectively. From memberships to marketplaces, these models will give you practical insights to expand and refine your business approach.

Conclusion

Whether you're selling a product, a service, or a mix of both, the key is to focus on creating value for your customers. By thinking creatively and leveraging innovative packaging strategies, you can transform your core offering into something that stands out in the marketplace. Remember, the boundaries between products and services are flexible—use this to your advantage.

Where does your profit come from?

Profit is the lifeblood of any business, but it doesn't always come from where you might expect. A business's revenue streams and profit drivers can be surprisingly different, and understanding this distinction is crucial for long-term success. Knowing where your profit comes from allows you to focus your resources strategically and make decisions that enhance profitability.

Beyond the Obvious: Hidden Profit Drivers

Many businesses generate revenue from one source but rely on another for profitability. Take the printer industry as an example. While printers themselves are often sold at or near cost, the real profit comes from ink cartridges. This model ensures customers return repeatedly to buy consumables, creating a steady and lucrative revenue stream.

Similarly, McDonald's doesn't rely heavily on coffee or ice cream to drive profits. While these items add to the menu's appeal, the real profit comes from their burgers and value meals. These high-margin items are designed to maximize earnings while keeping costs low.

Costco: The Membership Model

Costco is a masterclass in understanding profit drivers. While its hotdogs and other products are sold at razor-thin margins—or even at a loss—the company's real profits come from its membership fees. By offering unbeatable deals, Costco attracts loyal customers who renew their memberships year after year, ensuring a consistent and predictable profit stream.

This approach highlights the importance of thinking beyond individual transactions and focusing on the bigger picture. What seems like a low-margin business on the surface can be highly profitable when supported by complementary revenue streams.

Finding Your Profit Drivers

To identify where your profit comes from, start by analyzing your business model and customer behavior:

1. **Primary vs. Secondary Revenue**: Determine if your primary product or service is the actual profit driver or if secondary items or services contribute more to the bottom line.

2. **Customer Lifetime Value**: Consider not just the immediate sale but the long-term value of each customer. Are there opportunities for repeat business or upselling?

3. **Cost Structure**: Evaluate the margins on each product or service. High-volume, low-margin items can support profitability when paired with high-margin offerings.

Examples of Unconventional Profit Models

1. **Razor-and-Blade Model**: Similar to printers and ink, razor companies like Gillette sell razors cheaply while profiting heavily from replacement blades.

2. **Freemium to Premium**: Companies like Spotify and Dropbox offer free versions of their services, but their profits come from converting users to paid premium plans.

3. **Ecosystem Lock-In**: Apple generates significant revenue from its hardware, but its ecosystem of apps, accessories, and subscriptions drives long-term profitability.

Conclusion

Understanding where your profit comes from is essential for building a sustainable business. Sometimes, the products or services you think are your primary revenue sources are actually supporting another, more lucrative part of your business. By identifying and focusing on your true profit drivers, you can optimize your strategy, maximize earnings, and ensure long-term success.

What's Your Business Model?

A business model is the blueprint for how your company creates, delivers, and captures value. It defines not only how you generate revenue but also how you sustain profitability and provide value to your customers. While many entrepreneurs are familiar with basic models like selling products or services, there's a wide range of innovative options to consider.

Here's an expanded list of business models, blending traditional approaches with modern strategies. By exploring these, you'll gain clarity on how your business operates and uncover opportunities to refine or diversify your revenue streams.

1. Subscription Model

   A. **Description**: Customers pay a recurring fee to access a product or service.

   B. **Examples**: Netflix, Spotify, Adobe Creative Cloud.

   C. **Why It Works**: Predictable revenue streams and increased customer retention.

   D. **Considerations**: How can you provide consistent value to keep subscribers engaged?

2. Freemium Model

A. **Description**: Basic services are free, but premium features are charged.

B. **Examples**: Dropbox, Zoom, LinkedIn.

C. **Why It Works**: Attracts a large user base and converts a percentage into paying customers.

D. **Considerations**: What premium features will entice free users to upgrade?

3. Razor-and-Blade Model

A. **Description**: A primary product is sold at a low price (or given away) to drive sales of complementary, high-margin products.

B. **Examples**: Gillette (razors and blades), HP (printers and ink).

C. **Why It Works**: Creates long-term customer dependency on consumables.

D. **Considerations**: What complementary products can create consistent revenue?

4. Franchise Model

A. **Description**: Businesses license their brand and operations to franchisees.

B. **Examples**: McDonald's, Subway, Dunkin' Donuts.

C. **Why It Works**: Allows for rapid expansion with lower capital investment.

D. **Considerations**: Can your business be replicated while maintaining quality?

5. Licensing Model

A. **Description**: Grants other businesses the right to use your intellectual property for a fee or royalty.

B. **Examples**: Microsoft (software licensing), Disney (merchandising).

C. **Why It Works**: Generates recurring revenue with minimal additional effort.

D. **Considerations**: Is your intellectual property valuable and scalable?

6. Marketplace Model

A. **Description**: Connects buyers and sellers, earning revenue through transaction fees, commissions, or subscriptions.

B. **Examples**: Amazon, Etsy, Airbnb.

C. **Why It Works**: Low inventory risk and scalable across markets.

D. **Considerations**: How will you attract and balance supply and demand?

7. Aggregator Model

A. **Description**: Aggregates goods or services under one brand and connects providers directly to customers.

B. **Examples**: Uber, Zomato, TripAdvisor.

C. **Why It Works**: Simplifies user experience and scales efficiently.

D. **Considerations**: How can you maintain quality and consistency across providers?

8. Direct-to-Consumer (DTC) Model

A. **Description**: Sells products directly to consumers, bypassing intermediaries.

B. **Examples**: Warby Parker, Allbirds, Glossier.

C. **Why It Works**: Greater control over branding, pricing, and customer relationships.

D. **Considerations**: How will you build direct connections with your audience?

9. Pay-As-You-Go Model

A. **Description**: Customers pay only for what they use, such as metered services.

B. **Examples**: AWS (cloud computing), electricity providers.

C. **Why It Works**: Appeals to cost-conscious customers by eliminating upfront costs.

D. **Considerations**: How can you scale pricing without overcomplicating billing?

10. Affiliate Marketing Model

A. **Description**: Earns revenue by promoting third-party products and earning a commission for sales.

B. **Examples**: Amazon Affiliates, bloggers, influencers.

C. **Why It Works**: Minimal overhead and scalability.

D. **Considerations**: How will you build trust with your audience to drive conversions?

11. Data Monetization Model

A. **Description**: Generates revenue by collecting and selling data or leveraging it to improve other services.

B. **Examples**: Google, Facebook.

C. **Why It Works**: Capitalizes on user-generated data to create additional value streams.

D. **Considerations**: Are you transparent and ethical in data usage?

12. Product-as-a-Service Model

A. **Description**: Customers pay for access to a product instead of owning it.

B. **Examples**: Zipcar, Rent the Runway.

C. **Why It Works**: Reduces barriers to entry for customers and creates recurring revenue.

D. **Considerations**: Can you ensure seamless access and maintenance?

13. Crowdsourcing Model

A. **Description**: Engages a large group of people to contribute resources, content, or funding.

B. **Examples**: Kickstarter, Wikipedia.

C. **Why It Works**: Harnesses collective power for low-cost innovation or funding.

D. **Considerations**: How will you motivate and manage contributors?

14. Ad-Supported Model

A. **Description**: Provides free or low-cost products/services while generating revenue from advertisements.

B. **Examples**: Google Search, YouTube, free mobile apps.

C. **Why It Works**: Monetizes a large audience effectively.

D. **Considerations**: How will you balance user experience with ad revenue?

15. Ecosystem Model

A. **Description**: Creates a network of interconnected products or services that lock customers into the ecosystem.

B. **Examples**: Apple (hardware + App Store), Amazon (Prime + Marketplace).

C. **Why It Works**: Increases customer loyalty and lifetime value.

D. **Considerations**: Can you integrate multiple offerings seamlessly?

Finding Your Model

To identify your business model:

A. Assess your product/service and customer needs.

B. Consider how to deliver value consistently.

C. Align your revenue streams with your vision and capabilities.

Conclusion

Choosing the right business model is a mix of understanding your strengths, customer demands, and market dynamics. Whether you adopt a traditional model or innovate with a hybrid approach, the key is to ensure it aligns with your goals and can adapt as your business evolves. Let these models inspire you to define and refine your own path to profitability.

Do you need license or permit to sell?

Starting a business is exciting, but before you can legally operate, it's essential to ensure you have the proper licenses and permits. These requirements vary widely depending on your industry, location, and the type of product or service you're offering. Failing to obtain the necessary permissions can result in fines, closures, or even legal action—so it's critical to address this step early in your journey..

Understanding Licenses and Permits

A license grants you the legal right to operate your business, while a permit allows you to engage in specific activities. Depending on what you're selling, you may need one or both. Key considerations include:

1. **Business Location**: Local governments often require businesses to obtain general operating licenses, even for home-based businesses.

2. **Industry Requirements**: Certain industries, such as food, transportation, and healthcare, are highly regulated and require specific certifications or permits.

3. **Product-Specific Rules**: Selling alcohol, firearms, or hazardous materials usually involves stricter licensing procedures.

For example, opening a coffee shop typically requires a business license, a health permit, and potentially a food handler's certificate. Meanwhile, starting an online store selling handmade goods might only require a general business license, depending on your location.

Steps to Determine Your Requirements

To identify the licenses and permits your business needs:

1. **Research Local Regulations**: Check with your city, county, and state authorities. Many government websites have resources for small businesses outlining licensing requirements.

2. **Understand Industry Standards**: Some industries, like finance or construction, have national or state-level licensing boards.

3. **Consult Professionals**: An attorney or business consultant can help ensure you meet all legal requirements.

Take Amazon, for example. When Jeff Bezos started the company as an online bookseller, he ensured compliance with e-commerce regulations, including sales tax collection and intellectual property laws. This groundwork allowed Amazon to scale without regulatory setbacks.

Common Licenses and Permits

While requirements vary, here are some common types of licenses and permits:

1. **General Business License**: Required by most cities or counties for operating a business.

2. **Health and Safety Permits**: Necessary for food-related businesses to ensure compliance with hygiene standards.

3. **Sales Tax Permit**: Allows you to collect sales tax on goods or services.

4. **Professional Licenses**: Required for fields like law, accounting, and real estate.

5. **Signage Permits**: For businesses that display signs or banners in public spaces.

What Happens Without Proper Licenses?

Operating without the necessary licenses or permits can lead to:

1. **Fines and Penalties**: Local authorities can impose financial penalties for noncompliance.

2. **Closure**: Your business might be shut down temporarily or permanently.

3. **Legal Action**: In severe cases, you could face lawsuits or criminal charges.

Imagine a restaurant opening without a health permit. Even if the food is excellent, authorities can shut it down immediately, causing financial loss and reputational damage.

Conclusion

Licenses and permits may not be the most exciting part of starting a business, but they are among the most important. By ensuring compliance from the beginning, you protect your business from legal risks and set the stage for smooth operations. Take the time to research and secure the necessary permissions—it's a small investment that can save you from significant trouble down the line

CHAPTER 3: WHO'S BUYING? UNDERSTANDING YOUR MARKET

Every business exists to serve its customers. No matter how innovative your product or service is, its success depends on your ability to identify, understand, and connect with the people who need it. Chapter 3 delves into this fundamental question: Who is your customer?

When I started my moving company, I assumed my customers were simply "anyone who needed a mover." Over time, I realized how crucial it was to narrow down that broad audience into specific groups—whether it was families relocating across town or students moving on a tight budget. This focus allowed me to tailor my services, improve marketing efforts, and build stronger customer relationships.

This chapter isn't just about identifying your target audience; it's about understanding their behaviors, needs, and motivations. By knowing your customers deeply, you can create better solutions, communicate effectively, and ultimately, build a loyal customer base.

Why This Chapter Matters

Many startups fail because they don't fully understand their customers. They create products or services without validating whether they solve a real problem or meet a genuine need. Knowing your customer is the first step in creating value that resonates, and it influences everything from product development to marketing and sales strategies.

Take Airbnb, for example. Its founders initially targeted conference attendees looking for affordable lodging. By focusing on this niche, they built a strong foundation that later allowed them to expand to a broader audience. Their success came from knowing exactly who they were serving at the start.

What This Chapter Covers

In this chapter, we'll explore:

1. **Identifying Your Customer**: How to define and refine your target audience.

2. **Understanding Competitors**: Why analyzing your competition helps you understand your customers better.

3. **Customer Motivation**: What drives customers to choose your business over others?

4. **Finding Your Customers**: The channels and strategies to connect with your audience.

We'll also share actionable strategies for gathering customer insights, including surveys, interviews, and data analysis. By the end of this chapter, you'll have a clear picture of who your ideal customers are and how to reach them effectively.

Conclusion

Your customers are the lifeline of your business. Identifying and understanding them is not just an exercise—it's the foundation of everything you'll build. This chapter will equip you with the tools to define your audience, understand their needs, and position your business as the perfect solution. Remember, knowing your customer is not a one-time task; it's a continuous process that evolves as your business grows

Understanding Your Ideal Customer

Every successful business is built on a deep understanding of its customers. Knowing who your customers are goes beyond identifying the people who might buy your product or service—it's about understanding their needs, behaviors, and motivations. Without this clarity, even the most innovative ideas can fall flat.

Take Starbucks as an example. Initially, Starbucks wasn't just targeting coffee drinkers; it was targeting a specific experience. Their ideal customer was someone who valued a premium coffee experience—a place to sit, relax, or work while enjoying their beverage. This understanding allowed Starbucks to design their stores and products to cater to this need, setting them apart from competitors focused solely on selling coffee.

Defining Your Customer

To identify your customers, start by asking:

1. **Who Benefits the Most?**: Which group of people will find the greatest value in your offering?

2. **What Do They Need?**: What problems do they face, and how does your product or service solve them?

3. **Where Are They?**: Where do your customers live, work, or spend time, and how can you reach them?

For instance, Nike doesn't just sell athletic wear—they sell inspiration and performance. Their customers aren't just athletes; they're anyone who identifies with the idea of striving for greatness. By targeting this mindset, Nike appeals to a broad audience while still maintaining a strong identity.

Understanding Your Core Customer Segments

Your customers are rarely a single, homogenous group. Instead, they often fall into distinct segments, each with unique needs and preferences. Understanding these groups helps you craft targeted strategies.

Apple: Apple's core customers range from tech enthusiasts who value cutting-edge innovation to professionals who need reliable tools for their work. By serving these segments, Apple positions itself as a premium brand that appeals to diverse but specific audiences.

Amazon: Amazon's initial target was book buyers. Over time, they expanded to serve multiple customer groups, including casual shoppers, businesses using AWS, and sellers on their marketplace. This segmentation helped Amazon scale while maintaining relevance to each audience.

Different Types of Customers

Your business may serve more than one type of customer. Common categories include:

End Consumers: People who use your product or service directly, like families using moving services.

Businesses: Companies that purchase your offering to support their operations, such as office relocations.

Intermediaries: Distributors or partners who resell or promote your product.

How to Learn About Your Customers

To understand your customers deeply, you need more than assumptions—you need real data and insights. Here are some ways to do it:

Customer Feedback: Engage with your customers directly through surveys, reviews, or focus groups. This gives you firsthand insight into what they want and need.

Competitor Analysis: Study who your competitors are targeting and how they engage with their audience. This can help you identify gaps or opportunities in the market.

Data Analytics: Use tools to analyze customer behavior. For example, tracking website visits, purchase patterns, or social media engagement can reveal valuable trends.

Netflix, for example, leverages data analytics to understand its customers better. By analyzing viewing habits, Netflix doesn't just know what its audience likes—they predict what they'll want next, allowing them to recommend content and create original shows tailored to customer preferences.

Why It Matters

Understanding your customers is critical for several reasons:

1. It helps you create products or services that truly meet their needs.

2. It allows you to craft marketing messages that resonate with their desires and pain points.

3. It builds loyalty by showing that you understand and care about your audience.

Without a clear understanding of your customer, you risk wasting resources on ineffective strategies. Kodak's failure to adapt to the digital photography revolution is a cautionary tale of losing touch with customer needs. While customers were shifting to digital, Kodak clung to its film products, ultimately leading to its decline.

Conclusion

Your customers are the foundation of your business. Identifying who they are and understanding what drives them is not a one-time task but an ongoing process. Famous companies like Starbucks, Nike, and Netflix thrive because they continually refine their understanding of their audiences. By following their example, you can position your business to meet customer needs, build loyalty, and grow sustainably.

Your Competition: Who Are They and Why

Do They Matter?

Competition is an inevitable part of running a business. Whether you're launching a new product, opening a service-based company, or stepping into a niche market, chances are, someone is already doing something similar. Understanding your competitors isn't about copying their strategies or fearing their presence—it's about learning from them, identifying your unique edge, and finding ways to differentiate yourself in the marketplace.

When I started my moving company, I quickly realized that I wasn't the only one offering moving services in my area. Established companies dominated the market, and smaller players were constantly vying for customers. Rather than seeing this as a disadvantage, I used it as an opportunity to study their strengths, weaknesses, and gaps, which allowed me to craft a service that stood out for its professionalism and customer care.

Why Competitors Matter

Competition isn't just a challenge—it's a resource. Competitors can:

1. **Validate the Market**: Their presence confirms that there's demand for what you're offering.

2. **Reveal Opportunities**: By studying their weaknesses or areas they overlook, you can identify gaps to fill.

3. **Keep You Innovating**: Healthy competition motivates businesses to improve their offerings and customer experience.

Consider Coca-Cola and Pepsi. These two giants have been competing for decades, but their rivalry has driven both companies to innovate constantly, expand into new markets, and refine their branding strategies. Without competition, neither would be as dominant or as creative as they are today.

Types of Competitors

Your competitors may fall into several categories:

1. **Direct Competitors**: Businesses that offer the same product or service as you. For example, McDonald's and Burger King both target fast-food consumers.

2. **Indirect Competitors**: Companies offering different products or services that fulfill the same customer need. For instance, Netflix competes indirectly with traditional cable TV providers.

3. **Future Competitors**: Potential entrants to the market who might disrupt your space. Think about how Airbnb entered the hospitality market and became a competitor to traditional hotels.

Understanding these categories helps you assess who your true competitors are and how they might impact your business.

How to Analyze Competitors

Studying your competitors provides valuable insights into what works, what doesn't, and where your opportunities lie. Here's how to do it:

1. **Identify Them**: Use online tools, local directories, or industry reports to find competitors in your space.

2. **Study Their Offerings**: What are they selling? What's their pricing model? How do they position themselves in the market?

3. **Understand Their Strengths**: What do they do well? This could include superior branding, customer service, or product quality.

4. **Pinpoint Their Weaknesses**: What are they missing or failing to do? These gaps can become your opportunity to shine.

For example, when I launched my shipping business, I noticed that many competitors were focusing only on domestic routes. By offering reliable international shipping solutions, I was able to carve out a niche and attract customers who needed global logistics services.

Differentiating Yourself

Once you've analyzed your competitors, the next step is to determine what sets your business apart. This could be:

Superior Quality: Offering a product or service that outperforms others.

Better Pricing: Providing more value for money.

Unique Features: Adding benefits that competitors don't offer.

Exceptional Service: Delivering an unforgettable customer experience.

Apple is a prime example of differentiation. While many companies produce smartphones, Apple sets itself apart with its sleek design, intuitive user interface, and ecosystem of interconnected devices and services. This differentiation has made Apple a market leader despite fierce competition.

Conclusion

Competitors are not your enemies—they're your motivators and educators. By studying them carefully and positioning yourself uniquely, you can thrive even in a crowded market. Whether you're up against small local players or industry giants, the key is to focus on what you do best and consistently deliver value to your customers. Remember, competition drives innovation, and embracing it will only make your business stronger

Why do they pay you?

Understanding why customers are willing to pay for your product or service is one of the most crucial aspects of running a successful business. The answer lies not just in what you're offering but in the value you provide. People don't pay for products or services—they pay for solutions, experiences, and results. Identifying what drives customers to choose you over your competitors is essential for crafting a compelling value proposition and ensuring your business thrives.

When I started my moving company, I realized that customers weren't just paying for a truck and labor—they were paying for peace of mind, reliability, and the assurance that their belongings would be handled with care. This understanding shaped every aspect of my business, from how we trained our staff to how we communicated with clients.

The Core of Customer Payments: Value

Customers pay you when they perceive that the value they receive is greater than the price they pay. This value can take many forms, including:

1. **Convenience**: Saving them time or effort.

2. **Cost Savings**: Offering better prices or helping them avoid expensive mistakes.

3. **Quality**: Delivering superior products or services.

4. **Trust**: Providing reliability, consistency, or assurance.

5. **Experience**: Creating an enjoyable, memorable, or seamless interaction.

Consider Amazon. Customers pay for Prime memberships not just for faster shipping but for convenience, access to exclusive content, and the overall value of a seamless shopping experience. Amazon bundles multiple benefits, making the membership feel indispensable to many customers.

The Psychology Behind Payment

People don't part with their money lightly. Understanding the psychological reasons why they pay can help you refine your approach:

1. **Problem-Solving**: Customers will pay if you solve a pain point. For example, Starbucks customers pay a premium for coffee not just for the drink but for the comfortable atmosphere and consistent experience.

2. **Aspirations**: Sometimes, customers pay to achieve a goal or align with a certain image. Luxury brands like Louis Vuitton thrive because customers want to express status or taste.

3. **Emotional Connection**: People often buy from businesses they trust or feel connected to. Apple's loyal customers pay more because of the brand's reputation for innovation and quality.

Why Do They Choose You?

Customers will pay you instead of your competitors if you provide unique value that sets you apart. This could include:

Specialization: Offering something tailored to a specific audience, like Peloton's targeted fitness ecosystem for cycling enthusiasts.

Innovation: Delivering something new or better, like Tesla's electric vehicles disrupting the automotive market.

Customer Experience: Creating a seamless, delightful experience, such as Disney's ability to transport visitors into a magical world.

How to Ensure They'll Pay

To consistently attract paying customers, focus on:

1. **Understanding Their Needs**: Conduct surveys, gather feedback, and analyze behavior to learn what customers truly value.

2. **Communicating Value**: Make it clear why your product or service is worth the price. Highlight benefits, not just features.

3. **Delivering on Promises**: Ensure the customer experience aligns with their expectations. A broken promise can erode trust and drive customers away.

Netflix is a prime example of this. Its users pay for convenience, entertainment variety, and an ad-free experience. By continuously adding new content and improving usability, Netflix ensures that its subscribers perceive the service as worth the cost.

Conclusion

Customers pay you because they believe your business offers value that meets or exceeds their expectations. By understanding the reasons behind their decisions, you can refine your offerings, enhance customer satisfaction, and build loyalty. Remember, customers don't just pay for what you sell—they pay for what it does for them, how it makes them feel, and the problems it solves. Focus on delivering value, and the payments will follow

CHAPTER 4: TEAMWORK MAKES THE DREAM WORK: ASSEMBLING YOUR BUSINESS BACKBONE

No business can thrive without the right people behind it. While an entrepreneur's vision and determination are essential, it's the team that turns ideas into reality, overcomes challenges, and drives growth. Chapter 4 explores the critical question: who will be in your team?

Building a team isn't just about hiring employees—it's about creating a network of people who contribute to your business's success. This includes co-founders, employees, subcontractors, advisors, and even the partners who help you execute your vision. The goal isn't just to assemble a group of people but to bring together individuals with the right mix of skills, attitude, and commitment to take your business forward.

When I started my moving company, I quickly learned that the people I chose to work with made all the difference. Initially, I hired whoever was available, focusing on affordability rather than expertise. But as the business grew, I realized that having reliable, skilled team members was crucial for delivering quality service and maintaining my company's reputation. This realization reshaped how I built my teams in subsequent ventures.

Why Building the Right Team Matters

Your team is the backbone of your business. They're the ones executing your vision, interacting with customers, and ensuring operations run smoothly. A strong team can elevate your business, while the wrong team can lead to costly mistakes, inefficiencies, and even failure.

Take Apple as an example. While Steve Jobs was the face of the company, it was the collective brilliance of his team—visionaries like Steve Wozniak and Tim Cook—that made Apple the global powerhouse it is today. Building a team isn't about finding people who simply follow orders—it's about assembling individuals who bring unique strengths and perspectives to the table.

What This Chapter Covers

In this chapter, we'll explore:

1. **Defining Your Business Structure**: Understanding the roles and responsibilities needed to run your business effectively.

2. **Identifying Key Players**: Who do you need on your team, and why are they important?

3. **Attracting and Retaining Talent**: Strategies for finding the right people and keeping them motivated.

4. **Building Strong Relationships**: Fostering collaboration and trust among team members.

We'll also examine common challenges entrepreneurs face when building their teams, such as hiring too quickly, delegating too little, or struggling to balance cost and quality. These lessons will help you avoid pitfalls and create a team that's aligned with your goals.

Conclusion

Your team is more than just a collection of individuals—it's the driving force behind your business. Building the right team requires careful planning, strategic hiring, and a commitment to fostering a positive and productive work environment. In this chapter, we'll guide you through the process of identifying, attracting, and developing the people who will play a pivotal role in your business's success

Your Business Structure Shapes Your

Team

Your business structure does more than define your legal or financial obligations—it shapes the composition, dynamics, and responsibilities of your team. The structure you choose sets the framework for how decisions are made, who has authority, and how ownership and roles are distributed. From sole proprietorships to corporations, each structure creates unique team dynamics that influence how your business operates and grows.

The Link Between Structure and Team

Your business structure determines how people become part of your team and what their roles entail. For example, in a partnership, the partners are usually integral to the team, actively contributing to the business's day-to-day operations. In a corporation, shareholders might work in the company or remain passive investors, leaving the management to a dedicated team.

When I transitioned my moving company from a sole proprietorship to a corporation, the change impacted the team dynamics significantly. Incorporating meant formalizing operations, defining roles more clearly, and balancing the interests of shareholders who had varying levels of involvement. This shift highlighted the importance of aligning the structure with the team's goals and functions.

How Different Structures Shape Teams

The choice of business structure impacts the type of team you build:

1. **Sole Proprietorship**:
    In this structure, the business owner is often the sole decision-maker and primary worker. Any additional team members are usually hired employees. This setup works best for small businesses with limited operational complexity.
    Example: A freelance photographer who hires assistants for specific projects operates as a sole proprietor, with the team's involvement being temporary and task-specific.

2. **Partnership**:
    Partnerships involve two or more individuals sharing

ownership and responsibilities. Each partner typically brings unique skills or resources, making the partnership the core team. Effective communication and defined roles are essential to avoid conflicts.

Example: Ben & Jerry's started as a partnership, with both founders playing active roles in running the business.

3. **Corporation**:
    Corporations have a more formalized team structure, often including shareholders, a board of directors, and hired executives or managers. Shareholders may work in the business or take a hands-off role, leaving daily operations to professional managers.

    Example: Apple's structure includes a mix of involved executives, like Tim Cook, and passive shareholders who influence the company's direction through board decisions.

4. **Limited Partnerships (LPs) or Other Jurisdiction-Specific Entities**:
    In an LP, general partners manage the business, while limited partners invest capital but don't participate in operations. This setup provides flexibility in team composition.

    Example: Real estate development projects often use LPs, where developers act as general partners and investors as limited partners.

Why Structure Matters for Your Team

Your business structure defines:

Roles and Responsibilities: Who's involved in operations and who isn't.

Decision-Making Authority: Whether decisions rest with a single owner, partners, or a board.

Compensation and Incentives: How team members, shareholders, or partners are rewarded for their contributions.

Understanding these dynamics helps you build a cohesive team that aligns with your business goals.

Choosing the Right Structure

Selecting a business structure is not just a legal decision—it's a strategic one. Consider factors like:

1. The size and scope of your team.

2. Whether team members will also be owners.

3. How roles and authority will evolve as the business grows.

Take time to assess which structure best fits your vision and the needs of your team. Consulting with legal and financial advisors can provide clarity and ensure your structure supports your long-term goals.

Conclusion

Your business structure is a cornerstone of how your team operates and collaborates. It influences everything from hiring to decision-making, making it essential to align your structure with your team's needs and your business objectives. Whether you're a sole proprietor, a partnership, or a corporation, understanding the link between structure and team dynamics is critical for building a foundation that supports sustainable growth.

Beyond You: The Team That Builds

Success

No matter how driven or capable you are, building a successful business requires more than just your individual efforts. Beyond your vision and hard work, it's the expertise and contributions of others that transform an idea into a thriving enterprise. As the founder, you are the cornerstone, but your business will only reach its full potential with the right team and support network behind you.

Identifying who you need—and understanding why—goes beyond assembling a core team of employees. It involves recognizing the value of external professionals, advisors, and specialists who can address the gaps in your expertise and bring your business to the next level.

Legal Experts: Guardrails for Growth

Navigating the legal landscape of business can be complex, from drafting contracts to ensuring compliance with regulations. A skilled lawyer acts as a safeguard, protecting your business from costly mistakes and liabilities.

For instance, in the early days of Microsoft, Bill Gates relied heavily on legal expertise to secure intellectual property rights for the software that would become the foundation of the company's success. Without this foresight, Microsoft could have lost its competitive edge to rivals. Whether it's setting up a business entity, negotiating contracts, or addressing intellectual property issues, legal advisors are indispensable to protecting and scaling your business.

Financial Experts: Mastering the Numbers

Managing finances effectively is critical to staying afloat and achieving long-term success. Accountants and bookkeepers ensure accurate financial records, prepare taxes, and offer insights into budgeting and profitability.

Consider Starbucks, whose rigorous financial management helped it weather economic downturns while expanding globally. With financial experts monitoring its cash flow and optimizing costs, Starbucks maintained steady growth even during challenging periods. For a small business, having a knowledgeable accountant can mean the difference between thriving and struggling to make ends meet.

IT Specialists: Keeping the Engine Running

In today's digital world, technology is integral to most businesses. IT professionals ensure your systems are secure, functional, and optimized for efficiency. From building an e-commerce website to safeguarding customer data, their contributions are vital.

Amazon's early success was built on a robust IT infrastructure that allowed the company to scale operations and handle growing customer demands. Even small businesses benefit immensely from IT expertise, whether it's for setting up payment systems or managing cybersecurity threats.

Advisors: Trusted Guides for Strategic Decisions

Advisors bring a unique value to your business. They provide an external perspective, helping you navigate strategic decisions and avoid potential pitfalls. Whether you're determining a manager's salary or evaluating a major investment, an advisor's guidance can be invaluable.

Take Howard Schultz's journey with Starbucks, where seasoned advisors helped him refine his vision and craft strategies for scaling the company. Advisors bring experience and objectivity, asking the tough questions and ensuring decisions are based on sound reasoning rather than emotion.

Specialized Roles: Tailoring Support to Your Business

No matter how skilled or determined you are as an entrepreneur, your success hinges on the people you bring into your business. These are not just employees or partners—they are the specialists, advisors, and experts who help ensure that your business operates smoothly and efficiently. The right team fills gaps in your knowledge, manages complexities, and creates a system where every part of your business works seamlessly.

Each business has unique needs, and building the right team requires identifying roles that align with your industry, scale, and vision. In some cases, these roles may be obvious, such as hiring a marketing manager for a retail business. In other instances, specialized or hidden roles—such as a food safety consultant for a restaurant or a supply chain expert for a logistics company—are essential for long-term success. Recognizing these needs is the first step in assembling a team that will drive your business forward.

Critical Roles and Their Importance

The core team you build will likely include positions essential to daily operations and growth. For example, an operations manager oversees processes to ensure efficiency, while a customer service representative handles client inquiries, maintaining the reputation of your brand. Beyond these, your team might also include individuals like a compliance officer to navigate regulations or a quality control specialist to uphold standards. Each role contributes to the smooth running of your business, and understanding their importance allows you to structure your team effectively.

However, not every crucial role is immediately visible, especially in specialized industries. A new restaurateur might overlook the need for a food safety consultant, while a tech startup might miss the importance of a cybersecurity expert.Without these roles, businesses face unnecessary risks that could have been mitigated with the right expertise.

Take the example of Starbucks, where rigorous financial and operational management played a significant role in its expansion. Behind the scenes, financial analysts ensured profitability while operations managers refined processes to maintain quality and efficiency. These specialized roles weren't visible to customers but were critical to the company's success.

Learning Through Industry Knowledge

If you're entering a field where your expertise is limited, it's essential to seek guidance. One of the best ways to understand what roles are necessary is to gain hands-on experience. Spending time working in the industry can reveal hidden complexities and the need for specialized positions. For example, a logistics entrepreneur might work in the field to understand the importance of route optimization or inventory management roles.

Alternatively, hiring experienced advisors or consultants can provide you with insights into roles you might otherwise overlook. These professionals have a deep understanding of industry-specific challenges and can recommend positions that align with your business's needs. Their experience can save you time, money, and the potential pitfalls of trial and error.

Tailoring Your Team for Long-Term Success

As your business grows, the roles you need may evolve. A small coffee shop might initially require only a barista and a cashier, but as it expands, roles like a supply chain manager or social media strategist become vital to manage inventory and engage customers effectively. Similarly, a startup might begin with a founder and a few developers but eventually need a dedicated human resources professional to handle recruiting and employee relations.

The key is to regularly assess your operations to identify bottlenecks or inefficiencies. As your processes become more complex, more roles may be necessary to ensure smooth operations. This dynamic approach to team-building allows your business to adapt and thrive as it scales.

The success of your business depends not only on your vision but on the people who support it. Identifying the right roles—whether visible or hidden—and bringing in experienced individuals ensures that your business operates effectively. By tailoring your team to your specific industry and needs, seeking expert guidance when necessary, and adapting as your business grows, you can create a foundation for long-term success. A well-built team isn't just about filling positions—it's about creating a cohesive system that propels your business toward its goals

Knowing When and How to Build Your Team

As your business evolves, so will your team's composition. During the startup phase, you may rely on freelancers or part-time professionals to keep costs manageable. As you grow, full-time roles and strategic partnerships become more feasible. Balancing cost, expertise, and timing ensures you get the support you need without overextending resources.

Conclusion

Success isn't achieved in isolation. Beyond your efforts, it's the team you build—both internally and externally—that drives your business forward. From legal and financial experts to IT specialists and trusted advisors, these individuals fill the gaps in your knowledge and provide the tools to succeed. By recognizing who you need and why, you can create a support network that strengthens your business at every stage

Keeping Your Team Motivated

The success of any business relies on the people who work for it— shareholders, employees, and independent professionals. Their dedication and engagement stem from how fairly and thoughtfully you address their contributions, needs, and expectations. People want to feel that their work is valued and that they're part of something meaningful. Achieving this requires a balanced and fair approach tailored to the different roles they play in your business.

The Role of Shareholders in the Business

Shareholders who actively work in the business bring more than just financial investment; they contribute their time, skills, and effort to the company's growth. However, if their involvement isn't properly recognized—whether through salaries, dividends, or other incentives —it can lead to dissatisfaction. For instance, shareholders working without fair compensation may find their contributions outweigh the dividends they receive, especially when profits are low. This can erode their motivation and commitment.

A fair solution involves offering shareholders who work in the business an appropriate salary for their operational roles, supplemented by dividends tied to their equity. This ensures that their contributions are rewarded, regardless of short-term profitability. For example, when Larry Page and Sergey Brin transitioned from founders to active executives at Google, they were compensated both as leaders of the company and as shareholders. Clear agreements about compensation and roles, established from the outset, are critical to avoiding conflicts and maintaining harmony between active and non-active shareholders.

Engaging Regular Employees

For employees, financial compensation is important, but it's not the only factor that drives their commitment. They also want to feel valued, supported, and part of a larger purpose. Offering fair wages that align with market standards is the baseline. Beyond that, stock options, bonus, awards, rewards, benefits also can be used to motivate employees. Also creating opportunities for professional growth, providing clear career paths, and recognizing individual contributions all play a role in fostering a loyal workforce.

Consider how companies like Netflix and Southwest Airlines approach employee engagement. Netflix provides competitive salaries and empowers employees with autonomy, trusting them to make decisions and innovate. Southwest Airlines goes a step further, fostering a culture where employees feel like an integral part of the company's mission. By treating their staff as vital stakeholders, these businesses build loyalty and commitment that translates into exceptional performance.

Independent Professionals: The Pay-and-Go Approach

Not all contributors to your business need to be full-time employees or shareholders. Independent professionals, such as lawyers, accountants, and IT consultants, often operate on a pay-as-you-go basis, providing flexibility and cost efficiency. This model works well for specialized services that your business may not require on a daily basis but are critical during specific times, such as legal compliance, financial audits, or IT system upgrades.

For example, many startups engage freelance IT professionals to set up and maintain their systems, allowing them to control costs without sacrificing quality. Even large corporations rely on external legal firms for specialized cases, ensuring they receive expert guidance while maintaining flexibility. This arrangement allows businesses to access high-level expertise without incurring the long-term costs of full-time hires.

Creating a Culture of Fairness and Value

To ensure everyone working for your business feels engaged and motivated, fairness must underpin your approach. Shareholders need to see that their time and effort are valued. Employees should feel recognized for their contributions and have opportunities to grow. Independent professionals require clarity about their roles and respect for their expertise.

This balance requires thoughtful planning and transparent communication. Whether through structured salaries, performance-based incentives, or flexible arrangements with contractors, the goal is to match contributions with appropriate rewards. When people feel their work is valued and aligned with the company's success, they are more likely to remain committed and care deeply about the business.

Conclusion

Why do people work for you, and why do they care about your business? The answer lies in how you treat them. Shareholders, employees, and independent professionals all have unique motivations and expectations, and addressing these with fairness and thoughtfulness is the key to keeping them engaged. A successful business is built not just on great ideas but on the people who bring them to life. By fostering an environment of mutual respect, recognition, and value, you create a team that's invested in your success as much as you are.

CHAPTER 5: MONEY MATTERS: MANAGING CAPITAL AND CASH FLOW

Money is the lifeblood of any business. It fuels your operations, supports your growth, and ensures your survival during tough times. But managing capital and cash flow isn't just about having money—it's about understanding how to use it wisely, attract it strategically, and sustain it effectively. Chapter 5 dives into these essential financial foundations, providing you with the tools to assess, manage, and optimize your business's financial health.

Every entrepreneur faces critical questions about money: How much capital do you need to get started? Where will you find it? How can you ensure that cash keeps flowing in, not just out? And when will you finally break even? These are not just questions—they are milestones that determine whether your business thrives or struggles.

When we talk about capital and cash flow, we're discussing more than just numbers on a spreadsheet. This chapter explores the deeper story behind your finances—how to estimate your needs realistically, find the right funding sources, value your business fairly, and navigate the challenges of staying afloat.

Why This Chapter Matters

Many startups fail because of financial mismanagement—not due to lack of ideas or hard work, but because they underestimate costs, overestimate revenues, or lose track of cash flow. This chapter will help you avoid those pitfalls by providing practical strategies and actionable insights.

For instance, companies like Amazon, which famously operated at a loss for years, understood the importance of managing cash flow to sustain growth until profitability. Their success wasn't just about revenue—it was about strategically managing resources to achieve long-term goals.

What You'll Learn in This Chapter

This chapter will guide you through key financial concepts that every entrepreneur must master:

1. **How Much Capital is Enough?**: Learn to estimate your startup costs and create a realistic budget.

2. **Where Can You Get the Money and Why?**: Explore funding options and understand what each source expects in return.

3. **What's Your Business Really Worth Before Startup?**: Discover how to assess your business's pre-revenue valuation and why it matters to investors.

4. **The Break-Even Equation: When Will You Profit?**: Calculate when your revenues will cover your costs and how to plan for that milestone.

5. **Managing Cash Flow: Inflows, Outflows, and Staying Afloat**: Develop strategies to keep your cash flow positive and handle unexpected challenges.

Conclusion

Money matters because it shapes every decision you make in business. Whether you're figuring out how much capital you need, securing funding, or ensuring that cash flow remains steady, your financial management will determine the trajectory of your success. This chapter provides the knowledge and tools to approach these challenges with confidence, helping you lay a solid financial foundation for your business

How Much Capital is Enough?

Determining how much capital you need to start and sustain your business is one of the most critical questions for any entrepreneur. Get it wrong, and you could either run out of money too soon or overcommit to unnecessary expenses. The key is to strike a balance —identifying the exact amount required to launch and grow your business without overstretching your resources.

When I started my moving company, I didn't have a perfect formula for estimating costs. Instead, I borrowed $10,000 from the bank and three credit cards to buy a truck. This approach gave me just enough to get started while forcing me to manage my expenses carefully. Over time, I learned that a strategic approach to estimating capital needs can save you from unnecessary stress and financial pitfalls.

Estimating Your Startup Costs

The first step in determining how much capital is enough is understanding the expenses involved in launching your business. Startup costs can be broadly categorized into:

1. **One-Time Costs**: These include expenses like equipment, licenses, initial inventory, and marketing for your launch.

2. **Recurring Costs**: These are ongoing expenses such as rent, salaries, utilities, and subscription services.

Take Starbucks as an example. When Howard Schultz envisioned scaling Starbucks beyond a local coffee shop, he meticulously calculated costs for everything—from store buildouts to supply chain management. His planning ensured the company had the capital to grow steadily.

The Importance of a Buffer

It's not enough to calculate exact costs—you need a buffer for unexpected expenses. Entrepreneurs often face surprises like regulatory changes, delayed revenues, or unexpected repairs. Having an additional 20–30% of your estimated capital as a safety net can make the difference between survival and failure.

For example, Amazon operated at a loss for several years while building its e-commerce empire. Its founders anticipated the need for additional capital to sustain operations until revenues grew, ensuring the company didn't collapse under financial pressure.

Testing Your Estimates

Once you've estimated your capital needs, validate them by running small-scale tests. For instance, if you're starting a restaurant, calculate the costs of a pop-up or catering event to test your concept before committing to a full-scale launch. This approach helps refine your estimates and avoid overcommitting resources.

Your Unique Situation

The amount of capital required varies greatly depending on your business model, industry, and goals. A tech startup might need significant upfront investment in research and development, while a freelance consulting business could begin with minimal costs. The key is to tailor your calculations to your specific situation and goals.

Practical Steps to Determine Your Capital Needs

1. **List All Costs**: Categorize your expenses into one-time and recurring costs. Be thorough—missing even small details can lead to shortfalls.

2. **Research Benchmarks**: Look into similar businesses to understand typical startup costs in your industry.

3. **Add a Buffer**: Include additional capital for unforeseen expenses to ensure financial flexibility.

4. **Refine Through Testing**: Pilot your business idea on a small scale to validate your estimates and adjust as necessary.

Conclusion

"How much capital is enough?" isn't just a question of math—it's a question of strategy. By understanding your costs, planning for contingencies, and validating your estimates, you can approach funding with confidence. Whether you're launching a coffee shop, a tech startup, or a shipping company, the principles remain the same: plan wisely, stay flexible, and prepare for the unexpected. The right amount of capital isn't just a number—it's your first step toward building a sustainable business

Where can you get the money and why?

Securing funding is one of the most crucial steps in launching or scaling a business. The challenge isn't just finding the money—it's finding the right type of funding that aligns with your goals and your business's stage. Whether you're looking for startup capital, operational funding, or resources to expand, understanding your options and presenting a compelling case are key to success.

When I started my moving company, I pieced together funding from personal savings, bank loans, and credit cards. While it worked at the time, I quickly realized that each funding source comes with unique expectations and trade-offs. What's suitable for a small venture may not work for a high-growth startup, and understanding these nuances can make or break your funding journey.

Debt vs. Equity Financing

At the heart of any funding decision lies a choice: debt or equity. Debt involves borrowing money that must be repaid with interest, while equity means selling a share of your business in exchange for capital. Both approaches have advantages. Debt allows you to retain full ownership but adds repayment obligations that can strain cash flow. Equity brings in partners who share the risks and rewards but also dilutes your ownership.

Consider Amazon in its early days. Jeff Bezos relied on a $300,000 loan from his parents, a form of debt financing, to keep the company afloat. On the other hand, startups like Uber and Airbnb turned to equity financing, attracting venture capital to fuel their rapid growth. The right choice depends on your business's unique needs, risk tolerance, and growth potential.

Exploring Your Funding Options

Funding sources vary widely, and each comes with its own benefits and challenges. Personal savings are often the first resource for entrepreneurs, as they demonstrate commitment and avoid external obligations. Sara Blakely, the founder of Spanx, started her company with just $5,000 from her savings, proving the power of self-investment. However, not all businesses can rely solely on personal resources.

Friends and family are another common source of early funding, offering a mix of loans and informal investments. While these relationships often come with favorable terms, clear agreements are essential to avoid misunderstandings. Traditional bank loans remain a popular choice for small businesses, providing structured repayment plans but requiring collateral and a strong credit history.

For larger ventures or high-growth businesses, external investors like angel investors or venture capitalists are key players. These investors don't just provide funding—they bring expertise, connections, and credibility. For example, companies like Google and Facebook attracted venture capital in their early stages, enabling them to scale rapidly while gaining strategic insights.

Crowdfunding platforms like Kickstarter or Indiegogo offer a modern twist on raising capital. By directly engaging the public, businesses can validate demand and secure funding simultaneously. Pebble Technology, for instance, raised over $10 million through Kickstarter, highlighting the potential of this approach.

The Art of Convincing Investors

Securing funding requires more than just financial projections—it's about building confidence in your vision and your ability to execute it. Investors and lenders want to see why your business will succeed and how their involvement will yield returns. To achieve this, you must present a clear value proposition, demonstrate market demand, and showcase your strategic planning.

Howard Schultz's journey to scale Starbucks is a prime example. When seeking investors, Schultz didn't just talk about selling coffee; he painted a vivid picture of creating a "third place" between home and work, where customers could enjoy premium coffee in a welcoming atmosphere. This compelling narrative, backed by detailed financial plans and robust market research, inspired confidence and helped secure the funding needed to turn Starbucks into a global brand.

By crafting a clear and inspiring pitch, grounded in data and vision, you can show potential funders why your business is worth their trust and investment.

Howard Schultz leveraged experienced advisors when scaling Starbucks, ensuring his vision was backed by financial rigor and market insights. These advisors helped refine his strategy and present Starbucks as more than a coffee shop—a visionary concept that investors wanted to be part of.

Having advisors on your side can make the difference between a good pitch and a great one, giving you the credibility and confidence to secure the funding your business needs

Aligning Funding with Your Needs

Choosing the right funding source also depends on your business's stage and goals. A small retail shop may thrive with a modest loan, while a tech startup might require millions in venture capital. For businesses with fluctuating needs, hiring pay-as-you-go professionals like IT consultants or legal advisors can offer cost-effective solutions without long-term commitments.

Conclusion

Funding your business is as much about strategy as it is about numbers. The money you secure—and the source you choose—can shape the future of your company. Whether it's personal savings, loans, equity investment, or innovative options like crowdfunding, understanding the trade-offs and aligning them with your goals is essential. Remember, it's not just about where the money comes from but why someone believes in your vision. By presenting a clear, compelling case and choosing wisely, you set the foundation for sustainable growth

What's your business really worth before startup?

Before your business generates its first dollar, it already has a value —your "pre-revenue valuation." This valuation is crucial when seeking equity financing, as it determines how much of your business you need to offer in exchange for investment. Understanding your business's worth at this stage isn't just about numbers; it's about presenting your vision, assets, and potential in a way that convinces investors you're worth betting on.

Valuation before launch is a mix of art and science. Without tangible revenues, the focus shifts to factors like your business model, market potential, intellectual property, and the team behind the idea. When I explored funding options for one of my businesses, I realized that investors weren't just evaluating my concept—they were assessing the likelihood of my ability to execute it and turn it into a profitable venture.

How Pre-Revenue Valuation Works

Pre-revenue valuation involves estimating the potential worth of your business based on its projected future performance. This estimate forms the basis of negotiation with investors, who decide how much they're willing to invest and what percentage of ownership they want in return. For example, if an investor values your business at $1 million and offers $100,000 in funding, they would typically expect a 10% equity stake.

Several factors influence this valuation:

Market Size and Opportunity: Is the market for your product or service large and growing? Investors are drawn to businesses with significant potential for expansion.

Uniqueness and Intellectual Property: Do you have a unique product, service, or patented technology that gives you a competitive edge?

Founding Team: Investors often place great weight on the experience, skills, and track record of the founders. A capable team inspires confidence.

Early Traction: Even without revenue, metrics like social media engagement, customer sign-ups, or prototype feedback can demonstrate demand and validate your idea.

Business Model and Strategy: A clear, well-defined business model and growth strategy show investors how you plan to turn ideas into profits.

Real-World Examples of Pre-Revenue Valuation

Consider Uber in its early days. The company didn't own cars or have significant revenues, but its founders presented a compelling vision for disrupting the transportation industry. Investors evaluated the market potential, the scalability of the app-based model, and the strength of the founding team. These factors justified Uber's high valuation even before it became profitable.

Similarly, companies like Airbnb and Instagram secured millions in funding before generating revenue by convincing investors of their long-term potential. Their ability to articulate a clear value proposition and their plans for monetization were key to their success.

Why It Matters to Investors

Investors value your business before startup because they need to assess the risks and rewards of their investment. A clear understanding of your business's worth helps them decide:

1. How much capital they're willing to invest.

2. The percentage of equity they want in return.

3. Whether your business aligns with their investment strategy.

For you, understanding your pre-revenue valuation ensures you're offering a fair and reasonable stake in your company without undervaluing or overvaluing your business. Overvaluation can deter investors, while undervaluation may leave you with less equity and control than you deserve.

How to Approach Pre-Revenue Valuation

Since pre-revenue valuation is subjective, here's how you can prepare:

1. **Research Comparable Businesses**: Look at similar startups in your industry to understand their valuation benchmarks.

2. **Showcase Your Potential**: Highlight the size of your market, your unique value proposition, and any early traction.

3. **Build a Strong Team**: Surround yourself with experienced, capable individuals who can execute your vision.

4. **Work with Advisors**: Experienced advisors or consultants can help you craft a realistic valuation and negotiate with investors.

Conclusion

Before your business officially takes off, its valuation lays the foundation for equity financing and future growth. Knowing what your business is worth—and being able to justify that worth—is essential when negotiating with investors. By focusing on market potential, your team's strength, and a clear plan for success, you can present a compelling case for your valuation, ensuring that both you and your investors are set up for a rewarding partnership.

The Break-Even Equation: When Will You Profit

Profitability is the ultimate goal for any business, but before you can achieve profit, you need to reach your break-even point—the point at which your total revenue equals your total costs. Knowing when you'll break even isn't just about crunching numbers; it's a strategic tool that helps you understand your business's financial health, plan for growth, and make informed decisions.

Understanding your break-even point can save you from financial missteps and ensure you're focusing on what matters most: covering your costs and building a path toward profitability. Whether you're running a small café or launching a tech startup, the break-even analysis is a fundamental part of your business planning.

What Is the Break-Even Point?

The break-even point is the moment when your total revenue matches your total costs. It's the point where you're no longer operating at a loss but haven't yet started generating profit. This calculation includes two types of costs:

Fixed Costs: Expenses that don't change regardless of sales volume, such as rent, salaries(maybe), and equipment.

Variable Costs: Costs that fluctuate with production or sales, like raw materials or delivery fees.

For example, if you're running a coffee shop, your fixed costs might include rent and equipment leases, while your variable costs would include coffee beans, milk, and disposable cups.

The break-even equation is straightforward:

$$\text{Break-Even Point (Units)} = \frac{\text{Fixed Costs}}{\text{Price per Unit} - \text{Variable Cost per Unit}}$$

This formula tells you how many units of your product or service you need to sell to cover all your costs.

Why the Break-Even Point Matters

Knowing your break-even point gives you a clear target. It allows you to:

1. **Set Realistic Sales Goals**: Understand how much you need to sell to avoid losses.

2. **Plan Pricing Strategies**: Ensure your pricing covers costs while remaining competitive.

3. **Monitor Financial Health**: Quickly identify if you're on track or falling behind.

Take Amazon's early years as an example. The company operated at a loss for years because its break-even point was pushed forward by massive investments in infrastructure and logistics. However, Jeff Bezos understood this trade-off, focusing on long-term growth rather than immediate profitability. Today, Amazon's break-even strategy has paid off, turning it into one of the world's most valuable companies.

How to Calculate Your Break-Even Point

Let's walk through a simplified example:
Imagine you're selling custom-made candles at $20 each.

1. Fixed Costs: $5,000 per month (rent, utilities, marketing).

2. Variable Cost per Unit: $10 (materials, packaging).

Using the formula:

$$\text{Break-Even Point (Units)} = \frac{\text{Fixed Costs}}{\text{Price per Unit} - \text{Variable Cost per Unit}} = \frac{5000}{20 - 10} = 500 \text{ units}$$

This means you need to sell 500 candles per month to break even. Every candle sold beyond that point contributes directly to your profit.

Strategies to Reach Break-Even Faster

1. **Reduce Fixed Costs**: Negotiate better rent terms or use cost-effective marketing channels.

2. **Lower Variable Costs**: Source materials more efficiently or renegotiate supplier contracts.

3. **Increase Prices**: Raise prices slightly if the market allows, ensuring you still deliver value.

4. **Boost Sales Volume**: Invest in targeted marketing to increase sales without significantly raising costs.

For example, Tesla's early strategy focused on high-margin products like luxury electric cars. By targeting a premium market, Tesla reached break-even on its first models faster than if it had launched with mass-market vehicles.

The Bigger Picture

While the break-even point is critical, it's not the end of your financial journey. It's the starting line for building profitability. Reaching break-even gives you the confidence to expand, reinvest, and focus on scaling your business sustainably.

Conclusion

The break-even equation isn't just a financial calculation—it's a roadmap to sustainability and growth. By understanding when your business will break even, you can set realistic goals, make smarter decisions, and position your business for long-term success. Whether you're running a startup or an established company, knowing your break-even point is one of the most empowering tools you have as an entrepreneur.

Managing Cash Flow: Inflows, Outflows, and Staying Afloat

Cash flow is the lifeblood of your business. While profitability is the ultimate goal, maintaining a positive cash flow ensures that your business can survive and thrive in the short term. Even a profitable business can fail if it runs out of cash to cover day-to-day expenses. Managing inflows and outflows effectively is crucial for staying afloat and setting your business up for sustainable growth.

Cash flow is more than just tracking money—it's about timing, planning, and making strategic decisions to ensure that your resources are available when needed. It's a balancing act that requires both discipline and foresight.

Understanding Cash Flow

At its core, cash flow refers to the movement of money in and out of your business. There are two primary components:

1. **Inflows**: The money coming into your business, typically from sales, loans, or investments.

2. **Outflows**: The money going out of your business, including rent, salaries, inventory purchases, and utilities.

For example, a retail business might have steady inflows from daily sales but face large outflows at the beginning of each month for rent and inventory restocking. Timing mismatches between inflows and outflows can create cash flow problems, even if the business is profitable on paper.

Why Cash Flow Matters

Managing cash flow is critical for several reasons:

Daily Operations: Ensures you can pay employees, suppliers, and bills on time.

Flexibility: Allows you to take advantage of opportunities, such as bulk purchasing discounts or unexpected expansion possibilities.

Survival: Protects your business from unexpected downturns, such as a seasonal dip in sales or an economic slowdown.

Take Walmart as an example. The company's sophisticated cash flow management ensures it can pay suppliers promptly while reinvesting in inventory and operations. This discipline allows Walmart to maintain its low-price strategy and dominate the retail market.

Strategies for Managing Inflows

1. **Accelerate Receivables**: Encourage customers to pay promptly by offering incentives for early payments or requiring deposits upfront for large orders.

2. **Diversify Revenue Streams**: Relying on a single source of income can be risky. Explore complementary revenue streams to create consistent inflows.

3. **Monitor Payment Terms**: Avoid overly generous payment terms for customers that delay cash inflows unnecessarily.

For instance, Amazon's Prime membership program creates a steady inflow of subscription revenue, supplementing its traditional e-commerce sales and providing consistent cash flow.

Strategies for Controlling Outflows

1. **Negotiate Payment Terms**: Work with suppliers to extend payment deadlines without incurring penalties, freeing up cash for immediate needs.

2. **Prioritize Expenses**: Differentiate between essential and non-essential spending, especially during lean periods.

3. **Use Technology**: Automate expense tracking and budgeting to ensure timely and accurate records.

Tesla, for example, strategically delayed payments to suppliers in its early days to align outflows with its inflows from vehicle sales, allowing it to conserve cash during its growth phase.

Planning for Cash Flow Challenges

Even with the best planning, cash flow hiccups can occur. Preparing for these moments is critical:

Maintain a Cash Reserve: Set aside a portion of your earnings as a buffer for unexpected expenses or slow periods.

Use Credit Strategically: Accessing a line of credit can provide temporary relief during cash flow gaps, but use it wisely to avoid long-term debt.

Forecast Regularly: Continuously update your cash flow projections based on current trends and historical data to anticipate issues before they arise.

Many small businesses learned the importance of cash flow management during the COVID-19 pandemic when unexpected disruptions forced them to adapt quickly or face closure.

The Role of Cash Flow in Growth

Effective cash flow management doesn't just keep you afloat—it sets the stage for growth. By maintaining a healthy cash position, you can reinvest in marketing, hire additional staff, or expand into new markets without jeopardizing your financial stability.

Conclusion

Managing cash flow is about more than balancing books—it's about maintaining control over your business's lifeline. By understanding the dynamics of inflows and outflows, preparing for challenges, and making strategic decisions, you can ensure your business remains steady in the present and poised for growth in the future. Cash flow isn't just about staying afloat; it's about thriving in a competitive landscape

Pricing for Profit and Growth

Pricing is one of the most powerful tools in business, influencing not just revenue but customer perception, brand positioning, and market competitiveness. The right pricing strategy can attract loyal customers, generate steady profit, and establish your brand as a market leader. On the flip side, poor pricing decisions can alienate customers, harm your reputation, or leave money on the table.

Pricing strategies must balance cost, value, and long-term goals. They are rarely static; as markets evolve, so should your approach. Adjusting prices, however, requires careful planning to avoid backlash, maintain trust, and preserve your brand's reputation.

Strategic Choices for Pricing

Businesses use a variety of strategies to set prices, often tailored to their specific goals, customer base, and competitive landscape. Here are some of the most effective approaches, illustrated with real-world examples:

1. Value-Based Pricing

Value-based pricing sets the price based on the perceived value to the customer rather than the cost of production. Luxury brands like Rolex and Hermès excel at this strategy. A Rolex watch, for example, isn't just a timepiece—it's a symbol of status, craftsmanship, and exclusivity. Customers pay a premium for the value they perceive, which far exceeds the cost of production.

2. Loss-Leader Pricing

Some businesses sell key products at a loss to attract customers, betting that these customers will buy additional, higher-margin products. Costco's hot dog and soda combo, priced at $1.50 since 1985, is a prime example. Despite inflation, Costco has famously refused to raise the price, understanding that it draws customers to its warehouses, where they're likely to purchase other items with higher profit margins.

Similarly, fast-food chains like McDonald's use dollar menus to attract customers, expecting them to spend more on combo meals or desserts.

3. Razor-and-Blade Model

This approach involves pricing a primary product low while charging more for consumables or accessories. Printer companies, for instance, sell printers at attractive prices but make substantial profits on ink cartridges. Similarly, Nespresso coffee machines are affordable, but the pods generate significant ongoing revenue.

This strategy is particularly effective for businesses with repeat-use products. The low initial price lowers the barrier to entry, and consumables create a steady revenue stream.

4. Bundling and Upselling

Offering multiple products as a package at a discounted price encourages customers to buy more than they might otherwise. Adobe uses this strategy effectively with its Creative Cloud suite. Instead of purchasing individual apps, users can subscribe to the entire suite at a perceived discount, boosting overall revenue while offering value.

Upselling complements this by encouraging customers to buy a more expensive version of a product or add-ons, like airlines offering seat upgrades or priority boarding.

5. Skimming Pricing

Businesses with innovative products often set high initial prices to target early adopters, then lower prices over time to attract more customers. Apple has successfully used this strategy with products like the iPhone, capturing premium-paying customers at launch and gradually making the product more accessible.

However, this strategy can backfire if not executed carefully. Tesla, for instance, faced backlash when it dropped prices on certain vehicles shortly after launch. Early buyers felt alienated, leading to damaged trust and brand reputation. Similar issues have plagued condo developers who initially set high prices but later offer discounts to clear inventory.

6. Penetration Pricing

The opposite of skimming, penetration pricing involves setting low prices initially to gain market share and attract price-sensitive customers. Once established, businesses can raise prices. This strategy is common in subscription services like Netflix, which initially offer discounted plans to build a user base before increasing rates.

The Risk of Changing Prices

While price adjustments may be necessary as circumstances change, they carry significant risks. Lowering prices can upset loyal customers who paid more, while raising prices can drive away price-sensitive buyers if not handled carefully.

Tesla's pricing missteps are a cautionary tale. When Tesla reduced prices on its electric vehicles, many early adopters felt undervalued. This led to negative publicity and damaged trust. Similarly, when developers of high-end condos slash prices to sell remaining units, they risk undermining the perceived value of the property and eroding buyer confidence.

To navigate these challenges:

Communicate Clearly: Be transparent about the reasons behind price changes, emphasizing customer benefits.

Add Value: When raising prices, offer enhanced features or services to justify the increase.

Plan Gradually: Avoid abrupt changes; small, incremental adjustments are less likely to shock customers.

The Bigger Picture of Pricing

Pricing is not just about setting a number—it's about understanding your customers, market, and value proposition. Businesses like Costco demonstrate the long-term power of thoughtful pricing strategies. By keeping its hot dog combo at $1.50, Costco reinforces its brand promise of value, fostering customer loyalty and drawing foot traffic to its stores.

The strategy isn't always about maximizing profit on every product. Sometimes, it's about using pricing to attract customers and building relationships that lead to greater profitability down the line.

Conclusion

Pricing is both an art and a science. It requires careful consideration of costs, customer perception, and market dynamics. Strategies like value-based pricing, loss-leader approaches, and bundling can all be effective when aligned with your business goals. However, pricing isn't set in stone. Markets evolve, and so should your strategies—but changes must be handled with care to protect your reputation and maintain customer trust.

Ultimately, pricing is about more than just generating revenue. It's about creating a sustainable foundation for growth, building loyalty, and delivering value that resonates with your customers. Done thoughtfully, it's a powerful tool for long-term success

Your Business's First Impression: Name,

Logo, Colour, and Digital Footprint

Your business's first impression is more than just a name—it's a combination of elements that convey your brand's identity, values, and personality. From the moment potential customers encounter your business, they begin forming opinions based on its name, logo, colours, and online presence. These elements set the tone for your relationship with your audience, making it critical to design them thoughtfully.

Crafting a Memorable Name

Your business name is often the first interaction customers have with your brand. A great name should be simple, memorable, and reflective of what you do. Think of companies like Google, whose name has become synonymous with search, or Tesla, which conveys innovation and energy. Whether you're starting a coffee shop or a tech startup, your name should resonate with your target audience and evoke curiosity or trust.

When I chose the name for my moving company, I opted for something straightforward and professional that aligned with the reliable service I aimed to provide. Interestingly, some customers even thought the business had been established for a very long time, which added to its credibility.

When deciding on a name, several key considerations can help ensure it serves your business well:

Check Domain Availability: Before settling on a name, verify that the corresponding domain is available. A matching domain name makes it easier for customers to find you online and adds professionalism to your digital presence.

Legal Registration: Ensure that no other company in your industry is using the same or a confusingly similar name. This step is crucial for legally registering your business name and securing trademarks. It helps prevent potential legal disputes and protects your brand identity.

Cultural Sensitivity and Multilingual Appeal: If your business operates globally or in a culturally diverse area like Vancouver, consider how your name translates into other languages. Make sure it doesn't have unintended meanings or negative connotations in different cultures or linguistic communities. This sensitivity can enhance your brand's appeal to a broader audience.

Memorability and Neutrality: Choose a name that is easy to remember and pronounce. Avoid using slang or terms that might be offensive or exclusionary to any group. A neutral and inclusive name helps in building a positive brand image.

Overall, your business name should be memorable, culturally appropriate, legally available, and consistent across all platforms—including your website and social media channels. Taking the time to carefully select the right name lays a strong foundation for your brand identity and helps ensure that your first impression is a positive and lasting one.

Designing a Logo That Speaks for You

A logo is your brand's visual shorthand, often forming the cornerstone of your branding. It should be distinctive and easy to recognize. Consider Apple's minimalist logo, which is instantly recognizable worldwide and conveys innovation and simplicity. A well-designed logo doesn't have to be complex; it needs to align with your brand message and be versatile enough to work across various platforms.

Choose colors wisely, as they evoke emotions and play a key role in branding. Blue, for instance, is associated with trust and professionalism, which is why it's popular among financial institutions like PayPal and Chase. Green conveys growth and sustainability, often used by environmentally conscious companies like Whole Foods.

Your Digital Footprint: The Gateway to Your Brand

In today's digital-first world, your online presence is as important as your physical one. Securing a strong domain name that matches your business name makes it easier for customers to find you online. Social media accounts on platforms like Instagram, Facebook, or LinkedIn are equally vital to engage with your audience and showcase your offerings.

Your website serves as the cornerstone of your digital footprint. A well-designed website should be user-friendly, mobile-optimized, and reflective of your brand's personality. For example, Shopify's clean and intuitive website not only highlights its services but also builds trust with potential customers.

Consistency Is Key

All these elements—name, logo, colors, and digital presence— should work together cohesively to create a consistent brand identity. Whether a customer encounters your logo on social media, sees your website, or visits your storefront, the experience should feel unified. This consistency builds trust and helps customers remember your brand.

Conclusion

Your business's first impression can shape how customers perceive you and whether they choose to engage with your brand. A memorable name, a strong logo, a thoughtful color palette, and a well-executed digital footprint are essential elements for success. These choices are not just creative decisions; they are strategic tools to connect with your audience and leave a lasting impact. Invest the time to get them right, as they will serve as the foundation of your brand identity.

Identify Risks and Avoid Them

Every business faces risks, whether it's a small café or a multinational corporation. These risks can range from financial losses and legal issues to operational disruptions and market competition. Identifying potential risks early and creating strategies to mitigate them is critical to building a resilient business. While you can't eliminate risks entirely, proactive planning can help you avoid unnecessary pitfalls and respond effectively when challenges arise.

Types of Risks Businesses Face

Risks in business can be broadly categorized into several areas:

1. **Financial Risks**: These include cash flow problems, unexpected expenses, and difficulty securing funding. For example, startups often overestimate their initial revenue and underestimate operating costs, leading to cash shortages.

2. **Operational Risks**: These involve disruptions in day-to-day operations, such as supply chain delays, equipment failures, or staffing issues. A restaurant, for instance, might struggle if a key supplier suddenly goes out of business.

3. **Market Risks**: Changing consumer preferences, increased competition, or economic downturns can threaten a business's success. Think of how Netflix had to adapt when streaming competitors like Disney+ entered the market.

4. **Legal and Regulatory Risks**: Failure to comply with local laws, tax requirements, or industry regulations can result in fines, lawsuits, or even business closure. For example, Uber

has faced numerous legal challenges in different countries due to varying regulations.

5. **Reputational Risks**: Negative reviews, social media backlash, or public scandals can harm a brand's image. A single viral incident can damage years of hard-earned trust, as seen in cases where companies mishandled customer complaints or public relations crises.

How to Identify Risks

To manage risks effectively, you must first identify them. Here's how to approach this:

Conduct a Risk Assessment: Analyze every aspect of your business, from finances to operations, and list potential vulnerabilities. For instance, ask yourself: What happens if sales drop by 20%? What if a supplier fails to deliver?

Learn from Industry Trends: Study similar businesses in your industry to identify common challenges. For example, if you're starting a retail store, look at how others have handled economic downturns or shifts to e-commerce.

Engage Experts: Professionals such as accountants, lawyers, and consultants can provide valuable insights into risks specific to your business model or industry. They can help you spot risks you may have overlooked.

Use Scenario Planning: Think about "what if" situations and plan accordingly. For example, what's your strategy if a major competitor cuts their prices or a key employee leaves?

Strategies to Avoid Risks

Once risks are identified, the next step is to create strategies to avoid or mitigate them:

Build Financial Resilience: Maintain a cash reserve to handle unexpected expenses. Monitor your cash flow closely and avoid overleveraging debt.

Diversify Suppliers and Revenue Streams: Relying too heavily on one supplier or product line can be risky. A logistics company, for example, might secure multiple freight providers to ensure continuity if one fails.

Ensure Compliance: Stay updated on legal and regulatory changes in your industry. Hiring a legal advisor or consultant can save you from costly compliance errors.

Invest in Reputation Management: Actively manage your brand's image by addressing customer complaints promptly and transparently. Establish a social media policy to prevent public missteps.

Have a Contingency Plan: Prepare for emergencies with a detailed plan. For instance, an e-commerce business should have backup servers to avoid downtime during peak shopping seasons.

Examples of Risk Management in Action

Businesses that proactively address risks often emerge stronger. For example:

Apple: The company has diversified its manufacturing to multiple countries, reducing its reliance on a single region like China. This minimizes the impact of geopolitical tensions or local disruptions.

Starbucks: The coffee giant locks in future coffee prices through hedging contracts, protecting itself from sudden price spikes in the commodity market.

Amazon: The company invests heavily in logistics infrastructure to avoid reliance on third-party shipping, ensuring smoother operations during peak seasons.

Conclusion

Risks are an inherent part of doing business, but they don't have to be paralyzing. By identifying potential challenges early and implementing strategies to address them, you can protect your business from avoidable setbacks and prepare for unexpected ones. Whether it's through financial planning, compliance measures, or diversification, proactive risk management allows you to focus on growth while staying resilient in the face of challenges

STEP 2: RECONFIRM - SECOND CREATION

After crafting your initial plan in Step 1, Step 2 focuses on reconfirming your ideas with real-world insights. This phase —the second creation—is where your vision begins to meet reality. It's not enough to have a great concept; you need to validate, test, and refine it to ensure it's practical, impactful, and ready for execution. This process reduces risks and builds confidence as you prepare to move forward.

Step 2 is divided into four critical chapters that guide you through the essentials of reconfirmation:

1. **Validating Your Idea**: Testing your concept with potential customers and markets to ensure it solves a real problem and has the potential to succeed. This chapter will explore why validation matters, how to approach it, and why it's an ongoing process.

2. **Feedback Matters**: Feedback is the backbone of growth. It reveals blind spots, uncovers opportunities, and ensures you're on the right track. Gathering meaningful insights from customers, advisors, and stakeholders is crucial to refining your strategy.

3. **Refining Your Plan**: With validation and feedback, your initial plan evolves into something more robust. Refinement is not a one-time activity but a continuous process of improvement. This chapter will provide actionable steps to strengthen your business model and approach.

4. **Risk-Free Testing**: Before fully committing resources, it's essential to test your idea without overextending. Smart, cost-effective testing minimizes risks and ensures your concept is ready for the market.

Step 2 isn't about finding perfection — it's about creating confidence. It's a phase where you embrace learning, adapt to challenges, and ensure that your business is built on a foundation of knowledge, not assumptions. By the end of this step, you'll have not only reconfirmed your vision but also armed yourself with the clarity and resilience needed to move forward

CHAPTER 8: PROVE IT FIRST: THE POWER OF VALIDATION

Great business ideas often start with a spark of inspiration, but even the brightest ideas need to be tested before they can shine. Validation is the process of proving that your idea works—not just in theory, but in practice. It's about gaining confidence in your concept and reducing risks by gathering real-world insights. Skipping validation is like building a house without a foundation—it might look promising at first, but it's bound to face trouble as you move forward.

This chapter explores why validation is essential and how to approach it effectively. From identifying your target audience to testing your idea on a small scale, validation provides the clarity you need to make informed decisions. It's not about perfecting your idea overnight but about confirming that it solves a real problem and meets market demand.

Validation also saves time, money, and resources. Many businesses fail because they launch without understanding what their customers truly want. This chapter will help you avoid those pitfalls by showing you how to test and refine your idea before committing fully.

Remember, validation isn't a one-time task. It's an ongoing process that evolves with your business. As markets, technologies, and customer preferences change, so must your approach to validation. By embracing it as a continuous practice, you'll position yourself to adapt and succeed in a competitive landscape.

Let's dive in and explore how to prove your idea, avoid the costs of skipping validation, and set your business up for success

Proving Your Idea: Confidence and Risk

Reduction

Starting a business is inherently risky, but that doesn't mean you need to dive in blindly. Validation is the bridge between an idea and a successful venture. It's the process of proving that your concept solves a real problem, resonates with your target audience, and has the potential to thrive in the market. By testing your idea early, you can build confidence in your decisions while reducing the risks of costly mistakes.

Why Validation Matters

Many startups fail because they skip the validation stage, rushing to launch without confirming whether their idea meets customer needs. Validation helps you uncover potential flaws, refine your approach, and ensure you're addressing a problem that matters to your audience. It's like performing a dress rehearsal before opening night —it reveals what's working and what needs adjustment.

Consider Airbnb's early days. The founders tested their concept by renting out air mattresses in their own apartment during a conference in San Francisco. This small-scale experiment not only validated the demand for affordable, short-term accommodations but also helped them refine their platform before scaling. By proving their idea on a small scale, they built the confidence needed to attract investors and grow their business.

The Benefits of Proving Your Idea

1. **Risk Reduction**:
    Validation minimizes financial and reputational risks by identifying potential issues before they escalate. Instead of investing heavily in an unproven idea, you can test its viability with minimal resources.

2. **Building Confidence**:
   When you validate your idea, you gain clarity and assurance that your concept has merit. This confidence is invaluable when pitching to investors, building a team, or committing your own time and energy.

3. **Customer Alignment**:
   Validation ensures that your solution aligns with customer needs and expectations. It helps you fine-tune your offering to better meet their demands, increasing the likelihood of success.

4. **Resource Optimization**:
   By validating first, you can focus your efforts on what works and avoid wasting resources on ineffective strategies or products.

How to Approach Validation

Validation doesn't require a massive budget or a fully developed product. Instead, the key is to start small and focus on incremental tests that provide meaningful feedback. The goal is to gather real-world insights without overcommitting resources. Here are some practical methods to approach validation:

1. **Surveys and Interviews**:
   Directly engage with potential customers to understand their pain points and whether your solution resonates with them. Ask open-ended questions to uncover what they truly need and value. For instance, if you're considering launching a new coffee shop, ask customers in your target area about their preferences, such as hours of operation or menu options.

2. **Prototypes**:
   Develop a simple version of your product or service and test it with a small audience. Prototypes don't need to be perfect; they are meant to demonstrate functionality and gather feedback. For example, if you're creating a new app, a

clickable mock-up can help users visualize the concept without full development.

3. **Popup Stores or Market Trials**:
    A popup store or night market stall can be an excellent way to test a product without committing to a long-term lease or high overhead costs. If you're launching a food business, setting up at a local night market lets you test customer interest, gather feedback, and refine your offerings based on real-world interactions.

4. **Online Sales with Low Commitment**:
    Selling online can reduce overhead and long-term commitments. Platforms like Etsy, eBay, or even social media can help you test demand for a product with minimal investment. This method allows you to adjust your approach quickly based on customer feedback.

5. **Pre-Orders and Presales**:
    Offer your product or service for pre-order before it's fully developed. This approach not only gauges interest but also helps generate early revenue. For example, Tesla successfully validates demand for new vehicles through pre-order campaigns, securing customer commitments long before production begins.

6. **Landing Pages**:
    Create a simple webpage that describes your concept, its benefits, and a call to action, such as signing up for updates or placing a pre-order. Tools like Google Ads or social media can drive traffic to your landing page, giving you insights into customer interest and engagement.
    Example: Before building Dropbox, the founders created a short demo video explaining how their product would work. The overwhelmingly positive response validated their idea without writing a single line of code. The feedback also helped them prioritize features based on customer needs.

Why Start Small?

Starting small minimizes risks and keeps costs manageable. It allows you to test ideas quickly and refine them based on real feedback before scaling up. These incremental steps ensure you're solving a real problem for your audience while giving you the flexibility to pivot if necessary.

This iterative approach is particularly powerful because it keeps you connected to your target market throughout the process. Each test sharpens your understanding of what customers want, helping you shape a product or service that truly resonates

Validation: A Continuous Process

Proving your idea isn't a one-and-done task. Markets evolve, and customer preferences change. Continuous validation allows you to adapt and grow alongside your audience. Businesses that embrace this mindset—like Amazon, which constantly tests and refines its offerings—are better positioned to stay competitive.

Conclusion

Validation is your safety net in the high-stakes world of entrepreneurship. By proving your idea early, you reduce risks, build confidence, and ensure alignment with your target audience. It's not about eliminating uncertainty entirely but about making informed decisions that set your business up for long-term success. As you move forward, let validation guide you, helping you refine your concept and solidify your path to a thriving venture

The Cost of Skipping Validation

Skipping validation might seem tempting when you're eager to launch your business. After all, validation takes time, effort, and sometimes money. But failing to validate your idea is like setting sail without checking the weather forecast—it might look fine at first, but you're heading straight into unknown waters. The consequences of skipping validation can be dire, often leading to wasted resources, damaged reputations, and outright failure.

The High Price of Assumptions

When businesses skip validation, they base their decisions on assumptions rather than facts. This often leads to creating products or services that don't resonate with customers or solve the wrong problems. For example:

Segway: The self-balancing scooter was marketed as a revolutionary mode of transportation. However, the creators didn't validate whether people actually wanted or needed it. The product failed to meet sales expectations, largely because its use case wasn't clear to customers.

Pepsi's Crystal Pepsi: In the 1990s, Pepsi launched a clear cola, assuming customers would embrace it as a unique, health-conscious option. However, they didn't validate whether customers associated clarity with cola flavors. The product flopped because it confused rather than inspired.

These examples illustrate how assumptions can lead to products that miss the mark entirely, wasting time, money, and market opportunities.

Financial Losses

Skipping validation often results in financial losses that could have been avoided. Developing a product, building inventory, or creating marketing campaigns for an untested idea can drain resources without any return. For small businesses and startups, these losses can be catastrophic.

Take the example of **Juicero**, the high-tech juicer that raised millions in funding but didn't validate its value to consumers. Customers quickly discovered they could squeeze the juice packs by hand, rendering the $400 machine unnecessary. The company collapsed, leaving behind millions in unsold inventory and a cautionary tale for other entrepreneurs.

Damaged Reputation

A failed product or service doesn't just cost money—it can also damage your reputation. Customers who feel misled or disappointed are less likely to trust your brand in the future. This damage can take years to repair, especially for new businesses.

For instance, **MoviePass**, the subscription-based movie ticket service, gained rapid popularity but didn't validate whether its pricing model was sustainable. The company faced backlash when it couldn't deliver on its promises, leading to frustrated customers and a tarnished brand.

Lost Opportunities

Without validation, you risk investing in the wrong idea while missing opportunities for better ones. Validation not only uncovers flaws but also highlights areas of potential improvement or alternative paths. Many businesses pivot to success after realizing their initial concept wasn't viable, but those who skip validation may never see these opportunities.

For example, Slack originally started as an internal communication tool for a gaming company. Through validation, the founders realized the potential for broader use and pivoted to create one of the most successful workplace communication platforms in the world.

Why Entrepreneurs Skip Validation

Despite the risks, some entrepreneurs skip validation because they fear hearing negative feedback or believe their intuition is enough. Others may underestimate its importance or feel validation takes too much time. However, the time and effort spent validating upfront pale in comparison to the cost of failure down the road.

Conclusion

Skipping validation might seem like a shortcut, but it often leads to costly mistakes that could have been avoided with a little effort and foresight. The price of skipping validation isn't just financial—it can harm your reputation, waste opportunities, and jeopardize your business's future. Validation is not a luxury; it's a necessity. By proving your idea early, you set the stage for success while saving time, money, and credibility. It's a small investment with immense returns, ensuring your business is built on a foundation of facts rather than assumptions.

Validation in Action: Real-World Steps to Prove Your Idea

Turning your business idea into a viable venture requires more than enthusiasm—it demands proof. Validation in action means moving beyond assumptions and theoretical planning to test your concept in real-world scenarios. This is where you uncover whether your idea holds up under actual conditions, resonates with your target audience, and delivers value. Let's explore the practical steps to make validation a hands-on, actionable process.

1. Define What You're Testing

Every validation effort starts with a clear question: what do you need to know? Are you testing whether your product solves a specific problem, if your pricing is right, or if there's enough demand? Each test should have a focused objective. For example:

A new food delivery app might validate whether people are willing to pay for convenience over traditional takeout.

An innovative fitness product might test if the unique features attract customers compared to existing alternatives.

Defining the question keeps your efforts targeted and efficient.

2. Start with Small Experiments

The first steps in validation don't require full-scale operations. Instead, start small with low-cost, low-commitment tests. These could include:

Launching a single product line: A new fashion brand might start by selling one type of clothing to gauge demand before expanding.

Participating in local events: Food startups often test their offerings at farmers' markets or festivals, gathering direct feedback from customers.

For example, Warby Parker initially operated as an online-only glasses retailer. To validate their concept, they sent prototypes to friends and potential customers, gathering insights on preferences before committing to large-scale production.

3. Engage Directly with Your Audience

Customer feedback is invaluable during validation. It's one thing to test a concept; it's another to understand why customers respond to it. Use methods like:

Pop-Up Shops: Temporary setups allow you to observe how customers interact with your product in person.

Focus Groups: Gather a small group of potential customers to test your idea and provide detailed insights.

For instance, when Zappos wanted to validate online shoe sales, the founder started by listing shoes from local stores online and personally buying and shipping them when customers placed orders. This validated demand before they invested in inventory and logistics.

4. Simulate the Market Online

The digital world offers cost-effective ways to validate ideas in real time. Set up a basic landing page or e-commerce store and test your idea's appeal. Techniques include:

Pre-Sales Campaigns: If you're launching a new gadget, offer it for pre-order and gauge how many people commit to buying.

Social Media Ads: Use platforms like Facebook or Instagram to advertise your concept and track engagement or sign-ups.

Example: Pebble, the smartwatch company, validated demand through Kickstarter, raising over $10 million from early adopters. This overwhelming response provided proof of concept and funding to bring the product to life.

5. Measure, Analyze, and Adjust

Data is the lifeblood of validation. After running your experiments, measure the results and look for patterns. Key metrics might include:

1. Customer interest (e.g., clicks, sign-ups, or purchases).

2. Feedback on pricing or features.

3. Pain points or objections raised during testing.

Take the lessons learned and refine your approach. For instance, if customers showed interest but hesitated due to price, consider tweaking your pricing strategy or adding value to the offering.

6. Iterate Continuously

Validation isn't a one-time task; it's an ongoing process. As your business grows, re-test your assumptions to stay aligned with evolving market trends. Continuous validation ensures your product or service remains relevant and competitive.

Conclusion

Validation in action is about taking meaningful steps to prove your idea in the real world. Whether you're testing with a popup shop, engaging customers through surveys, or running online campaigns, each step brings clarity and reduces uncertainty. By defining your focus, starting small, and continuously learning from your experiments, you build a foundation for a business that's not only viable but ready to thrive.

Validating is not one time thing

Validation isn't a task you check off your list and forget about—it's an ongoing process that evolves with your business. Markets shift, customer preferences change, and competitors emerge. What worked yesterday may not work tomorrow, and businesses that fail to adapt risk being left behind. Continuous validation ensures your business stays aligned with the needs of your audience, the realities of your industry, and the opportunities for growth.

Why Validation is Ongoing

1. **Changing Market Dynamics**:
   Industries rarely remain static. A trend or demand that propels your business today could fade away tomorrow. For instance, Blockbuster thrived on physical movie rentals until streaming services like Netflix validated and dominated a more convenient delivery model. Netflix continues to validate its approach by analyzing viewer preferences and adapting its offerings to maintain relevance.

2. **Evolving Customer Expectations**:
   Customers' needs and behaviors are constantly evolving, influenced by new technology, cultural shifts, or economic changes. For example, Starbucks continually validates its menu by introducing seasonal items and testing innovative concepts like mobile ordering to enhance the customer experience.

3. **Your Business Grows and Changes**:
   As your business scales, what worked for a small startup may no longer be effective. A small local restaurant might validate menu changes through direct customer interaction, but as it grows into a franchise, validation may need to involve larger-scale surveys or data-driven insights.

Practical Steps for Continuous Validation

1. **Monitor Key Metrics**:
   Keep an eye on sales data, customer retention rates, and other performance indicators. If these numbers start to dip, it's a signal to revisit your assumptions and validate whether your offerings still meet market needs.

2. **Regularly Gather Feedback**:
   Establish systems to collect customer feedback on an ongoing basis. This could include post-purchase surveys, online reviews, or social media engagement. Actively listen to what your customers are saying and use their insights to refine your strategies.

3. **Test New Ideas Frequently**:
   Treat your business as a living experiment. Whether it's a new product, marketing strategy, or operational change, validate these ideas with small-scale tests before rolling them out widely.

4. **Benchmark Against Competitors**:
   Watch what your competitors are doing and analyze why their strategies succeed or fail. This helps you validate your own approach in the context of the broader market.

Examples of Continuous Validation

Amazon: One of the reasons Amazon dominates is its commitment to constant validation. By continuously testing and refining its user interface, delivery options, and product recommendations, Amazon stays ahead of competitors and ensures a seamless customer experience.

Coca-Cola: While the classic Coca-Cola formula remains unchanged, the company consistently validates its product lineup through market research and limited releases of new flavors, such as Cherry Coke or Vanilla Coke.

The Risks of Stopping Validation

If you stop validating your ideas, you risk becoming out of touch with your market. For example:

Kodak failed to validate the impact of digital photography, sticking to traditional film even as the market shifted. The result? A once-dominant company fell behind, unable to adapt to customer demands.

MySpace, once a leading social media platform, didn't validate its approach against emerging competitors like Facebook, which led to its decline.

Conclusion

Validation is not a one-time checkpoint; it's a continuous process that ensures your business remains relevant, competitive, and customer-focused. By regularly testing your assumptions, gathering feedback, and adapting to change, you build a business that can thrive in the face of uncertainty. Remember, the journey of validation never ends—it evolves with your business, keeping you aligned with the ever-changing world.

CHAPTER 9: FEEDBACK: THE COMPASS FOR GROWTH

Feedback is one of the most powerful tools for growth in any business. It acts as a compass, guiding you toward improvement, innovation, and alignment with your customers' needs. No matter how brilliant your initial idea may seem, the real test lies in how it resonates with the people you aim to serve. Feedback bridges the gap between your vision and reality, providing the insights needed to adapt, improve, and thrive.

This chapter focuses on making feedback an integral part of your business strategy. Gathering feedback isn't just about listening to customers—it's about truly understanding their needs, desires, and frustrations. When used effectively, feedback can reveal blind spots, uncover new opportunities, and even inspire breakthroughs you hadn't considered.

But feedback alone isn't enough. It's about asking the right questions, analyzing the information thoughtfully, and acting on it decisively. A structured approach to feedback ensures you don't just collect data but turn it into actionable insights that drive your business forward. Whether you're just starting out or scaling to new heights, mastering the art of feedback is essential for staying relevant and competitive.

In this chapter, you'll learn why feedback matters, how to gather meaningful insights, and how to turn those insights into actions that propel your business forward. Feedback isn't just a tool for troubleshooting; it's your secret weapon for continuous growth and lasting success. Let's explore how to use it to your advantage

Feedback is Your Business's Lifeline

In the ever-changing landscape of business, feedback serves as your lifeline—a critical tool that keeps your business connected to the people it serves. Without feedback, even the most innovative ideas risk falling short, misaligned with customer needs or market demands. Feedback is more than just data; it's a bridge between your vision and the real world, offering clarity, guidance, and an opportunity to improve.

Why Feedback Matters

Feedback ensures you're solving the right problems for your audience. It helps answer essential questions: Are customers satisfied? Does your product or service meet their expectations? Are there ways to improve? Ignoring feedback is like sailing without a compass—you might move forward, but you'll have no idea if you're heading in the right direction.

Consider Amazon, one of the most customer-focused companies in the world. Its success is largely due to its commitment to listening to customers. From the early days, Amazon collected feedback on everything from website navigation to delivery times. This relentless focus on feedback allowed Amazon to refine its processes, introduce features like one-click ordering, and build unmatched customer loyalty.

Feedback for Every Stage of Business

Feedback isn't just for established companies—it's vital at every stage of a business's journey:

For Startups: Feedback can validate your idea, refine your product, and ensure you're solving real customer problems.

For Growing Businesses: Feedback highlights areas for improvement and helps you adapt to a larger or more diverse audience.

For Established Companies: Feedback keeps you competitive, revealing emerging trends and shifting customer preferences.

Netflix, for example, uses customer data and feedback to continually refine its content offerings. By analyzing viewer preferences, it shifted from a DVD rental service to a global leader in streaming and original programming. This evolution wasn't guesswork—it was feedback-driven innovation.

The Risk of Ignoring Feedback

Ignoring feedback can lead to missteps, lost customers, and reputational damage. Blockbuster, for instance, failed to adapt to the digital shift in entertainment because it didn't heed the feedback customers gave indirectly through their actions—like switching to Netflix. Feedback, when ignored, becomes a missed opportunity for growth and innovation.

Conclusion

Feedback is not just a tool; it's the lifeline that keeps your business aligned with its audience. By embracing feedback, you gain clarity, reduce risks, and ensure your efforts are directed toward what truly matters. Whether it's through direct conversations, surveys, or data analysis, feedback keeps your business grounded in reality while empowering it to grow. Recognize it as a gift—a compass that points you toward long-term success

Getting Real Insights: Gathering

Meaningful Feedback

Feedback is only as valuable as the quality of the insights it provides. Gathering meaningful feedback means going beyond surface-level questions to uncover deep, actionable insights that help you refine your business and better serve your audience. It's not just about collecting opinions—it's about understanding the why behind those opinions and using that knowledge to make informed decisions.

The Importance of Meaningful Feedback

Meaningful feedback serves as the foundation for growth and improvement. It highlights what's working, what needs adjustment, and what opportunities might be hiding just below the surface. For example:

When Starbucks introduced its mobile app, it didn't stop at launch. Through user feedback, the company refined the app's interface, improved the payment system, and added features like rewards tracking. These changes were directly informed by meaningful feedback from customers.

Gathering meaningful feedback ensures you're focusing on the right areas, saving time and resources that might otherwise be wasted on ineffective changes.

Methods to Gather Feedback

There are numerous ways to collect feedback, each with its strengths. The key is to choose methods that align with your goals and audience.

1. **Direct Conversations**
   Face-to-face discussions or phone calls provide rich, detailed insights. They allow you to ask follow-up questions and clarify responses in real time. For instance, if you're launching a new product, talking directly with potential customers can reveal their expectations and concerns.

2. **Surveys and Questionnaires**
   Surveys are a scalable way to collect feedback from a larger audience. Platforms like Google Forms, SurveyMonkey, or Typeform make it easy to design and distribute surveys. Keep your questions specific and concise to encourage honest and useful responses.

3. **Customer Reviews and Social Media**
   Monitor online reviews and social media mentions to understand how customers perceive your brand. Tools like Hootsuite or Google Alerts can help track mentions and sentiments, giving you a pulse on public opinion.

4. **Usability Testing**
   For products or digital platforms, usability testing provides direct insights into how customers interact with your offerings. Watch how users navigate your website, app, or service to identify pain points or areas for improvement.

5. **Focus Groups**
   Bringing together a small group of customers to discuss your product or service can provide qualitative feedback and spark ideas you hadn't considered.

Best Practices for Gathering Feedback

Be Specific: Ask targeted questions that address specific areas of your business. For instance, instead of asking, "Do you like our service?" ask, "What aspect of our service do you find most valuable?"

Make It Easy: Simplify the feedback process to encourage participation. Short surveys, easy-to-navigate forms, or casual conversations work better than lengthy or complicated methods.

Incentivize Participation: Offering small rewards, like discounts or gift cards, can increase response rates without compromising the quality of feedback.

Examples of Feedback in Action

Apple's dedication to gathering customer feedback has been central to its success. Before launching new features or products, Apple conducts extensive testing and collects user insights to ensure their offerings meet expectations. This commitment to meaningful feedback has helped the company consistently deliver innovative and user-friendly products.

Similarly, Toyota's success with its Kaizen philosophy—continuous improvement—is built on collecting and acting on employee and customer feedback. This approach ensures every aspect of the company aligns with its goals and customer needs.

Conclusion

Gathering meaningful feedback isn't about asking for opinions; it's about seeking real insights that inform your business decisions. By choosing the right methods, asking the right questions, and making the process seamless for your audience, you can gain the clarity and direction needed to improve and grow. Remember, feedback isn't just data—it's a conversation with your customers, and every meaningful insight brings you closer to long-term success.

Mastering the Craft of Effective Feedback

Questions

The quality of feedback you receive depends largely on the quality of the questions you ask. Poorly framed or vague questions can lead to generic responses, while well-crafted questions open the door to meaningful insights that can guide your business decisions. Asking the right questions is an art, one that requires clarity, focus, and empathy for the person providing feedback.

Effective feedback questions can help you identify what's working, what isn't, and what opportunities might exist for improvement. For instance, when Netflix wanted to refine its platform, they didn't just ask users if they liked the service. Instead, they delved into specifics: what content they enjoyed, how they navigated the platform, and what features they wanted. These targeted inquiries allowed Netflix to personalize its offerings and maintain its position as a market leader.

The Core Principles of Effective Feedback Questions

Clarity is key when crafting feedback questions. Ambiguous or overly broad questions often confuse respondents, leading to unclear answers. A question like "What do you think about our business?" might yield vague responses such as "It's good" or "It's fine," which offer little actionable insight. Instead, specific questions like "How satisfied are you with our delivery speed, and why?" guide the respondent to provide focused feedback.

Another important principle is focusing on one idea per question. Overloading a single question with multiple components can overwhelm respondents and produce incomplete answers. For example, instead of asking, "Do you like our product and customer service?" it's more effective to split this into two distinct questions: "How satisfied are you with our product quality?" and "How would you rate our customer service?"

Encouraging open-ended responses is equally important. While yes-or-no questions are quick and easy, they often miss the nuances of customer sentiment. Asking, "What did you like or dislike about your experience with our service?" invites customers to elaborate, providing richer, more detailed insights that can lead to actionable changes.

When appropriate, consider using scenario-based questions. These questions help respondents think about real-life situations, making their feedback more practical and grounded. For instance, an app developer might ask, "If you were using our app to book a service, what feature would make the process easier for you?" This approach helps you understand user behavior in context.

Avoiding Pitfalls in Feedback Questions

It's critical to avoid leading or biased questions that might influence the respondent's answer. For example, a question like "Don't you think our service is great?" is likely to elicit a positive response regardless of the customer's true feelings. A better alternative would be, "How would you describe your experience with our service?" Neutral language ensures that feedback is authentic and unbiased.

Furthermore, always make the feedback process simple and convenient. If customers find it tedious or time-consuming to provide their input, they're less likely to do so. Short, clear questions delivered through accessible formats—such as online surveys or casual in-person conversations—are far more effective.

Real-World Examples of Effective Feedback

Businesses that master the art of asking the right questions often find themselves ahead of the competition. Amazon is a prime example. After a purchase, Amazon doesn't simply ask, "Did you like the product?" Instead, they ask targeted questions like, "Did this product meet your expectations?" and "How would you rate the delivery experience?" These specific queries provide actionable insights for improving both products and services.

Another example is Slack, which tailors its platform based on customer feedback. During onboarding, they ask new users, "What features are most important for your team?" This focused question helps Slack refine its offerings to meet the unique needs of different businesses, ensuring customer satisfaction and loyalty.

The Impact of Thoughtful Questions

Crafting effective feedback questions is not a one-time effort but an ongoing practice. As your business evolves, so will the questions you need to ask. Thoughtful questions foster a dialogue between you and your customers, building trust and demonstrating that you value their opinions. This trust, in turn, encourages more honest and detailed feedback, creating a virtuous cycle of improvement.

Conclusion

Mastering the craft of effective feedback questions is essential for any entrepreneur. By asking clear, focused, and meaningful questions, you can unlock insights that guide your business forward.

The right questions don't just collect data—they create a connection between you and your audience, empowering you to build a business that truly meets their needs. Whether you're refining a product, enhancing a service, or exploring new opportunities, the way you ask for feedback shapes the answers you receive—and ultimately, the success you achieve.

Creating a Framework for Continuous Feedback

Feedback is not a one-time exercise—it's a continuous process that evolves with your business. To remain competitive and relevant, you need a structured system for consistently collecting, analyzing, and acting on feedback. A well-designed framework ensures that feedback isn't scattered or ignored but becomes a tool for growth and adaptability.

A feedback framework is more than just gathering opinions; it's about creating a reliable system that keeps your business aligned with customer needs, market trends, and operational goals. For example, companies like Amazon and Apple have embedded feedback loops into their core processes, allowing them to refine products, enhance customer experiences, and stay ahead in their industries.

Building the Foundation of Your Feedback Framework

The first step in creating a feedback system is to define your objectives. Are you trying to improve customer satisfaction, refine a product, or identify operational inefficiencies? Having clear goals helps you focus your efforts and ensures the insights you gather are actionable.

Feedback can come from multiple sources—customers, employees, suppliers, or even competitors. It's important to set up consistent channels for collecting this feedback. For example, direct conversations, customer surveys, and online reviews are excellent ways to engage customers, while internal feedback systems can help you gather ideas from employees. A restaurant might solicit feedback through comment cards, while an e-commerce business may use post-purchase surveys to understand the customer experience better.

Integrating feedback collection into your regular operations is crucial. If you gather feedback sporadically, you risk missing trends or failing to act on critical insights. A company like Starbucks ensures regular customer engagement through platforms like "My Starbucks Idea," which allows customers to submit ideas and feedback, creating an ongoing dialogue.

Turning Feedback Into Action

Collecting feedback is only the beginning. The real power lies in analyzing the data and acting on it. Start by organizing the feedback into themes or categories, such as product features, customer service, or delivery efficiency. Tools like customer relationship management (CRM) software can help streamline this process, making it easier to identify recurring issues or opportunities.

Once you've analyzed the data, prioritize the changes based on their potential impact. For example, if multiple customers mention that your website is difficult to navigate, addressing this issue should take precedence over minor aesthetic changes.

Closing the loop is an essential part of the feedback framework. Customers want to know their voices are heard. By communicating the actions you've taken based on their input—such as introducing a new feature or improving a process—you build trust and encourage more engagement. Similarly, within your team, recognizing employees for valuable suggestions fosters a culture of innovation and collaboration.

Keeping Your Framework Dynamic

A feedback system should be flexible, adapting as your business grows or market conditions change. Continuous improvement is the cornerstone of successful companies like Toyota, whose Kaizen philosophy emphasizes learning and innovation driven by feedback from all levels of the organization. Similarly, Netflix consistently refines its offerings based on viewer preferences, ensuring it stays relevant in a competitive market.

Creating a framework for continuous feedback requires effort and commitment, but the rewards are immense. It provides a steady stream of insights that guide decision-making, enhance customer satisfaction, and strengthen your business against unforeseen challenges. With this system in place, you're not just responding to change—you're staying ahead of it.

From Feedback to Action: Closing the Loop

Collecting feedback is essential, but its true value lies in what you do with it. Turning feedback into meaningful action is the ultimate goal of any feedback system. Closing the loop means acknowledging the insights you've received, implementing changes based on that feedback, and communicating those actions back to the stakeholders who contributed. This process not only drives improvement but also builds trust and loyalty among your customers, employees, and partners.

The Importance of Closing the Loop

When customers or team members provide feedback, they're offering their time, thoughts, and ideas. Ignoring that feedback—or failing to act on it—can leave them feeling undervalued, eroding trust and reducing their willingness to engage in the future. On the other hand, closing the loop demonstrates that you value their input and are committed to using it for positive change.

Take Starbucks as an example. Through its "My Starbucks Idea" platform, the company invites customers to share suggestions and then implements the best ones, such as introducing new drink options or loyalty program enhancements. By publicly acknowledging these contributions, Starbucks shows that it listens and acts, reinforcing customer loyalty.

How to Turn Feedback Into Action

The journey from feedback to action involves several key steps. First, you need to analyze the feedback you've gathered to identify recurring themes or critical issues. For example, if multiple customers highlight long wait times at your restaurant, it's clear that this area needs attention. Prioritize feedback based on its potential impact—what changes will most significantly improve the customer or employee experience?

Next, develop a plan to address the issues raised. If the feedback is about product quality, this might involve revisiting your manufacturing process or supplier agreements. If it's about service, it could mean retraining staff or revising workflows. The key is to take tangible, measurable steps that address the core concerns.

Finally, ensure you communicate the actions you've taken. Transparency is vital here. Let customers and team members know how their feedback influenced your decisions. For example, a software company might release an update with a note saying, "Based on your feedback, we've added this feature to improve usability." This kind of communication not only closes the loop but also encourages further engagement.

Examples of Feedback-Driven Change

Some of the most successful companies have built their reputations on effectively turning feedback into action. For instance:

Amazon: Constantly refines its platform based on customer reviews and preferences, from introducing one-click ordering to optimizing delivery times.

Toyota: Embraces a culture of continuous improvement (Kaizen), where feedback from employees and customers is actively implemented to enhance product quality and operational efficiency.

Slack: Regularly updates its platform with features requested by users, ensuring the tool stays relevant and user-friendly.

These companies don't just listen; they act. This commitment to closing the loop keeps them ahead of the competition and builds long-term loyalty.

The Challenges of Acting on Feedback

Closing the loop can be challenging, especially when feedback is conflicting or involves significant resources to address. For example, customers might request a feature that's difficult to implement within your current budget or timeline. In these cases, it's crucial to be honest and manage expectations. Communicate what you can do now and what might be possible in the future, showing that you take the feedback seriously even if immediate action isn't feasible.

Conclusion

Feedback without action is a missed opportunity. By closing the loop —analyzing feedback, implementing changes, and communicating your efforts—you demonstrate that you value the voices of your customers, employees, and stakeholders. This process drives continuous improvement, strengthens relationships, and sets your business on a path to sustained success. Remember, feedback is only the beginning; the real transformation happens when you take action.

CHAPTER 10: ADAPT, IMPROVE, THRIVE: REFINE AND REDEFINE TO PERFECT YOUR PLAN

Creating a business plan is a vital step in building your entrepreneurial journey, but no plan is ever perfect from the outset. Refinement is where good plans become great and where great plans evolve to meet the demands of reality. This chapter focuses on the critical process of adapting, improving, and redefining your plan to ensure it stays relevant, actionable, and aligned with your goals.

The road to success is rarely linear. Markets shift, customer needs change, and new challenges arise. A static business plan can quickly become outdated in this dynamic environment. Refinement allows you to address these changes proactively, transforming obstacles into opportunities and ensuring your plan reflects the latest insights and feedback.

In this chapter, we'll explore why refinement is essential, guide you through the practical steps to enhance your plan, and emphasize that refinement is an ongoing journey. By committing to this process, you can ensure your business plan remains a living document—one that adapts, improves, and evolves alongside your ambitions.

Let's delve into how refining and redefining can bring you closer to perfection and position your business for long-term success.

Refinement is Essential for Success

In the world of business, a plan is never truly finished—it's a living document that evolves alongside your goals, market conditions, and customer needs. Refinement is the process of revisiting, rethinking, and enhancing your plan to ensure it stays relevant and effective. Without refinement, even the most promising ideas risk becoming stagnant or misaligned with the realities of the market.

Why Refinement Matters

Refinement bridges the gap between theory and practice. While your initial business plan outlines your vision, the real world often presents challenges and opportunities you couldn't have anticipated. Refinement allows you to adapt to these changes, making your plan stronger and more actionable. It's not a sign of failure—it's a mark of growth.

Consider how businesses like Tesla have embraced refinement. Tesla's initial plan to revolutionize electric vehicles began with the high-end Roadster, which allowed the company to test its technology and validate its market. Over time, Tesla refined its approach, introducing more affordable models like the Model 3 to broaden its audience. This iterative process of refinement enabled Tesla to stay ahead of competitors and achieve its ambitious vision.

Refinement as a Tool for Innovation

Refinement isn't just about fixing problems; it's a tool for innovation. By continuously revisiting your plan, you can uncover new opportunities, streamline processes, and enhance your offerings. Apple's success with the iPhone is a testament to the power of refinement. Each new iteration of the iPhone builds on customer feedback, technological advancements, and market trends, keeping the product fresh and desirable.

Similarly, small businesses can use refinement to improve efficiency and customer satisfaction. A restaurant might start with a basic menu, then refine it over time based on customer preferences, seasonal ingredients, and operational feedback. This process ensures the business stays relevant and competitive.

The Risk of Skipping Refinement

Failing to refine your plan can leave you vulnerable to unforeseen challenges. Kodak, for example, was a pioneer in photography but didn't refine its strategy to embrace the digital age, leading to its decline. Refinement isn't just a luxury; it's a necessity for survival and growth in an ever-changing business landscape.

Conclusion

Refinement is not an admission of imperfection—it's an essential part of achieving success. By embracing refinement as a continuous process, you can adapt to change, seize new opportunities, and ensure your business stays on the path to growth. Remember, the most successful businesses aren't those with flawless plans but those with the willingness and ability to refine and improve continuously. Let refinement be your ally as you navigate the challenges and opportunities of entrepreneurship.

The Refinement Process: Practical Steps

to Polish Your Plan

Refinement is the bridge between a good plan and a great one. It's the process of identifying gaps, addressing weaknesses, and leveraging opportunities to ensure your business plan is as effective and resilient as possible. Polishing your plan is not about starting over but about making thoughtful adjustments that bring it closer to perfection. Let's explore practical steps to refine your plan into a powerful tool for success.

1. Review Your Plan with Fresh Eyes

The first step in refinement is to revisit your plan with a critical perspective. Step away for a while and return with fresh eyes, or involve a trusted mentor, advisor, or colleague who can offer an unbiased review. Ask yourself:

1. Are the assumptions you made initially still valid?

2. Does the plan reflect the latest market trends and customer needs?

3. Are there any gaps in your strategy or execution timeline?

For example, when Amazon first launched as an online bookstore, Jeff Bezos reviewed his original business plan and recognized a broader opportunity in e-commerce. By refining the plan to include other product categories, Amazon became the global marketplace it is today.

2. Integrate Feedback from Validation and Experience

Feedback from customers, employees, and market research is a treasure trove of insights for refinement. Use the lessons learned from validation and testing phases to address weaknesses or enhance areas of your plan that need improvement. For instance:

A. If customers express concerns about pricing, consider refining your pricing model to better reflect value without compromising margins.

B. If team members highlight inefficiencies in operations, adjust workflows or allocate resources more effectively.

Slack's journey is a perfect example of refinement based on feedback. Originally developed as an internal communication tool, Slack's founders refined the product based on user input, evolving it into a platform that revolutionized workplace communication.

3. Reassess Financial Projections and Resources

Your financial projections are likely based on assumptions made during the early stages of planning. Refinement involves reassessing these numbers to ensure they align with current realities. Evaluate:

A. Are your revenue projections realistic based on market validation?

B. Have your costs changed due to new insights or scaling plans?

C. Is your funding sufficient to achieve your goals, or do you need additional investment?

Revisiting these elements ensures that your plan is financially sound and adaptable to potential challenges.

4. Test Adjustments on a Small Scale

Before making sweeping changes, test refinements on a small scale to gauge their effectiveness. For example:

A. Introduce a new product or service feature to a limited audience before a full rollout.

B. Pilot a revised marketing strategy in a specific region to measure its impact.

This approach minimizes risk and provides data to support your refinements. Toyota's Kaizen philosophy exemplifies this iterative process, where continuous small improvements lead to significant long-term gains.

5. Align with Long-Term Goals

While making refinements, ensure that your adjustments align with your broader vision and goals. It's easy to get sidetracked by short-term trends or pressures, but staying true to your mission will keep your business on track. For instance, if your goal is sustainability, refine your supply chain or product design to align with eco-friendly practices.

6. Document and Communicate Changes

Refinements are only effective if they're clearly documented and communicated. Update your business plan to reflect new strategies, timelines, or goals. Share these updates with your team to ensure alignment and accountability. When Tesla adjusted its strategy to focus on scaling production for the Model 3, the team's clarity and alignment were instrumental in executing the plan.

Conclusion

The refinement process is an essential step in turning your business plan into a dynamic tool that grows with your vision. By revisiting your plan, integrating feedback, and testing changes, you can adapt to challenges and seize opportunities. Refinement isn't about perfection—it's about progress. With each iteration, your plan becomes more resilient, actionable, and aligned with success.

Refinement is a Journey, Not a Destination

In the world of business, there's no such thing as a perfect plan. Markets evolve, customer needs shift, and unforeseen challenges arise. The key to long-term success isn't creating a flawless blueprint —it's continuously refining your plan to adapt to new realities. Refinement is an ongoing journey that keeps your business relevant, competitive, and aligned with its goals.

The Nature of Continuous Refinement

A business plan isn't a static document; it's a living, breathing guide that evolves as your company grows. What worked yesterday may not work tomorrow, and the ability to pivot and improve is what separates thriving businesses from stagnant ones. Refinement is about staying flexible and open to change while maintaining focus on your core mission.

Consider how Netflix has approached refinement. Originally a DVD rental service, Netflix recognized the shift toward digital streaming early on. By continuously refining its business model and adapting to emerging trends, Netflix transitioned into a global leader in streaming and original content. This transformation didn't happen overnight—it was the result of ongoing refinement driven by market changes and customer feedback.

Embracing a Growth Mindset

Viewing refinement as a journey requires adopting a growth mindset. Instead of seeing changes as corrections or admissions of failure, treat them as opportunities to learn and improve. Every challenge, feedback point, or market shift is a chance to revisit your plan and make it better.

For example, when Slack first launched as a workplace communication tool, it wasn't immediately perfect. The team continuously refined the product based on user feedback, adjusting features, improving usability, and enhancing integrations. This iterative process turned Slack into one of the most popular and effective collaboration platforms in the world.

Refinement Through Every Stage of Growth

Refinement isn't just for startups; it's a critical practice at every stage of a business's lifecycle.

Startups refine their initial plans as they validate ideas and gather early feedback.

Growing businesses refine to scale operations, expand into new markets, and address increasing complexities.

Established companies refine to stay competitive, innovate, and meet changing customer demands.

Take Coca-Cola as an example. Despite its long-standing success, the company continuously refines its product lineup, marketing strategies, and global operations. This ongoing process ensures it remains a leader in the beverage industry.

The Risk of Stopping Refinement

Complacency can be a business killer. Companies that fail to refine risk falling behind competitors or becoming irrelevant in their markets. Kodak is a cautionary tale of this—despite inventing the digital camera, the company stuck to its traditional film business model and failed to refine its strategy to embrace the digital revolution. The result was a loss of market dominance and a long struggle to regain relevance.

Conclusion

Refinement is not a one-time task; it's an ongoing journey that keeps your business resilient, adaptable, and forward-looking. By embracing the mindset that there's always room for improvement, you position your business for sustainable growth and success. Remember, it's not about achieving perfection—it's about consistently striving to be better. In this journey, refinement is your most valuable tool for staying ahead in an ever-changing world.

CHAPTER 11: SMART AND RISK-FREE TESTING

Testing your business idea is one of the most critical steps in your entrepreneurial journey. It's the moment where theory meets reality—where you find out if your concept resonates with your target audience, if your processes work as expected, and if your pricing is sustainable. However, testing doesn't have to be expensive or high-risk. A smart and risk-free approach allows you to validate your ideas without jeopardizing your resources or reputation.

This chapter focuses on how to test efficiently and strategically. Smart testing means using creative, low-cost methods to evaluate your concept and gather real-world insights. Whether it's through small-scale experiments, pilot programs, or customer feedback, each test provides valuable information to refine your idea and minimize risks.

We'll explore practical ways to test without breaking the bank, strategies for testing smartly, and how to measure success through key metrics. By the end of this chapter, you'll have a clear framework for running meaningful tests that help you move forward with confidence. Testing isn't just about proving your idea—it's about learning, improving, and building a solid foundation for growth. Let's dive in.

Testing Your Idea Without Breaking the

Bank

Testing your business idea is essential, but it doesn't have to cost a fortune. Many entrepreneurs assume that validating a concept requires substantial investment, but smart and resourceful strategies can provide meaningful insights without draining your budget. The goal is to gather enough evidence to confirm your idea's viability while keeping your risks and expenses low.

Start Small to Learn Big

The best way to test an idea affordably is to start on a small scale. Instead of launching with a fully developed product or service, focus on creating a minimum viable product (MVP) or a simplified version of your offering. This approach allows you to test core elements of your idea while saving money on unnecessary features or complexities.

For example, when Dropbox launched, its founders didn't build the entire platform upfront. Instead, they created a simple explainer video showing how the service would work. The overwhelmingly positive response validated their concept and helped secure funding for full development. This low-cost test provided clarity without significant upfront expenses.

Leverage Free or Low-Cost Tools

Digital tools and platforms offer incredible opportunities for testing ideas affordably. From setting up basic landing pages to running social media campaigns, there are countless ways to gauge interest and collect feedback without significant investment:

Landing Pages: Use free or low-cost tools like Wix, Squarespace, or Carrd to create a simple webpage describing your product or service. Include a sign-up form or call-to-action to measure interest.

Social Media Ads: Platforms like Facebook and Instagram allow you to target specific demographics with minimal budgets. A small ad campaign can reveal how your audience responds to your idea.

Pre-Sales: Offer your product or service for pre-order to test demand and secure upfront funding. Platforms like Kickstarter and Indiegogo make this process accessible to anyone.

Collaborate and Share Resources

Testing doesn't have to be a solo endeavor. Partnering with other businesses or utilizing shared resources can help you validate your idea at a fraction of the cost. For example:

A. A food startup might test recipes in a shared commercial kitchen or partner with a local café to feature its dishes temporarily.

B. A fashion brand could collaborate with a boutique to test designs and gather customer feedback before committing to large production runs.

By leveraging existing networks and partnerships, you can reduce costs and gain access to valuable customer insights.

The Value of Creativity and Experimentation

Sometimes, the most affordable testing methods are also the most creative. For instance:

Pop-Up Shops: Temporary setups at local markets or events allow you to interact directly with customers and test pricing, packaging, and messaging.

Online Marketplaces: Platforms like Etsy, eBay, or Amazon let you sell products with minimal overhead, testing demand without committing to long-term investments.

Social Media Engagement: Share your idea with your audience and invite feedback. Polls, Q&A sessions, and surveys can provide invaluable insights for free.

Consider Costco's famous hot dog strategy. Before expanding its food court offerings, the company tested pricing and demand through specific locations, refining its approach until they achieved the perfect balance of quality, price, and profitability—all without risking large-scale rollout costs.

Conclusion

Testing your idea doesn't have to break the bank. By starting small, leveraging affordable tools, collaborating with others, and embracing creativity, you can gather meaningful insights that guide your next steps. Testing is about working smarter, not harder, and these strategies help you validate your concept while keeping your resources intact. Remember, a thoughtful, low-cost test can provide the clarity and confidence you need to move forward with success.

How to Test Smartly

Testing smartly is about maximizing the value of your experiments while minimizing costs and risks. It's not just about running tests—it's about designing them in a way that provides meaningful, actionable insights. Smart testing allows you to validate your ideas efficiently, using creativity, strategy, and a clear focus on your goals.

Define Your Testing Objectives

The first step in smart testing is knowing what you want to learn. Every test should have a clear objective. Are you validating demand, testing pricing strategies, or evaluating customer preferences? By focusing on a specific question, you ensure that your test yields relevant and actionable insights.

For instance, when Airbnb was in its early stages, the founders tested their idea by renting out space in their own apartment to travelers. Their goal wasn't just to see if people would stay—it was to understand the pain points in the process and refine their platform accordingly. This clear objective helped them create a service tailored to their audience.

Choose the Right Testing Methods

Smart testing involves selecting the methods that best align with your objectives and resources. Some effective approaches include:

A/B Testing: Compare two versions of a product, webpage, or advertisement to determine which performs better. This method is particularly useful for refining messaging or design elements.

Pilot Programs: Launch your product or service to a small, targeted audience to gather feedback and identify improvements.

Surveys and Focus Groups: Engage with potential customers directly to understand their needs, preferences, and willingness to buy.

For example, before launching its famous spicy chicken sandwich nationwide, Popeyes tested the product in select locations. The enthusiastic response confirmed demand and helped the company prepare for a larger rollout.

Use Real-World Scenarios

Testing in a real-world context provides the most accurate insights. Theoretical tests or artificial environments might not capture the complexities of actual customer behavior. Smart testing replicates real-world conditions as closely as possible.

Pop-up shops are an excellent example of real-world testing. A clothing brand might set up a temporary store to test its designs, pricing, and customer interactions. The feedback from these interactions is invaluable for refining the product and strategy before a full-scale launch.

Measure the Right Metrics

Testing without tracking results is like navigating without a map. Identify the key metrics that will determine the success or failure of your test. These metrics might include:

1. Conversion rates for online sales or sign-ups.

2. Customer satisfaction scores from surveys.

3. Retention rates for repeat purchases or interactions.

By focusing on relevant data, you can objectively evaluate your test's outcome and make informed decisions.

Learn and Iterate

Smart testing isn't a one-and-done process—it's an iterative cycle. Each test provides insights that help refine your approach for the next round. If a test reveals unexpected challenges, use that knowledge to adjust your strategy and run a new experiment. This iterative approach allows you to continuously improve and adapt.

Tesla is a master of this principle. Before releasing a new model, the company gathers extensive data from its previous versions. Customer feedback on the Model S influenced design improvements for the Model 3, demonstrating how learning and iteration can lead to success.

Minimize Risk Through Scaling

When testing smartly, it's essential to start small. Scaling up too quickly without enough data can lead to costly mistakes. Instead, begin with limited resources and expand gradually as your confidence in the idea grows. A restaurant might test a new menu item in a single location before introducing it chain-wide, ensuring the concept is refined and ready for broader adoption.

Conclusion

Smart testing isn't about running as many experiments as possible—it's about designing tests with purpose and precision. By defining clear objectives, using real-world scenarios, tracking key metrics, and embracing an iterative approach, you can gather meaningful insights that drive your business forward. Testing smartly ensures you're not just learning but learning efficiently, making every test a stepping stone to success.

Real-World Testing: Trying Before

Committing

The ultimate goal of testing is to see how your idea performs in the real world. While theoretical planning and market research are valuable, there's no substitute for putting your concept to the test with actual customers in real environments. Real-world testing provides critical insights into customer behavior, operational challenges, and market demand, helping you make informed decisions before committing significant resources.

Why Real-World Testing Matters

Real-world testing allows you to move beyond assumptions and see how your product or service operates under real conditions. Even the best-laid plans can fail to account for the unpredictable nature of human behavior or external factors like competition and market dynamics. Testing in real-world settings bridges the gap between theory and practice, helping you refine your offering and reduce risks.

Consider how Warby Parker approached real-world testing. Before opening physical stores, the company tested its concept with pop-up shops and small showrooms. This allowed them to understand customer preferences, test their logistics, and refine their in-store experience without the costs and risks of a full-scale launch.

Methods of Real-World Testing

1. **Pop-Up Shops or Temporary Locations**
   Pop-up shops are an effective way to test products, services, and branding in a real-world setting. These temporary setups allow you to interact directly with customers, gather feedback, and observe buying behaviors. For example, a new bakery could sell its items at a weekend farmer's market to gauge demand before committing to a permanent location.

2. **Pilot Programs**

    A pilot program lets you roll out your product or service to a limited audience or region. This smaller-scale test provides valuable insights into customer responses, operational challenges, and areas for improvement. Many tech companies, like Google, use pilot programs to test new features or platforms before a full release.

3. **Collaborations with Existing Businesses**

    Partnering with established businesses can help you test your concept in a low-risk environment. For example, a new coffee brand might collaborate with a local café to feature its blends temporarily, gathering customer feedback and measuring demand before launching its own storefront.

4. **Online Marketplaces**

    Platforms like Amazon, Etsy, or eBay provide an excellent opportunity for real-world testing without requiring a physical presence. Selling through these marketplaces allows you to test pricing, product descriptions, and customer service while reaching a broad audience.

The Benefits of Trying Before Committing

Real-world testing delivers insights that are difficult to replicate in theoretical or controlled environments. It shows you:

How customers interact with your product or service: Are they using it as intended? What challenges do they face?

What pricing strategies work best: Are customers willing to pay your asking price, or is there resistance?

Operational strengths and weaknesses: Are your supply chains, staffing, or technology systems ready to handle real demand?

By testing in real-world conditions, you can identify and resolve these issues early, saving time, money, and frustration down the road.

Learning from Failures

Real-world testing may reveal flaws in your concept, but these failures are opportunities to learn and improve. For example, Coca-Cola famously launched "New Coke" in the 1980s to compete with Pepsi. Despite extensive market research, the product failed when tested on a large scale. However, the company learned from the backlash and leveraged the experience to strengthen its branding for "Classic Coke," ultimately regaining its market position.

Conclusion

Real-world testing is an invaluable step in the entrepreneurial process. By trying your idea in real conditions, you gain insights that can't be obtained from planning alone. Whether through pop-up shops, pilot programs, or online marketplaces, testing before committing helps you refine your offering, minimize risks, and build a foundation for success. Remember, the lessons you learn from real-world testing aren't just about proving your idea—they're about improving it to ensure it thrives

Tracking Success: Key Metrics for Testing

Testing is only effective if you can measure its outcomes. Tracking success requires identifying and monitoring key metrics that align with your testing objectives. These metrics serve as benchmarks to evaluate whether your idea is viable, needs adjustment, or should be reconsidered. Without a clear understanding of what success looks like, testing can become aimless and unproductive.

Defining Success Before You Start

Before you begin testing, define what success means for your specific experiment. Success metrics will vary depending on the type of test you're conducting. For example:

1. Are you testing demand? Measure customer interest through pre-orders or sign-ups.

2. Are you validating pricing? Look at sales volume relative to your pricing structure.

3. Are you gauging usability? Track customer engagement and satisfaction levels.

Setting clear goals ensures you know what to look for and provides a framework for analyzing the results.

Key Metrics to Monitor During Testing

1. **Customer Engagement**
   Engagement metrics reveal how customers interact with your product or service. This includes website visits, time spent on your platform, or interactions at a pop-up shop. For example, a new app might track the number of downloads and daily active users to assess initial interest and usability.

2. **Conversion Rates**
   Conversion rates indicate the percentage of people who take a desired action, such as making a purchase, signing up for a service, or completing a survey. A high conversion rate suggests your offer resonates with your audience, while a low rate highlights areas for improvement.

3. **Customer Feedback and Satisfaction**
   Direct feedback from customers provides qualitative insights to complement quantitative metrics. Monitor customer reviews, survey responses, and social media mentions to understand their experience and satisfaction levels.

4. **Revenue and Profit Margins**
   For tests involving sales, track your revenue and profit margins to ensure your pricing model and operational costs are sustainable. For instance, a food truck testing a new menu item might analyze sales volume and the cost-to-profit

ratio to determine whether the dish should remain on the menu.

5. **Retention and Repeat Engagement**
   If you're testing an ongoing service or subscription model, retention rates are crucial. How many customers return after their initial interaction? Retention is often a stronger indicator of long-term success than one-time sales.

Using Metrics to Drive Decisions

Tracking metrics is only the first step. The real value comes from analyzing the data and translating it into actionable insights. Look for patterns and trends that reveal what's working and what needs adjustment. For instance:

1. If conversion rates are high but customer satisfaction is low, your marketing might be effective, but the product or service could require improvement.

2. If customer engagement is strong but sales are weak, your pricing or value proposition may need refinement.

Tesla, for example, closely monitors metrics like reservation numbers and production costs when testing new models. These insights guide decisions about scaling production or introducing design changes.

Iterate Based on Results

Metrics are not just a scorecard—they're a tool for continuous improvement. Use the data from your tests to refine your idea and repeat the process. Each iteration brings you closer to a market-ready product or service. Testing and tracking are cyclical processes, with each round of analysis informing the next phase of development.

Conclusion

Tracking success through key metrics is essential for making informed decisions during testing. By focusing on customer engagement, conversion rates, feedback, financial performance, and retention, you can gain a comprehensive understanding of your idea's potential. Metrics provide clarity, direction, and the confidence to move forward—or pivot—when necessary. Remember, testing isn't just about proving your idea; it's about using data to refine and perfect it. With the right metrics in place, you're equipped to turn your vision into a thriving reality.

Risk-Free Testing: Minimize Risks, Maximize Insights

Testing is a critical step in turning your business idea into a reality, but it doesn't come without risks. Mismanaged testing can lead to wasted resources, tarnished reputations, or misguided decisions based on incomplete data. Risk-free testing is not about eliminating every potential challenge—it's about designing your experiments thoughtfully to minimize potential downsides while maximizing the value of the insights you gather.

The first step to risk-free testing is recognizing that every test carries inherent risks. These could range from financial losses due to poorly allocated resources, to reputation damage from negative customer experiences. Understanding these risks allows you to design your tests with safeguards in place, ensuring you learn what you need to without jeopardizing your business's future.

A smart way to reduce financial risks is to keep your tests small and controlled. Instead of investing heavily in a large-scale rollout, start with a prototype or pilot program. For example, a restaurant might test a new menu item as a special in one location before adding it to the menu chain-wide. This allows the business to gauge customer interest and gather feedback without committing to extensive changes or expenses.

Another critical aspect of risk-free testing is ensuring that you're working with accurate and meaningful data. Tests that are poorly designed or based on faulty assumptions can lead to incorrect conclusions, resulting in wasted effort or misguided decisions. To avoid this, establish clear goals for your testing phase. Define what success looks like and identify the key metrics you'll use to measure outcomes. For instance, if you're testing a new product, your metrics might include sales figures, customer feedback, and repeat purchase rates.

Communication also plays a significant role in minimizing testing risks. Be transparent with your test participants, whether they're customers, team members, or partners. Explain that you're in a testing phase and invite their honest feedback. Setting the right expectations can help manage potential dissatisfaction or misunderstandings during the process.

Risk-free testing also involves creating contingency plans. Not every test will yield positive results, and that's okay—as long as you're prepared to respond. If a test fails, analyze the reasons behind it and use those insights to refine your approach. Remember, a failed test isn't a wasted effort if it provides valuable lessons that guide your next steps.

For example, when Airbnb first tested its concept, the founders faced initial challenges in convincing users to trust strangers with their homes. Instead of abandoning the idea, they refined their platform based on user concerns, adding features like guest reviews and host guarantees. This iterative approach turned what could have been a significant risk into a key strength of their business.

Finally, be mindful of the impact your testing may have on your reputation. Even during a test phase, customers expect a certain level of quality and professionalism. Ensure that the product or service you're testing meets a baseline standard to avoid alienating potential customers or damaging your brand image.

In conclusion, risk-free testing is about being strategic, adaptable, and prepared. By starting small, defining clear objectives, using accurate data, and having contingency plans in place, you can minimize risks while gathering the insights needed to move forward confidently. Testing isn't just a step in the process—it's an opportunity to learn, adapt, and strengthen your business foundation for long-term success.

STEP 3: IGNITE - THE REAL CREATION

Step 3, **Ignite**, is where your vision takes its first tangible form. This stage transitions your business from an idea into a functioning entity, blending preparation with action. It's about more than just starting—it's about launching with purpose, precision, and sustainability. The decisions you make here lay the operational foundation that will support your growth and define your early success.

Ignite encompasses the practical steps of setting up your business space, assembling a strong team, and establishing a reliable network of suppliers and subcontractors. These elements ensure your operations run smoothly and position you to deliver exceptional value to your customers. Each decision you make at this stage— whether it's about location, team dynamics, or supplier relationships —has long-term implications.

But the ignition phase is not just about logistics. It's also about timing and strategy. A well-planned soft opening allows you to test your processes in a controlled environment, while a carefully executed grand opening introduces your business to the world with impact. These milestones mark your transition from preparation to operation, offering opportunities to fine-tune your approach before scaling.

Profitability, marketing, and compliance are equally vital in this step. Understanding the difference between income and profit, protecting your cash flow, and diversifying revenue streams ensure your financial health. Meanwhile, a targeted marketing strategy keeps your efforts focused, efficient, and impactful. And throughout it all, staying compliant with legal and tax obligations protects your business from unnecessary risks.

Finally, this step emphasizes risk-free creation. Launching is inherently risky, but with the right strategies in place, you can minimize potential pitfalls and maximize the chances of success. By approaching this phase thoughtfully and strategically, you set the stage for a business that's built to thrive.

Step 3 isn't just about starting—it's about starting smart. Let's explore each chapter in detail to ensure your business ignition is as smooth and successful as possible.

L aunching a business is a moment of transformation—a time when plans turn into action and ideas take on a physical or operational presence. But the launch isn't just about opening your doors; it's about setting up a foundation that ensures smooth operations and future growth. Chapter 13, **The Essentials for Launch**, focuses on the critical elements you need to establish before introducing your business to the world.

This chapter addresses the fundamental building blocks of your launch: securing and preparing the right physical or virtual space, equipping your business with the tools and technology it needs to operate efficiently, and navigating the legal and regulatory requirements that safeguard your venture. Each of these aspects requires careful planning and execution to ensure you're not just starting, but starting strong.

We'll also explore the art of prioritization. Not everything needs to be perfect at the beginning, and understanding what matters most right now can save you time, money, and stress. Some tasks and investments can wait until your business is up and running, allowing you to focus on what truly matters for a successful launch.

The launch phase is where dreams meet reality. By addressing these essentials thoughtfully and strategically, you can lay a solid foundation for your business, minimizing risks and maximizing your potential for success. Let's dive into the first steps of turning your vision into a thriving operation.

Setting Up Your Space: Office, Store, or

Warehouse

Your business's physical or operational space is one of the first significant decisions you'll face. Whether it's a retail store, a warehouse, an office, or a mix of these, the choice you make will profoundly impact how your business operates and how it's perceived. But this decision isn't just about securing a location—it's about aligning your space with your business model, goals, and growth trajectory.

Learning from Innovators: Apple's Bold Retail Move

Before Apple opened its first retail store in 2001, the idea of a tech company investing heavily in exclusive, branded retail locations was virtually unheard of. Most phone companies relied on third-party retailers or carrier outlets to sell their devices. Apple, however, recognized that their products needed a dedicated space where customers could experience the full Apple ecosystem—design, innovation, and functionality—in a carefully controlled environment.

This decision wasn't just about selling products; it was about creating a unique customer experience that reinforced Apple's brand and philosophy. The Apple Store became a destination, offering hands-on interaction with products, personalized service, and a space for customer education. By rethinking what a tech company needed in terms of space, Apple revolutionized retail in the tech industry and built one of the most profitable retail chains in the world.

The Rise of Warehouse Giants: JD.com and Amazon

On the other end of the spectrum, e-commerce platforms like JD.com and Amazon redefined how businesses approach warehousing and logistics. While early e-commerce relied heavily on third-party delivery services, both companies realized that owning their warehouses and delivery networks could streamline operations and enhance customer satisfaction.

JD.com built an extensive network of distribution warehouses across China, allowing for fast, reliable delivery, even in remote areas.

Amazon, meanwhile, developed its iconic fulfillment centers, where technology and efficiency drive their operations. By taking control of their warehouses and delivery, these companies didn't just meet customer expectations—they set new ones, offering same-day or even two-hour delivery in many regions.

For startups, these examples highlight the importance of thinking critically about your space needs. Do you need a retail presence to engage customers directly? Or is a warehouse essential for managing inventory and ensuring smooth logistics? Or perhaps your business is best served by a small office to handle administrative tasks while relying on virtual platforms to connect with customers.

What Do You Really Need Right Now?

As a startup entrepreneur, it's easy to get caught up in the allure of a shiny retail space or a sprawling warehouse. But the real question is: do you need it at this stage? For instance:

1. If you're launching an online clothing store, you might start with a home office and use a third-party fulfillment service before investing in your own warehouse.

2. If you're opening a coffee shop, choosing a small, cozy space in a high-traffic area might make more sense than a large, expensive location.

Think about the core functions your space needs to serve. Will it be primarily customer-facing, like Apple Stores? Or operationally focused, like Amazon's fulfillment centers? Understanding what you need—and what you don't—can save you significant resources and set you up for smarter growth.

Timing is Everything

The space you need today may not be the space you need tomorrow. Many successful companies started small, focusing on functionality and scalability. Amazon, for example, began in a garage before expanding into warehouses as their business grew. Similarly, JD.com started as a single physical store before transitioning to e-commerce and investing in a robust warehouse network.

The key is prioritization. Not every business needs a dedicated retail store or warehouse immediately. Some needs can be outsourced or delayed until the business achieves a stable revenue stream. Assessing your current stage and long-term vision ensures you make informed decisions about your space requirements.

Conclusion

Choosing the right space for your business isn't just about where you'll operate—it's about how you'll serve your customers, manage your operations, and position your brand for growth. Whether you're inspired by Apple's focus on exclusive retail experiences or Amazon's dedication to operational excellence, the lesson is clear: your space should align with your business goals and adapt as you grow. Start smart, think strategically, and build a foundation that supports your vision.

Equipping Your Business: Tools, Software, Equipment

Equipping your business is a crucial step in launching your operations successfully. Whether it's tools for production, software for management, or equipment for logistics, having the right resources in place can make or break your efficiency and productivity. However, equipping a business isn't just about buying everything outright—it's about making thoughtful decisions that balance functionality, cost, and timing.

Buy, Lease, or Subcontract?

The first decision when equipping your business is whether to buy, lease, or subcontract. Each option has its benefits and trade-offs:

Buying: Ownership provides long-term value but comes with significant upfront costs. It's a good choice for essential equipment that you'll use consistently.

Leasing: Leasing equipment spreads out costs over time, preserving cash flow while allowing you to access high-quality tools or machinery. For example, many small businesses lease office printers or heavy machinery to save on upfront expenses.

Subcontracting: For occasional or specialized needs, subcontracting can be the smartest move. Instead of investing in expensive equipment, hire professionals who already own and maintain the necessary tools. This approach is common in industries like construction and digital marketing, where expertise and equipment often go hand in hand.

Take Tesla as an example. In its early days, the company outsourced manufacturing to third-party suppliers for certain components rather than building factories for everything. This allowed Tesla to focus its resources on developing its core technology.

The Hidden Challenges of Developing Your Own Software

When it comes to software, the temptation to develop a custom solution can be strong. While having proprietary software tailored to your needs sounds appealing, it's a massive undertaking. Building your own software often leads to unforeseen challenges:

Cost Overruns: Development frequently exceeds budget estimates due to unforeseen complexities or changes in requirements.

Delays: Software projects often take longer than expected, delaying your business operations.

Functionality Gaps: The initial version may lack features or stability, requiring ongoing investments to fix bugs and enhance usability.

Instead, consider starting with off-the-shelf solutions. Software-as-a-Service (SaaS) platforms like QuickBooks for accounting, Shopify for e-commerce, and Slack for team communication offer affordable, reliable tools that are easy to implement. For startups, these tools often provide all the functionality you need without the headaches of custom development.

Create a Comprehensive Equipment List

Before purchasing or leasing anything, create a detailed list of the tools, software, and equipment you'll need. This process helps you identify what's essential, what can wait, and what alternatives exist. For example:

1. **Tools and Equipment**: Machinery, office furniture, vehicles, or production tools.

2. **Software**: Accounting software, inventory management systems, customer relationship management (CRM) platforms.

3. **Specialized Equipment**: Industry-specific tools like commercial ovens for a bakery or diagnostic machines for a medical practice.

With your list in hand, research costs, including options for second-hand equipment. Used equipment can save you a significant amount of money, especially for items like office desks, chairs, or production tools. Many businesses start with second-hand items to conserve capital for other needs.

Think in Stages

Equipping your business doesn't mean you need everything on day one. Consider your business's immediate needs versus what can be added later as you grow. For instance:

1. A coffee shop might start with basic espresso machines and expand to include cold brew equipment as demand increases.

2. An e-commerce store might begin with manual inventory tracking and later invest in an automated inventory system as sales volume grows.

This staged approach preserves cash flow, reduces upfront investment, and allows you to make adjustments based on real-world needs.

Think Creatively About Alternatives

Sometimes, the best solutions aren't the most obvious. For example:

Co-Sharing Resources: Join co-working spaces or shared industrial facilities that provide access to equipment like 3D printers, meeting rooms, or commercial kitchens.

Open-Source Software: Free software like GIMP for image editing or LibreOffice for document creation can save money without compromising functionality.

Short-Term Rentals: For seasonal businesses, renting equipment during peak periods can be more economical than owning it year-round.

Conclusion

Equipping your business requires more than just a shopping list—it requires strategic thinking. By evaluating whether to buy, lease, or subcontract, understanding the challenges of software development, and creating a comprehensive, staged plan, you can optimize your resources while preserving cash flow. Be smart about what you need, when you need it, and how to acquire it. With thoughtful planning, you can set up your business for efficiency and growth without overspending.

Navigating Legal and Regulatory

Requirements

Complying with legal and regulatory requirements is one of the most critical aspects of starting and running a business. While it may not be the most glamorous part of entrepreneurship, neglecting these responsibilities can lead to fines, legal disputes, or even the closure of your business. Understanding and addressing the legal landscape ensures that your operations are built on a solid foundation, protecting both your company and your customers.

Understanding Your Legal Obligations

Every business operates within a framework of laws and regulations that govern its activities. These requirements vary by location, industry, and the nature of your business. For example:

Business Registration: You may need to register your business with local, state, or national authorities, depending on your jurisdiction.

Licensing and Permits: Specific industries, such as food services, healthcare, or construction, often require special permits to operate legally.

Tax Registration: Ensure you register for the appropriate tax accounts, including sales tax, income tax, or payroll taxes if you employ staff.

When Uber first expanded its ride-sharing services, it encountered legal challenges in multiple markets due to unclear regulations for non-traditional taxis. By engaging with policymakers and adapting their model, Uber navigated these hurdles and reshaped the industry. This example underscores the importance of understanding the regulatory environment and being prepared to adapt.

Seek Professional Guidance

Legal requirements can be complex, and it's often challenging for entrepreneurs to navigate them alone. Hiring a lawyer or legal advisor can help ensure compliance and save you from costly mistakes. Professionals can assist with:

1. Drafting contracts and agreements for employees, partners, and suppliers.

2. Advising on intellectual property (IP) protections, such as trademarks or patents.

3. Reviewing lease agreements for office or retail spaces.

Patagonia, the outdoor clothing company, has built its brand around sustainability and environmental ethics. To align its operations with its values, the company relies heavily on legal experts to navigate certifications, environmental laws, and sustainable sourcing regulations. This proactive approach helps Patagonia maintain its credibility and commitment to its mission.

The Cost of Non-Compliance

Failing to adhere to legal requirements can have severe consequences, including fines, lawsuits, or reputational damage. For instance, in 2019, Facebook faced a $5 billion fine from the Federal Trade Commission for privacy violations. While most small businesses won't encounter penalties of this scale, even minor infractions can disrupt operations and erode customer trust.

To avoid these pitfalls:

1. Regularly audit your compliance with laws and regulations.

2. Stay informed about changes in legislation that may impact your business.

3. Invest in systems and processes that make compliance easier, such as payroll software for accurate tax calculations.

Tailor Compliance to Your Industry

Different industries come with unique regulatory challenges. For example:

Food and Beverage: Restaurants and cafes must comply with health and safety standards, such as obtaining food handling certifications and passing health inspections.

E-Commerce: Online businesses need to address data privacy laws like the General Data Protection Regulation (GDPR) in Europe.

Real Estate: Realtors and brokers must adhere to licensing requirements and disclosure laws.

If you're entering a regulated industry, familiarize yourself with both the general and specific rules that apply.

Preparing for International Operations

If you plan to expand globally, additional legal considerations come into play. These may include:

1. Import/export regulations.

2. Adhering to labor laws in different countries.

3. Registering trademarks internationally to protect your brand.

Amazon's expansion into global markets required careful navigation of varying tax laws, labor standards, and product regulations. By investing in legal expertise and local partnerships, Amazon built a global presence while remaining compliant with diverse regulatory frameworks.

Conclusion

Navigating legal and regulatory requirements may feel daunting, but it's a vital part of building a sustainable business. By understanding your obligations, seeking professional guidance, and tailoring compliance to your industry, you can avoid costly mistakes and operate with confidence. Remember, compliance isn't just about avoiding penalties—it's about building a trustworthy, reputable business that can thrive in any market

What matters now, What Can Wait

Launching a business is an exciting and challenging process, but it's easy to get overwhelmed by the endless to-do list. While there are many tasks to tackle, not everything needs to be done on day one. One of the keys to a successful and efficient launch is prioritizing what matters most and deferring non-essential tasks to a later stage. This approach helps conserve resources, maintain focus, and reduce unnecessary stress.

Focus on Essentials First

When starting out, prioritize tasks that directly impact your ability to deliver your product or service to customers. These are the elements that will enable you to start generating revenue and building a reputation:

Legal and Regulatory Requirements: Ensure your business is registered, licensed, and compliant with all necessary regulations.

Core Equipment and Tools: Invest in the essential tools, software, and equipment needed to run your business operations smoothly.

Customer Access Points: Set up your sales channels, whether that's a physical store, an online platform, or a service hotline.

Consider how Amazon began as an online bookstore. Jeff Bezos focused on building a simple, functional e-commerce platform and establishing relationships with book distributors. Fancy branding, advanced logistics, and diversified product offerings came later, but the essentials for selling books were the foundation.

What Can Wait

Some aspects of your business, while important, don't need immediate attention. These are tasks that can be phased in over time as your business grows:

Perfecting Branding: While a name and logo are crucial, you don't need to invest heavily in branding design right away. Focus on delivering value to your customers; your brand identity can evolve.

Expanding Offerings: Resist the urge to launch with a wide array of products or services. Start with a core offering, refine it, and expand based on customer demand.

Office Upgrades: A sleek office or showroom can wait until your cash flow stabilizes. Many successful startups begin in garages, shared spaces, or even at kitchen tables.

When Tesla launched its first vehicle, the Roadster, the company didn't build its gigafactories immediately. Instead, Tesla focused on testing its concept and generating revenue, later investing in production infrastructure once the demand and funding were secure.

Create a Phased Plan

To avoid the pitfalls of trying to do everything at once, create a phased plan for your business development. Break down tasks into immediate needs, short-term goals, and long-term projects. For example:

1. **Immediate Needs**: Legal setup, essential equipment, and customer access points.

2. **Short-Term Goals**: Building a marketing strategy, optimizing operations, and expanding customer outreach.

3. **Long-Term Projects**: Investing in proprietary software, scaling operations, and diversifying revenue streams.

This phased approach ensures that your resources are used efficiently and that you can adapt as new opportunities or challenges arise.

Conserving Resources for Growth

By focusing on what matters now and deferring non-essential tasks, you preserve cash flow and energy for future growth. Overcommitting resources too early can strain your budget and leave you vulnerable to unexpected expenses.

Costco's approach to its food courts is a great example. While the chain offers a limited but popular menu, it prioritizes efficiency and customer satisfaction rather than expanding offerings unnecessarily. This focus allows Costco to deliver value while maintaining profitability.

Conclusion

Launching a business is as much about prioritization as it is about execution. By focusing on immediate needs, deferring non-essentials, and adopting a phased approach, you can set your business up for success without overextending yourself. Remember, what matters most today is building a strong foundation—everything else can come in time. Let's move forward with purpose and patience, ensuring every step strengthens your business.

CHAPTER 13: BUILDING A TEAM THAT BUILDS YOUR BUSINESS

Behind every successful business is a team that shares its vision, drives its goals, and handles its day-to-day operations with skill and dedication. Building such a team is not just about hiring people—it's about assembling a group of individuals whose talents, values, and work ethic align with your business objectives. Your team isn't just an expense; it's an investment in your company's future.

The process of building your team is multifaceted. It begins with defining roles and responsibilities to ensure clarity and efficiency. From there, you must make strategic decisions about who to hire and how to compensate them fairly. The balance between experience and potential, or between hiring full-time staff versus outsourcing tasks, requires thoughtful consideration of both immediate needs and long-term goals.

But creating a strong team goes beyond recruitment. Cultural fit, loyalty, and engagement are essential for fostering an environment where employees feel valued and motivated. Providing opportunities for career growth not only enhances your team's capabilities but also strengthens their commitment to your business. On the flip side, knowing when and how to part ways with team members who aren't contributing effectively is equally crucial for maintaining a productive workforce.

In this chapter, we'll explore the key elements of building a team that doesn't just work for your business but actively helps it thrive. Whether you're assembling your first group of employees or scaling an established team, these insights will guide you in creating a workforce that's aligned with your vision and ready to contribute to your success.

Defining Positions and Roles: Building a

Solid Team Structure

A well-defined team structure is the backbone of any successful business. Clearly outlining positions and roles ensures that every team member knows their responsibilities, minimizes confusion, and optimizes productivity. Without a solid structure, even the most talented team can struggle to work cohesively, leading to inefficiencies and missed opportunities.

Why Defining Roles Matters

Clarity in roles provides direction. Employees perform better when they understand what is expected of them and how their work contributes to the overall goals of the business. For example, in the early days of Amazon, Jeff Bezos meticulously defined roles for his initial team, ensuring each member focused on specific tasks, such as website development, supply chain management, or customer service. This clarity allowed the team to operate efficiently, even as the company scaled rapidly.

A defined structure also prevents overlap and redundancy. Without clear boundaries, team members may duplicate efforts or leave critical tasks unattended. In a restaurant, for instance, assigning specific roles—such as head chef, line cook, server, and host— ensures smooth operations and excellent customer service.

Steps to Define Positions and Roles

1. **Understand Your Business Needs**
   Begin by identifying the tasks and functions your business requires. This will vary depending on your industry. For example:

   A. A coffee shop might need baristas, cashiers, and a manager.

B. A tech startup might prioritize developers, marketers, and customer support.

2. **Group Similar Functions**
   Organize related tasks into roles. For instance, administrative duties like scheduling and bookkeeping might be grouped under an "Operations Manager," while tasks related to brand outreach and campaigns could fall under a "Marketing Coordinator."

3. **Write Detailed Job Descriptions**
   For each role, create a clear job description that outlines:

   A. Responsibilities: What the person is accountable for.

   B. Required Skills: The qualifications needed to excel.

   C. Reporting Structure: Who they report to and who reports to them, if applicable.

4. **Account for Growth**
   Design your structure with scalability in mind. As your business grows, roles may need to evolve, or new positions may become necessary. For instance, a small online store might initially combine marketing and customer service into one role, later splitting them into separate positions as sales increase.

Adapting to Your Team's Strengths

While defining roles is crucial, flexibility is equally important. As you build your team, consider the unique strengths and skills of your employees. For example, if you hire a barista who is also great at social media, you might assign them additional marketing responsibilities, blending roles to suit your business's needs and leveraging their talents.

Examples of Successful Structures

Tesla's Cross-Functional Teams: Tesla emphasizes a flat organizational structure with cross-functional teams. This approach encourages collaboration across departments and enables faster problem-solving, particularly in product development.

Costco's Operational Roles: At Costco, every role is clearly defined, from cashiers and stockers to membership managers. This precision ensures that each aspect of their warehouse operations runs smoothly, contributing to their reputation for efficiency.

Avoiding Common Pitfalls

Overloading Roles: Avoid creating "catch-all" positions that combine too many responsibilities. This can lead to burnout and poor performance.

Neglecting Accountability: Ensure that every task has a designated owner. Ambiguity can result in important work falling through the cracks.

Ignoring Team Input: Engage your employees in discussions about their roles. They may provide valuable insights into how tasks can be structured more effectively.

Conclusion

Defining positions and roles is not just an administrative task—it's a strategic foundation for your business's success. By aligning your team structure with your business goals and being open to evolution, you create an environment where every member contributes effectively. A clear, well-thought-out structure enables your business to operate smoothly, adapt to challenges, and achieve long-term growth.

Why they work for you?

Building a committed and motivated team is about more than just hiring the right talent—it's about understanding what drives people to join your business, stay with it, and give their best effort. Employees, partners, and contractors bring their time, skills, and energy to your venture, and in return, they expect not just fair compensation but also meaningful rewards, growth opportunities, and recognition. A strong balance of financial, emotional, and professional incentives ensures your team remains engaged and invested in your success.

Compensation: More Than Just a Paycheck

The foundation of why people work for you starts with fair pay. Compensation isn't just about meeting basic needs—it's a reflection of the value you place on their contributions. But pay structures can take many forms, and tailoring them to your team and industry can give you an edge.

Base Salary + Commission: This is popular in sales-driven roles, like real estate agents or retail associates. Employees receive a stable income and are motivated to excel through commission-based rewards. For example, real estate agents often earn a percentage of each sale, which incentivizes them to close deals and maximize revenue for the business.

Performance-Based Bonuses: Rewarding employees for meeting or exceeding specific goals aligns their interests with the business's success. Tesla, for instance, ties executive compensation to performance milestones, driving results that benefit the company and its employees.

Dividends and Stock Options: For shareholders or key employees, offering dividends or stock options provides long-term financial incentives. Early employees at Amazon benefited significantly from stock options, which grew in value alongside the company. This not only attracts talent but also ensures their commitment to the business's growth.

Additional Benefits: Beyond pay, offering extras like dental and vision insurance, retirement plans, or housing allowances can make your business more attractive. For example, Google provides extensive employee benefits, including free meals, on-site healthcare, and generous vacation policies. These perks foster loyalty and create a positive work environment.

Purpose and Recognition: The Emotional Drivers

While financial incentives are critical, many employees are motivated by the purpose and recognition they receive from their work. People want to feel that they are contributing to something meaningful and that their efforts are acknowledged.

Clear Purpose: Businesses like Tesla inspire employees by aligning their work with a mission—accelerating the world's transition to sustainable energy. Employees are driven by the belief that they are part of a larger goal.

Recognition Programs: Acknowledging contributions through awards, public recognition, or small tokens of appreciation builds morale. For example, Starbucks encourages managers to recognize employee milestones, creating a culture of appreciation.

Career Growth Opportunities: Employees who see a clear path for advancement are more likely to stay engaged. Offering training programs, promotions, or mentorship demonstrates your commitment to their development.

Flexibility and Lifestyle Perks

Creating a supportive and accommodating work environment can set your business apart. People value flexibility and quality of life, and offering these benefits can make your business a more appealing place to work.

Vacation and Time Off: Generous vacation policies or unlimited leave programs, like those offered by Netflix, show trust in employees and help prevent burnout.

Transportation and Housing Perks: Providing company cars, housing allowances, or commuter benefits eases personal expenses and enhances job satisfaction. For example, many tech companies offer housing stipends to attract talent in high-cost areas like Silicon Valley.

Work-Life Balance: Flexible hours or remote work options appeal to employees juggling professional and personal responsibilities. Post-pandemic, businesses that offer hybrid or remote work setups have become particularly attractive.

Tailored Rewards for Partners and Shareholders

When shareholders or partners are actively involved in your business, compensation requires additional nuance. If they are working in the company, their efforts should be fairly rewarded through:

Salaries: Paying a salary ensures they are compensated for their time and expertise.

Profit Sharing or Extra Dividends: Offering an additional share of profits acknowledges their dual role as investors and contributors.

Long-Term Incentives: Options or shares align their success with the company's future performance.

Without these rewards, shareholders may feel undervalued, particularly if the company isn't generating significant profits in its early stages.

Pay-As-You-Go Professionals

Not every role needs to be filled by a permanent employee. Certain functions, such as legal counsel, accounting, or IT support, can be handled on an as-needed basis. For example:

Lawyers: Hire legal professionals for specific tasks, such as drafting contracts or handling disputes.

Accountants: Use part-time accountants during tax season or to manage payroll.

Freelancers and Contractors: For project-based work, freelancers provide flexibility and expertise without the long-term commitment.

This approach helps manage costs while ensuring that critical tasks are handled by professionals.

Conclusion

Why people work for you comes down to a blend of fair compensation, meaningful rewards, and an engaging work environment. Whether through competitive salaries, commissions, dividends, benefits, or recognition programs, the goal is to make your team feel valued and motivated. When you prioritize their growth, well-being, and purpose, they'll be inspired to give their best—and that's the key to building a strong, committed team.

Experience vs Potential: Hiring Pros or Training Newbies

Building a strong team often presents a fundamental question: Should you hire experienced professionals or invest in training promising but less-experienced newcomers? Both approaches have their advantages and challenges, and the decision depends on your business's specific needs, goals, and resources. Understanding the trade-offs between experience and potential can help you craft a balanced hiring strategy that aligns with your company's vision.

The Case for Hiring Experienced Professionals

Experienced professionals bring immediate value to your business. They've honed their skills in previous roles and require minimal training to hit the ground running. For startups, where time and expertise are often in short supply, hiring seasoned talent can be a game-changer.

Efficiency and Expertise: Professionals know how to navigate challenges, avoid common pitfalls, and deliver results quickly. For example, when Howard Schultz took over Starbucks, he hired experienced managers from established retail chains to bring operational efficiency to the company's rapid expansion.

Credibility: Experienced hires lend credibility to your business, especially if you're operating in industries where expertise is critical, such as finance, law, or technology. A skilled team can inspire confidence in investors, customers, and partners.

However, experienced hires often come with higher salary expectations, and their established ways of working may require adjustment to fit your company culture or innovative processes.

The Value of Hiring Newbies with Potential

New hires, especially those with minimal experience, bring energy, enthusiasm, and a fresh perspective to your business. While they may require more training and mentorship, they often excel in environments that value creativity and adaptability.

Cost-Effective Talent: Hiring and training less-experienced candidates can be more affordable, making it an appealing option for startups with limited budgets. Many companies, such as McDonald's, have successfully implemented training programs to turn entry-level employees into highly skilled team members.

Moldable Talent: Newbies are less likely to carry habits from previous roles and are more open to adopting your company's culture and systems. For example, Airbnb hired young talent early on, fostering a team that could embrace the company's unconventional approach to hospitality.

Long-Term Commitment: Employees who grow with your company are more likely to remain loyal, creating a stable workforce over time.

The challenge lies in dedicating the time and resources needed to train new hires while managing the risk that some may not adapt or meet expectations.

Finding the Right Balance

Many successful businesses adopt a mix of experienced professionals and fresh talent, leveraging the strengths of both. For example:

Amazon combines seasoned executives with a pipeline of new graduates trained through internal development programs. This blend ensures that the company benefits from both deep expertise and fresh ideas.

Tesla recruits world-class engineers while also developing internal talent, ensuring continuity and innovation.

To strike this balance, consider these factors:

1. **Immediate Needs**: If your business requires specialized skills or needs to meet tight deadlines, prioritize experienced hires.

2. **Budget Constraints**: For non-critical roles, consider hiring less-experienced candidates with high potential.

3. **Growth Plans**: Invest in training programs to build a talent pool that can grow with your company.

Mentorship and Collaboration

Regardless of whom you hire, fostering collaboration between experienced professionals and newer team members creates a dynamic environment where knowledge is shared. Experienced employees can act as mentors, transferring their expertise while benefiting from the fresh perspectives of younger colleagues.

Google's internal training programs, for instance, pair experienced employees with newer hires to create a mutually beneficial learning environment. This approach not only enhances skills but also strengthens team cohesion.

Conclusion

Choosing between experienced professionals and high-potential newcomers isn't a one-size-fits-all decision. It requires an understanding of your business's current needs, long-term goals, and resources. Experienced hires bring credibility and efficiency, while newer talent offers adaptability and enthusiasm. By striking the right balance and fostering collaboration, you can build a team that combines the best of both worlds, driving your business toward sustained success.

Hiring vs Outsourcing: Finding the Right Balance

When building your business, one of the most important decisions you'll face is whether to hire employees or outsource tasks to external professionals or firms. Each approach has its benefits and challenges, and the right choice depends on your business model, stage of growth, and the specific tasks involved. Striking the right balance between hiring and outsourcing can save costs, increase efficiency, and ensure that your business runs smoothly.

When to Hire

Hiring full-time or part-time employees is often the best choice for roles that are integral to your business operations. These roles typically require deep alignment with your company's goals, culture, and day-to-day activities.

Core Business Functions: Tasks critical to your operations, such as product development, customer service, or sales, are best handled in-house. These functions directly influence your business's reputation and success.

Long-Term Needs: If a role requires consistent attention or development over time, hiring ensures continuity. For example, a restaurant will need chefs and waitstaff regularly, making hiring the logical choice.

Building Expertise and Loyalty: Employees develop institutional knowledge, creating efficiency and expertise over time. For example, Starbucks focuses on hiring and training baristas to uphold its brand's consistency and quality.

However, hiring comes with costs beyond salaries, including benefits, training, and overhead. It's a long-term commitment that requires careful consideration, especially for startups with limited resources.

When to Outsource

Outsourcing is ideal for tasks that are specialized, temporary, or not part of your business's core operations. By leveraging external expertise, you can save time and resources while accessing high-quality services.

Specialized Skills: For complex or niche tasks like legal counsel, graphic design, or IT support, outsourcing to experts is often more efficient than building in-house capabilities.

For example, many startups outsource app development to professional firms to save time and access experienced developers.

Seasonal or One-Time Projects: Tasks like tax preparation, event planning, or website design may not require ongoing attention, making outsourcing a cost-effective option.

Flexibility and Scalability: Outsourcing allows you to scale resources up or down based on demand. For instance, during the holiday season, many e-commerce businesses outsource customer service to handle increased inquiries without committing to permanent staff.

One of the best-known examples of outsourcing is Nike. The company focuses on product design and brand management while outsourcing manufacturing to specialized factories. This model allows Nike to scale production globally without the burden of managing factories directly.

Finding the Right Balance

The decision to hire or outsource isn't binary—many successful businesses use a combination of both approaches. Here's how to find the right balance:

1. **Assess Your Needs**: Identify the tasks critical to your business and those that can be handled externally. For example, if your strength is in marketing but you lack technical expertise, you might hire marketers in-house and outsource IT support.

2. **Consider Cost vs. Control**: Outsourcing can save costs but may limit your control over how tasks are performed. Hiring, on the other hand, provides control but requires a higher investment.

3. **Start Small**: For startups, outsourcing can provide flexibility while you grow. As your business stabilizes, you can gradually bring more functions in-house.

For example, Amazon initially outsourced many of its logistics tasks but later built its own delivery network to gain greater control over the customer experience.

Building Hybrid Teams

In some cases, a hybrid approach works best. You might hire an in-house team for core functions and outsource specialized or supplemental tasks. For instance:

1. A marketing team might handle strategy and content creation in-house but outsource graphic design or paid ad campaigns to external agencies.

2. A restaurant might hire full-time chefs and servers but outsource food delivery to services like Uber Eats.

This approach allows you to optimize both cost and quality while maintaining flexibility.

Conclusion

The choice between hiring and outsourcing depends on your business's priorities, resources, and long-term vision. By understanding the strengths and limitations of each approach, you can build a team that combines in-house expertise with external flexibility, ensuring that your business operates efficiently and effectively. The right balance will empower your business to grow, adapt, and succeed in a competitive landscape.

Culture matters for team and customer, loyalty and profit

A company's culture isn't just about values on a poster or the atmosphere in the office — it's the driving force behind team cohesion, customer loyalty, and ultimately, profitability. A strong culture acts as a glue that binds your team together and as a magnet that draws customers in. Whether you're a startup or an established business, investing in a positive and well-defined culture can have a significant impact on your bottom line.

Why Culture Matters for Your Team

A team that shares common values and beliefs is more likely to work harmoniously, stay motivated, and contribute to the company's success. Culture shapes the way employees interact, solve problems, and tackle challenges.

Retention and Engagement: A healthy culture fosters loyalty among employees, reducing turnover and the costs associated with hiring and training new staff. For example, Patagonia has built a culture around environmental stewardship, which resonates deeply with its employees and keeps them committed to the company's mission.

Improved Collaboration: A positive culture encourages open communication and trust, making it easier for teams to collaborate. For instance, Google's culture of innovation empowers employees to share ideas freely, leading to groundbreaking products and solutions.

Attracting Top Talent: In competitive industries, culture can be a decisive factor for job seekers. Companies like Netflix emphasize their unique culture of freedom and responsibility to attract high-performing candidates who thrive in such an environment.

Culture's Role in Customer Loyalty

A strong internal culture often translates to exceptional customer experiences. When employees are engaged and aligned with the company's mission, it shows in the way they interact with customers.

Brand Consistency: A well-defined culture ensures that every customer interaction reflects the company's values. Apple, for example, has cultivated a culture of excellence and innovation that's evident in every product launch, store experience, and support interaction. Customers trust Apple not just for its products but for the consistent experience it delivers.

Emotional Connection: Customers are drawn to brands that align with their own values. Starbucks' culture of community and sustainability resonates with its loyal customer base, creating more than just transactions—relationships.

Customer-Centric Approach: Companies that prioritize a culture of service, like Zappos, consistently exceed customer expectations. Zappos' commitment to delivering "WOW" through service has earned it a fiercely loyal customer base and glowing reputation.

How Culture Drives Profitability

While culture might seem intangible, its impact on the bottom line is very real. A cohesive and positive culture creates a ripple effect throughout the organization:

Higher Productivity: Motivated employees are more productive, delivering better results with greater efficiency.

Reduced Costs: Loyal employees and customers save businesses the expense of constant recruitment and customer acquisition efforts.

Innovation and Growth: A culture that encourages creativity and collaboration can lead to innovative solutions, opening up new revenue streams and market opportunities.

Consider Southwest Airlines, which has long prioritized a culture of fun and employee empowerment. This culture not only boosts employee satisfaction but also enhances customer experiences, leading to sustained profitability in a highly competitive industry.

Building a Culture That Works

Creating a winning culture requires intentionality and effort. Here are some key steps:

1. **Define Your Values**: Clearly articulate what your company stands for and ensure these values are reflected in your policies, practices, and leadership.

2. **Lead by Example**: Culture starts at the top. Leaders must embody the values they want their teams to uphold.

3. **Align Actions with Words**: If your company values sustainability, show it through environmentally conscious operations and products.

4. **Foster Inclusivity**: Build a culture where everyone feels valued and respected, regardless of their role or background.

Conclusion

Culture is a powerful force that shapes your team, influences your customers, and drives your profitability. By cultivating a culture that aligns with your mission and values, you create an environment where employees thrive, customers stay loyal, and profits follow naturally. Remember, culture isn't just something you build—it's something you live every day. Let it be the foundation of your team's success and the secret behind your brand's loyalty and growth.

Creating Career Growth Opportunities

Investing in your team's career growth is one of the smartest decisions a business can make. Employees who see a clear path for advancement are more likely to stay engaged, motivated, and loyal to your company. Beyond benefiting your team, fostering career growth opportunities also enhances your business's productivity, reputation, and ability to attract top talent. When you help your employees grow, your business grows with them.

Why Career Growth Matters

Employee Retention: Talented employees are less likely to leave if they believe they can advance within your company. Offering growth opportunities signals that you value their contributions and see them as part of your long-term vision. For example, Microsoft's career development programs allow employees to explore diverse roles within the company, fostering loyalty and engagement.

Enhanced Skills and Productivity: Employees who invest in their skills through training or education bring new capabilities to the business. A well-trained workforce doesn't just perform better—it innovates, adapts, and drives business success. Starbucks exemplifies this by offering tuition reimbursement, helping employees pursue higher education while building their careers.

Attracting Top Talent: A reputation for promoting growth makes your company more attractive to ambitious, high-performing candidates. Companies like Google and Amazon are known for providing robust career development programs, which draw top talent from around the world.

Ways to Foster Career Growth

Creating growth opportunities doesn't necessarily mean spending vast sums of money on formal programs. There are many effective ways to support your team's development, regardless of your business's size or budget:

Internal Promotions: Whenever possible, promote from within. This practice rewards loyalty and provides employees with tangible examples of growth within the company. Walmart, for instance, emphasizes promoting store associates into managerial positions, showing employees that upward mobility is attainable.

Training and Skill Development: Offer access to workshops, certifications, or online courses. A small business could arrange monthly training sessions, while a larger enterprise might sponsor employees' participation in industry conferences.

Cross-Training: Expose employees to different roles within the organization to broaden their skills and perspectives. This practice not only benefits employees but also strengthens your team's adaptability during periods of change or growth.

Mentorship Programs: Pairing less experienced employees with seasoned mentors creates opportunities for learning and relationship-building. Companies like Intel have formal mentorship initiatives that help employees navigate their careers while fostering a sense of community.

Customized Growth Plans: Collaborate with employees to design individualized career paths that align with their goals and your business needs. This might include setting clear milestones for raises, promotions, or new responsibilities.

Aligning Career Growth with Business Goals

Career growth isn't just about individual development; it should align with your company's goals and vision. For example:

1. A technology startup might focus on cultivating technical leaders who can guide product innovation.

2. A retail business might develop store associates into district managers to support expansion.

3. A shipping company might train logistics staff to oversee operations in new regions.

By aligning career growth opportunities with your business objectives, you ensure that investments in your team also drive strategic outcomes.

Balancing Growth and Business Constraints

While growth opportunities are essential, they must be balanced with your business's realities. Not every employee will want—or need—a leadership role, and that's okay. Recognize and reward contributions at all levels. For example:

1. Offering incentives like bonuses or additional responsibilities can show appreciation without creating unnecessary managerial positions.

2. Providing non-monetary perks, such as extra vacation days or public recognition, can make employees feel valued.

Conclusion

Creating career growth opportunities is a win-win strategy: it empowers your employees while driving your business forward. By investing in their development, you build a loyal, skilled, and motivated team ready to tackle new challenges and seize opportunities. Whether through training, mentorship, or promotions, fostering growth ensures that your team doesn't just work for your business—they grow with it, paving the way for mutual success.

When and How to Let Go

Letting go of a team member is one of the toughest decisions a business owner or manager can face. Yet, holding on to someone who isn't contributing effectively—or worse, is negatively impacting your team—can harm your business, morale, and culture. Understanding when and how to part ways is essential for maintaining a healthy and productive workplace.

Recognizing when it's time to let go starts with identifying key challenges. Performance issues are a common indicator. If an employee consistently fails to meet expectations despite training, guidance, and opportunities to improve, it's a sign that the role may not be the right fit. Cultural misalignment can also create significant disruptions. Even high-performing individuals can harm a team if their behavior or values clash with the company's culture. Sometimes, external factors like restructuring or automation make certain roles redundant, while unethical behavior, such as dishonesty or harassment, is a clear non-negotiable.

For instance, when Apple decided to remove Steve Jobs from his leadership position in 1985, it was a difficult yet necessary move to address internal conflicts and the company's performance struggles. Though controversial, it ultimately allowed Apple to evolve and set the stage for Jobs' transformative return years later. Similarly, Netflix's philosophy of only keeping employees that managers would actively fight to retain has become a benchmark for balancing high standards with team cohesion.

Letting someone go requires care and professionalism. Preparation is key—documenting performance issues and any attempts to address them ensures transparency and fairness. During the conversation, it's important to be direct yet compassionate. Acknowledge the individual's contributions while clearly explaining the reasons for the decision. For example, saying, "We appreciate your efforts, but ongoing challenges have made it necessary to part ways," combines clarity with empathy.

The process doesn't end with the conversation. Offering support, such as severance, references, or outplacement services, can ease the transition for the individual. At the same time, communicating with the remaining team about the decision helps maintain morale and trust. It's essential to strike a balance between transparency and privacy, ensuring that the team understands the rationale without disclosing unnecessary details.

Each termination is an opportunity to learn and refine your processes. Were expectations communicated effectively? Could additional support or training have made a difference? Reflecting on these questions helps reduce the likelihood of similar challenges in the future. For instance, General Electric under Jack Welch adopted a transparent performance review system, pairing coaching with fair evaluations to ensure underperformers had a chance to improve before being let go.

Letting go is a challenging but sometimes necessary step for the health of your business. By approaching it with integrity, empathy, and a focus on the long-term vision, you can navigate these situations effectively. Every decision should align with your company's values and mission, ensuring that your team remains strong, focused, and ready to grow.

CHAPTER 14: MANAGING YOUR SUPPLIERS, SUBCONTRACTORS, AND BEYOND

Behind every successful business is a reliable network of suppliers and subcontractors working behind the scenes to keep operations running smoothly. From delivering materials and goods to providing specialized services, these external partners are an essential part of your business ecosystem. But managing this network effectively requires more than signing contracts and hoping for the best—it demands strategic thinking, proactive planning, and regular oversight.

Suppliers and subcontractors can make or break your operations. Poor-quality materials or missed deadlines can disrupt production, harm customer satisfaction, and even jeopardize your reputation. On the other hand, strong partnerships built on trust and mutual benefit can drive efficiency, reduce costs, and create opportunities for growth.

This chapter explores the key elements of managing these relationships. First, it's about making strategic choices: balancing price and quality to find partners who meet your needs without overburdening your budget. Next, you'll learn the importance of having backup plans to safeguard your business against unexpected disruptions, whether due to supply chain issues, economic shifts, or unforeseen emergencies. Finally, we'll discuss ongoing oversight, emphasizing how regular reviews and performance evaluations can ensure accountability and foster continuous improvement.

By mastering these aspects, you'll not only create a stable and efficient supply chain but also build a foundation for long-term success. A well-managed network of suppliers and subcontractors isn't just a supporting element—it's a competitive advantage. Let's dive into how to make it work for your business.

Balancing Price and Quality: Making Strategic Choices

In business, the balance between price and quality is often the difference between success and failure. While low costs might seem appealing, sacrificing quality can lead to dissatisfied customers, damaged reputations, and higher long-term expenses. Conversely, prioritizing top-notch quality at an unsustainable price may erode your profits and put your business at financial risk. Finding the right balance is a strategic necessity.

Why Quality Matters

Quality is the foundation of customer trust and satisfaction. A well-made product or reliable service keeps customers returning and builds a positive reputation. For example, Apple's commitment to high-quality materials and craftsmanship has allowed it to charge premium prices, creating a loyal customer base willing to pay for the perceived value.

However, quality isn't just about impressing customers—it impacts every aspect of your operations. High-quality inputs reduce errors, waste, and the need for rework. For instance, a restaurant sourcing fresh, reliable ingredients ensures not only better-tasting dishes but also smoother kitchen operations and fewer complaints.

The Role of Price in Your Decision

While quality is essential, it must align with your financial goals. Overpaying for materials or services can strain your budget and undermine your profitability. Businesses like Walmart demonstrate the power of negotiating competitive prices while maintaining sufficient quality to meet customer expectations. Walmart's scale and purchasing power allow it to balance affordability with a reliable supply chain.

Startups and small businesses, however, must approach price negotiations carefully. Unlike larger corporations, you may not have the leverage to demand steep discounts but can often secure better terms through relationship building or bulk commitments.

How to Strike the Right Balance

1. **Understand Your Priorities**: Define what quality means for your business and what your customers expect. For example, if you run a coffee shop, sourcing premium beans might be non-negotiable, even if it costs more. On the other hand, choosing mid-range furniture instead of luxury decor could free up funds for other priorities.

2. **Research and Compare**: Take the time to evaluate multiple suppliers or subcontractors. Don't just compare costs—examine reviews, performance records, and quality samples. Tools like Alibaba for product suppliers or specialized platforms for freelancers can help you weigh options effectively.

3. **Negotiate Strategically**: Negotiation isn't just about lowering costs—it's about creating value for both parties. Discuss ways to optimize the partnership, such as extended payment terms or bundled discounts, without compromising quality.

4. **Test Before Committing**: Consider conducting a trial order or project with a supplier to assess quality and reliability before signing long-term contracts. This approach minimizes risk and gives you confidence in your decision.

5. **Focus on Relationships**: Building strong relationships with suppliers can lead to better terms and flexibility. Treating suppliers as partners rather than transactions encourages collaboration and long-term loyalty.

Learning from Successful Models

Costco's Hotdog Strategy: Costco famously keeps its hotdog combo at $1.50, maintaining quality while absorbing costs in other areas to attract and retain customers. This loss-leader strategy exemplifies the balance between price and quality as a long-term business tactic.

Tesla's Supply Chain: Tesla initially faced challenges with quality in outsourced components but shifted to building in-house production for critical parts. This decision ensured tighter control over quality while optimizing costs in the long run.

Avoiding Common Pitfalls

Choosing the Cheapest Option: A low price tag often hides hidden costs, like delays, lower reliability, or increased maintenance. For example, outsourcing software development to the cheapest vendor might result in poor code quality, requiring costly fixes later.

Overestimating Quality Needs: Paying for unnecessary premium features or services can strain your budget without providing proportional value. Evaluate whether the top-tier option is truly necessary for your needs.

Conclusion

Balancing price and quality is a dynamic process requiring thoughtful consideration of your business priorities, financial constraints, and customer expectations. By strategically selecting suppliers and subcontractors who meet your standards without exceeding your budget, you set the stage for sustainable growth and long-term success. Remember, the cheapest option isn't always the best, and the most expensive isn't always necessary. Instead, focus on finding value—where price and quality align to create the greatest benefit for your business.

Backup Plans: Ensuring Continuity with

Alternative

In business, disruptions are inevitable. A trusted supplier might face production issues, a subcontractor could miss deadlines, or unexpected global events might disrupt the entire supply chain. Without a backup plan, these situations can halt operations, disappoint customers, and damage your reputation. A well-thought-out contingency strategy involving alternative suppliers and subcontractors is essential for maintaining business continuity.

Backup plans are your safety net, ensuring your operations can adapt to unforeseen changes. During the COVID-19 pandemic, companies with pre-established alternative suppliers managed to stay afloat despite global disruptions, while others faltered. These plans not only safeguard against crises but also build resilience, allowing businesses to respond swiftly to challenges like economic shifts, natural disasters, or sudden changes in customer demand.

To develop effective backup plans, start by analyzing your operations to identify areas of vulnerability. For example, if your business depends heavily on a single supplier for raw materials, a disruption in their service could cripple your operations. Diversifying your supplier base reduces this risk. Similarly, maintaining a network of potential subcontractors ensures you're not overly reliant on a single provider for critical services.

Establishing relationships with alternative suppliers and subcontractors in advance is key. Even if you don't engage their services immediately, maintaining communication and testing their capabilities ensures they can step in if needed. For instance, Apple sources the same components from multiple vendors, creating a robust network that mitigates risks from supplier-specific disruptions. Similarly, Amazon's extensive logistics network allows it to pivot between providers during peak demand or emergencies.

Implementing a backup strategy requires practical measures. Conduct trial orders to evaluate the quality and reliability of potential alternatives. For critical supplies, consider keeping a buffer inventory to handle short-term interruptions. Additionally, cross-training your team to handle various roles can fill gaps if a subcontractor becomes unavailable. These steps ensure your business remains operational, even under challenging circumstances.

The importance of balance cannot be overstated. While having multiple backups is prudent, overcomplicating your supply chain can lead to inefficiencies and unnecessary costs. Focus on quality over quantity, ensuring your backups meet your standards and can deliver seamlessly when activated.

A robust backup plan isn't just a safeguard; it's a strategic advantage. By preparing for the unexpected, you protect your operations, uphold customer trust, and position your business for long-term success. In an unpredictable world, resilience is not optional—it's essential.

Ongoing Oversight: Evaluating Supplier and Subcontractor Performance

Building a reliable network of suppliers and subcontractors is essential, but the work doesn't end once contracts are signed. Continuous oversight and performance evaluation are critical to maintaining quality, ensuring timely deliveries, and fostering strong relationships. A lack of ongoing evaluation can lead to inefficiencies, higher costs, and customer dissatisfaction. Regular oversight helps you identify potential issues early, optimize processes, and maintain alignment with your business goals.

Why Ongoing Oversight Matters

Suppliers and subcontractors play a crucial role in your operations. Their performance directly impacts your ability to deliver products or services to your customers. For example, if a supplier consistently delivers subpar materials, it can compromise the quality of your offerings. Similarly, delays from a subcontractor can disrupt timelines, damaging your reputation and customer relationships.

Oversight isn't about micromanagement—it's about partnership. By regularly evaluating performance, you can identify areas for improvement, provide constructive feedback, and build a stronger working relationship. This proactive approach ensures that your external partners continue to meet your standards as your business evolves.

Key Elements of Effective Oversight

Regular monitoring should focus on both quantitative and qualitative aspects of performance. For instance, track metrics like delivery times, defect rates, and cost efficiency. These indicators provide a clear picture of how well suppliers and subcontractors are meeting expectations. However, don't overlook qualitative factors such as communication, problem-solving capabilities, and alignment with your company's values.

Consider the example of Toyota's supply chain management. Toyota emphasizes long-term relationships with its suppliers, regularly assessing performance to ensure quality and reliability. This approach has allowed Toyota to maintain its reputation for excellence while adapting to changing market demands.

In addition to evaluating performance, it's important to provide consistent feedback. Share both strengths and areas for improvement, creating an environment where your partners feel valued and motivated to enhance their services. For instance, a logistics company that delivers on time but frequently damages goods might benefit from targeted feedback and collaborative problem-solving.

Addressing Underperformance

Even with regular oversight, issues may arise. When performance falls short, address the situation promptly and constructively. Start by identifying the root cause—whether it's resource constraints, miscommunication, or a lack of understanding about your expectations. Collaborate with the supplier or subcontractor to find solutions, such as additional training, revised processes, or adjusted timelines.

However, if underperformance persists despite efforts to resolve it, it may be necessary to reconsider the partnership. Replacing a supplier or subcontractor is never ideal, but sometimes it's essential to protect your business's integrity and operations.

Building Long-Term Partnerships

The goal of ongoing oversight isn't just about catching mistakes—it's about fostering collaboration and growth. By investing in strong relationships with your suppliers and subcontractors, you create a network of trusted partners who are invested in your success. Companies like Starbucks exemplify this approach, working closely with coffee growers to ensure sustainable practices and high-quality products. This collaborative relationship benefits both parties and strengthens the entire supply chain.

Conclusion

Ongoing oversight is a vital part of managing your suppliers and subcontractors. By regularly evaluating performance, addressing issues proactively, and fostering collaborative relationships, you ensure that your business operates smoothly and efficiently. Strong partnerships, built on trust and accountability, are the foundation of a resilient and successful business. Oversight isn't a one-time task—it's an ongoing commitment to excellence.

CHAPTER 15: THE STRATEGIC START: PERFECTING YOUR LAUNCH WITH A SOFT OPENING

Every business dreams of a flawless grand opening, with excited customers, smooth operations, and immediate success. However, a soft opening—a quieter, controlled pre-launch— can be the key to ensuring that dream becomes reality. By testing your operations, gathering feedback, and addressing challenges before going fully public, you can fine-tune your business and set yourself up for long-term success.

A soft opening is like a dress rehearsal for your business. It allows you to experiment with processes, train your team in real-world conditions, and identify any gaps in your planning. Whether you're opening a coffee shop, launching a software platform, or starting a retail store, this phase gives you a chance to adapt and improve without the pressure of a full-scale launch.

This chapter explores why soft openings are a vital step for any business. You'll learn how they help you catch and correct mistakes, adjust your approach based on real customer feedback, and refine your offerings. We'll also discuss why it's best to hold off on major marketing efforts during this stage, letting you focus on perfecting your business rather than managing overwhelming demand. A strategic start leads to stronger first impressions, happier customers, and a foundation for lasting success.

Soft Opening Can Make or Break Your Launch

A soft opening is not just a warm-up—it's a critical step that can determine the success of your grand launch. While a grand opening aims to dazzle the public and generate excitement, a soft opening is your opportunity to refine and perfect your operations in a controlled environment. This approach minimizes risks, provides invaluable insights, and ensures you're ready to meet the demands of your market.

The importance of a soft opening lies in its ability to expose potential issues before they escalate into larger problems. Imagine launching a restaurant without testing your kitchen workflow, or opening a retail store without gauging how your inventory system handles real customer traffic. A soft opening allows you to catch these problems early and resolve them without the pressure of a full-scale launch.

For example, Starbucks often uses soft openings when entering new markets. Instead of immediately rolling out all stores, they open a select few to test customer preferences and operational efficiency. This strategy allows them to tweak their offerings, train their staff, and adapt to local demands before scaling up. It's a practical and strategic way to ensure their brand delivers on its promise from day one.

Soft openings are also essential for building team confidence. Your staff gets to practice their roles, learn from real-world interactions, and become more comfortable with the processes and systems in place. This period of adjustment can make a significant difference in how smoothly your team operates when the grand opening arrives. For a restaurant, it might mean perfecting the flow between the kitchen and servers. For a tech company, it could involve troubleshooting user feedback during a beta launch.

That said, a soft opening is not without its challenges. If done hastily or without proper planning, it can backfire. Overcrowding, unclear objectives, or inadequate preparation can create unnecessary stress and leave you with more issues than solutions. The key is to approach a soft opening with the mindset of testing and learning, rather than rushing to impress.

Ultimately, a soft opening sets the tone for your business's long-term success. It's a chance to identify weaknesses, implement improvements, and build confidence in your team. While it may seem like a quieter start, the lessons and adjustments made during this phase can make the difference between a rocky launch and a seamless one. By treating your soft opening as a critical step in your launch strategy, you lay the groundwork for a business that can thrive in any market.

Making Adjustments Before Grand

Opening

The grand opening of your business is a pivotal moment—a chance to make a strong first impression and capture the attention of your target audience. However, to ensure that day runs smoothly, the adjustments you make during the soft opening phase are critical. This is your time to refine operations, resolve any issues, and optimize processes based on real-world feedback. By making the necessary adjustments before the big day, you set the stage for a successful and seamless launch.

Identifying Issues During the Soft Opening

A soft opening acts as a real-world test, exposing challenges you might not have anticipated during the planning stages. For example, a restaurant might discover that its kitchen layout slows down service during peak hours, or a retail store might realize that its checkout system struggles to handle multiple transactions efficiently. These issues, while manageable during a soft opening, could lead to customer dissatisfaction during a grand opening.

This phase also reveals gaps in employee training or workflows. Perhaps your team needs more practice using a point-of-sale system, or your inventory process isn't as intuitive as expected. The insights gained during the soft opening provide a roadmap for improvements, allowing you to address potential pain points before they impact your broader customer base.

Implementing Feedback from Early Customers

Early customers during your soft opening are a valuable source of feedback. Listen carefully to their comments about your products, services, or overall experience. For example, if customers frequently mention that a particular product is confusing to use or that wait times are too long, it's a signal to make adjustments. Engaging with these early customers not only helps you refine your business but also builds goodwill and loyalty.

Consider how companies like Amazon continuously refine their customer experience based on feedback. From improving website navigation to optimizing delivery logistics, Amazon's success lies in its relentless focus on adapting to customer needs. Your soft opening is your chance to adopt a similar approach, ensuring your grand opening delivers a polished and satisfying experience.

Fine-Tuning Processes and Systems

Adjustments before your grand opening often involve optimizing the systems and processes that keep your business running. For example:

1. If you run a coffee shop, you might experiment with different workflows behind the counter to speed up service.

2. A software company could use this time to address bugs and enhance user interface design based on beta testing feedback.

Refining these details can make the difference between a business that struggles to keep up and one that operates seamlessly, even under pressure.

Building Confidence in Your Team

Your employees play a crucial role in your business's success, and a well-prepared team is essential for a smooth grand opening. Use the soft opening period to address any knowledge gaps, provide additional training, and clarify roles and responsibilities. This not only ensures your team is ready but also boosts their confidence, making them more effective and enthusiastic when interacting with customers.

Conclusion

Adjustments made before your grand opening aren't just about fixing mistakes—they're about perfecting your business. By leveraging the insights gained during your soft opening, you can refine your operations, optimize your team's performance, and ensure every detail is ready for your big debut. The time and effort you invest in this phase will pay off in the form of a grand opening that impresses customers and sets the tone for your future success. Let your soft opening be the foundation of a launch that leaves a lasting, positive impression.

Why Marketing Can Wait: Focus on Getting It Right First

The temptation to dive into marketing before your grand opening can be strong. After all, generating excitement and attracting customers seems like a no-brainer when launching a new business. However, during your soft opening phase, the focus should be on perfecting your operations, ensuring quality, and addressing any issues. Premature marketing can create unnecessary pressure and expose your business to risks that could have been resolved in a controlled environment.

The Risks of Early Marketing

Marketing too soon can overwhelm your team and operations. Imagine hosting a flood of customers during your soft opening only to discover that your systems are not prepared for the demand. A coffee shop might run out of key ingredients, or an e-commerce site might crash due to unanticipated traffic. These hiccups can lead to customer frustration and damage your reputation before you've even officially launched.

Consider the experience of Tesla during its early Model 3 rollout. High-profile marketing created massive demand before the company could scale production efficiently. The resulting delays led to customer dissatisfaction and a blow to Tesla's reputation. The lesson is clear: marketing should align with your readiness to deliver on your promises.

Why Focusing on Operations First Pays Off

The soft opening phase is your opportunity to test and refine every aspect of your business. Without the distractions of heavy customer volume or intense public scrutiny, you can dedicate time to:

1. Streamlining processes to improve efficiency.

2. Training your team to handle real-world scenarios with confidence.

3. Gathering feedback to identify and resolve issues.

For example, when Shake Shack started as a hot dog stand in Madison Square Park, it focused on perfecting its product and customer experience. Only after building a loyal local following did it expand into a global brand. This patient approach allowed Shake Shack to establish a strong foundation for growth.

Building a Reputation Through Word-of-Mouth

Delaying large-scale marketing doesn't mean you can't generate awareness. During your soft opening, focus on creating exceptional experiences for your early customers. Word-of-mouth recommendations can be incredibly powerful and often carry more weight than advertising. Early advocates of your business can become loyal customers and help build organic buzz for your grand opening.

Starbucks, for example, relied heavily on word-of-mouth in its early days. By focusing on creating a cozy, welcoming environment and high-quality coffee, it attracted repeat customers who spread the word about the brand's unique value. This grassroots approach helped Starbucks grow without heavy reliance on advertising.

When It's Time to Market

Once you've addressed the challenges identified during your soft opening and feel confident in your operations, it's time to amplify your efforts through marketing. At this point, you can highlight your refined offerings, smooth processes, and well-trained team, ensuring a positive experience for your new customers. With everything in place, your marketing will work harder for you, converting interest into loyalty.

Conclusion

Marketing is an essential part of any business's success, but it's most effective when your operations are ready to support the attention it generates. Use the soft opening phase to focus on refining your processes, training your team, and resolving issues. By delaying marketing until you've perfected your business, you'll be better positioned to make a lasting impression and build a loyal customer base. Sometimes, patience is the most strategic move you can make.

CHAPTER 16: THE GRAND OPENING: UNLEASHING YOUR BUSINESS TO THE WORLD

Your grand opening is more than just a celebration—it's your business's introduction to the world. It's the moment when you transition from preparation to full operation, showcasing everything you've built to your community and target audience. A well-executed grand opening can create buzz, attract customers, and set the tone for long-term success.

This chapter is about making the most of your grand opening. It's not just about drawing a crowd—it's about delivering an experience that leaves a lasting impression. The excitement you generate on this day should translate into meaningful engagement and customer loyalty. The strategies you employ now can build momentum for your business, turning first-time visitors into repeat customers and advocates for your brand.

We'll explore effective marketing strategies to ensure your grand opening is a memorable event. From promotions to partnerships, you'll learn how to capture attention and create a buzz that reaches beyond the event itself. Additionally, we'll discuss how to use this opportunity to establish connections, gain customer insights, and lay the groundwork for a loyal clientele.

Your grand opening is more than a one-day event—it's the launchpad for your business's future. With the right planning and execution, it can be the start of a journey filled with growth, impact, and success. Let's dive into how to make it count.

Marketing Strategies for Your Grand

Opening

Your grand opening is a unique opportunity to introduce your business to the world with a splash. It's a chance to showcase your brand, attract customers, and create buzz that resonates long after the event. A well-crafted marketing strategy ensures that your big day doesn't just draw attention—it lays the foundation for long-term success.

Set the Stage with Pre-Event Buzz

The excitement for your grand opening should start well before the doors officially open. Creating anticipation is key to attracting a crowd and generating interest. Use social media, email campaigns, and local community connections to spread the word.

For instance, companies like Tesla build anticipation for new product launches by teasing features and benefits through videos and updates on social media. Similarly, you can share behind-the-scenes glimpses of your preparation, introduce your team, or highlight unique aspects of your business to engage your audience.

Consider partnering with local influencers, bloggers, or community groups to amplify your reach. Hosting small preview events or offering exclusive invitations can create a sense of exclusivity and excitement around your launch.

Leverage Promotions and Incentives

Promotions are a tried-and-true method for attracting customers. Whether it's a discount, a giveaway, or a special offer, a well-thought-out promotion can incentivize people to visit your business on opening day.

For example, when Shake Shack opens new locations, they often offer free items to the first 100 customers, creating a buzz that draws in crowds. Similarly, your promotions could include discounts for the first day, free samples, or loyalty program sign-ups with added benefits for early adopters.

Ensure that your promotions align with your brand and target audience. If you're launching a premium service, focus on highlighting quality rather than steep discounts. If you're in retail, bundle offers or exclusive launch-day products can drive sales and build excitement.

Create a Memorable Event

A grand opening is more than just an introduction—it's an experience. Think of ways to make your launch memorable and engaging. Consider hosting live entertainment, interactive activities, or demonstrations that showcase what makes your business unique.

For instance, Apple often uses product demonstrations during store openings to emphasize its innovation and customer experience focus. Similarly, a bakery might host a live baking demonstration, or a fitness studio could offer free trial classes on the opening day. The goal is to create a connection with your audience that leaves a positive and lasting impression.

Involve the Community

Connecting with your local community adds a personal touch to your launch. Partner with local businesses, charities, or organizations to show your commitment to the area. Hosting a charity fundraiser or donating a portion of your opening day's proceeds to a cause can create goodwill and align your brand with positive values.

When Tim Hortons expands to new locations, they often engage with the community by collaborating with local schools or sponsoring events. This approach not only builds relationships but also embeds the brand into the fabric of the community.

Capture the Moment

Don't let your grand opening end without capturing the excitement. Document the event with photos and videos that can be shared on social media and your website. Highlight customer testimonials, memorable moments, and the overall energy of the day.

Creating a buzz online allows your opening day's impact to extend far beyond those who were present. Encourage attendees to tag your business in their posts and offer incentives for sharing their experiences. This user-generated content acts as authentic word-of-mouth promotion.

Conclusion

Your grand opening is a once-in-a-lifetime event for your business, and a thoughtful marketing strategy can make all the difference. By building anticipation, offering compelling incentives, creating a memorable experience, and engaging with your community, you can ensure that your launch day is not only a celebration but also the start of a strong and successful relationship with your customers. Plan wisely, execute with enthusiasm, and watch your business take its first big step toward lasting success.

Turning Visitors Into Loyal Customers

Attracting visitors to your grand opening is an important milestone, but the true measure of success lies in transforming those first-time visitors into loyal, returning customers. Loyalty isn't built overnight —it's the result of consistent value, meaningful engagement, and an exceptional experience that keeps customers coming back.

Make a Memorable First Impression

Your grand opening is your chance to make a lasting impact. The way you present your business and interact with customers during their first visit sets the tone for future relationships. Focus on creating an environment that is welcoming, professional, and aligned with your brand values.

For example, Disney theme parks are known for their "magic moments," where every detail is designed to exceed visitor expectations. From the friendliness of staff to the cleanliness of the parks, Disney prioritizes a seamless and memorable customer experience. Similarly, ensure that your team is trained to deliver excellent service, anticipate customer needs, and resolve any issues quickly and efficiently.

Engage Customers with Value

Visitors are more likely to return if they feel valued. Offering personalized interactions, exclusive perks, or meaningful engagement can make customers feel connected to your brand. For instance, providing small tokens of appreciation—such as a free sample, a discount on their next purchase, or a loyalty program enrollment—can leave a positive impression.

Consider the success of Starbucks' loyalty program, which encourages repeat visits by rewarding customers with points for every purchase. Whether it's a rewards program or a simple thank-you email, showing appreciation for your customers' support can foster lasting loyalty.

Listen and Adapt

Your grand opening is also an opportunity to gather valuable feedback from your first customers. Engage with them, ask for their thoughts, and make adjustments based on their input. Customers appreciate businesses that listen to their needs and act on their feedback.

Zappos, for instance, built its reputation on exceptional customer service by actively seeking and implementing feedback. When customers feel heard, they're more likely to develop a deeper connection with your brand and become loyal advocates.

Stay Connected

The relationship with your customers doesn't end after their first visit—it's just the beginning. Use follow-up communication to keep them engaged. Send thank-you notes, special offers, or updates about your business. Build a presence on social media to maintain ongoing interaction and encourage customers to share their experiences.

Email marketing is another powerful tool. Sending personalized messages or updates about upcoming promotions can keep your business top of mind. For example, if you own a coffee shop, emailing regular customers about seasonal drinks or events can encourage them to return.

Deliver Consistent Value

Consistency is the cornerstone of customer loyalty. Visitors who experience the same high level of quality and service on every visit are more likely to become loyal customers. Inconsistency, on the other hand, can erode trust and push customers toward competitors.

Think about brands like Costco, which consistently delivers value through its product offerings and famously low-priced hotdog combo. Customers trust Costco to maintain its standards, which fosters long-term loyalty.

Conclusion

Turning visitors into loyal customers requires effort, strategy, and a genuine commitment to providing value. By making a strong first impression, engaging meaningfully, adapting based on feedback, and maintaining consistent quality, you can build lasting relationships that drive the growth of your business. Your grand opening may bring customers in the door, but it's the actions you take afterward that will keep them coming back.

CHAPTER 17: TAXATION AND COMPLIANCE

Taxation and compliance are the backbone of any legitimate and sustainable business. While they may not be the most glamorous aspects of running a company, they are crucial for maintaining your business's integrity, avoiding legal trouble, and ensuring long-term growth. Ignoring or mishandling these responsibilities can lead to fines, audits, or even the closure of your business.

Navigating the world of taxes and regulatory requirements can feel overwhelming, especially for startups. Different jurisdictions have varying rules about income taxes, sales taxes, payroll taxes, and corporate reporting. In addition, there may be industry-specific regulations you need to comply with, such as health and safety standards, environmental rules, or licensing requirements. For example, a restaurant must adhere to food safety regulations, while an e-commerce store may need to consider international shipping laws and online sales taxes.

The key to managing taxation and compliance effectively is to seek professional guidance. Accountants, tax advisors, and legal experts specialize in these areas and can help you understand your obligations, prepare necessary documentation, and avoid costly mistakes. They can also assist in planning for tax efficiency, ensuring you maximize deductions and credits while staying within the law.

For instance, Starbucks operates in multiple countries, each with its own tax regulations. The company employs a team of experts to ensure compliance across jurisdictions, allowing it to focus on its core business operations without disruptions. As a small business owner, you don't need a global tax team, but working with a local accountant or tax specialist can provide similar peace of mind.

Compliance goes beyond taxes. It includes adhering to labor laws, maintaining proper records, and meeting reporting deadlines. Neglecting these areas can harm your reputation and erode trust with stakeholders. A commitment to compliance demonstrates professionalism and reliability, key factors in building customer and partner relationships.

Ultimately, taxation and compliance should not be afterthoughts. They are essential components of running a responsible and successful business. By prioritizing these areas and relying on the expertise of professionals, you can focus on growing your business with confidence, knowing that your legal and financial foundations are secure.

L aunching a business is an exhilarating moment, but it comes with inherent risks. Mistakes during the ignition phase can lead to financial losses, damaged reputations, or even complete failure. The concept of "risk-free igniting" is not about eliminating all risks—that's impossible—but about minimizing unnecessary risks and managing unavoidable ones with foresight and strategy.

When starting your business, it's easy to get caught up in the excitement and overlook critical details. For instance, overcommitting to inventory before understanding customer demand can tie up capital unnecessarily. Similarly, investing heavily in marketing without fully testing your product or service can backfire if operational issues arise. The key is to proceed cautiously, making calculated decisions that protect your resources while allowing your business to grow steadily.

One of the most effective ways to ignite risk-free is through small-scale testing and incremental growth. Instead of diving headfirst into large-scale operations, consider starting small and scaling up as you gain confidence in your systems, products, and market response. For example, companies like Dropbox and Airbnb started with minimal offerings, using customer feedback to refine their services before expanding. This approach not only reduces risk but also ensures that your business evolves in line with customer needs.

Another important aspect of risk-free igniting is understanding your financial limits. Create a realistic budget and stick to it, avoiding unnecessary expenses that could drain your resources early on. Focus on areas that directly impact your customers' experience, such as product quality, customer service, and operational efficiency, while deferring less critical expenses to a later stage.

It's also essential to anticipate and plan for potential challenges. Identify the risks specific to your industry and business model, and develop strategies to address them. This might include diversifying suppliers, securing adequate insurance, or building a cash reserve to handle unforeseen expenses. By proactively preparing for setbacks, you can navigate them more effectively and keep your business on track.

Lastly, seek advice from those who have successfully launched businesses before. Mentors, advisors, and industry professionals can provide valuable insights and help you avoid common pitfalls. Learning from the experiences of others can save you time, money, and unnecessary stress during this critical phase.

Risk-free igniting is about balancing ambition with caution. It's about moving forward with confidence, knowing that you've taken steps to protect your business from avoidable mistakes while staying prepared to handle the challenges that arise. By approaching your launch strategically and thoughtfully, you set the stage for a stable and successful future.

STEP 4: SCALE: GROWING STRONGER AND BIGGER

S caling a business is about more than just getting bigger—it's about growing stronger, smarter, and more sustainable. Step 4 is where your foundation meets opportunity, and your business starts to expand its reach, revenue, and reputation. But growth isn't just a matter of increasing sales or hiring more people. It's a strategic process that requires careful planning, resource management, and adaptability.

At this stage, you're not just trying to survive—you're aiming to thrive. This means optimizing your operations, deepening customer relationships, and finding new revenue streams. It also means managing the complexities that come with growth, like maintaining cash flow, preserving quality, and ensuring your team and infrastructure can handle the increased demands.

Scaling doesn't happen in isolation. It's about understanding your market, adapting to trends, and staying ahead of the competition. Whether it's leveraging technology, refining your marketing strategies, or building stronger teams, Step 4 focuses on taking your business to the next level without losing sight of what made you successful in the first place.

This step is also about balance. Growing too fast can lead to instability, while growing too slow can mean missed opportunities. The goal is to scale in a way that's both ambitious and calculated, ensuring your business remains profitable, resilient, and ready for the future.

In Step 4, you'll learn how to measure and prioritize growth, harness the power of your team and technology, and scale smartly while minimizing risks. This is the phase where your business truly begins to take shape as a scalable, sustainable enterprise capable of reaching its full potential.

CHAPTER 19 : REVENUE, PROFIT, AND SIZE: THE POWER TRIO OF BUSINESS METRICS

Success in business isn't determined by a single number; it's a delicate balance of revenue, profit, and size. These three metrics together form the foundation of any thriving enterprise, each representing a distinct but interconnected aspect of growth and sustainability. While they are often discussed independently, the interplay between them reveals the true health and potential of a business.

Revenue showcases your business's ability to generate sales, providing an outward sign of demand and market presence. Profit, on the other hand, digs deeper into the core of financial health—it's what remains after expenses, reflecting your efficiency and ability to create value. Size, measured by your scale, reach, or market share, highlights the scope of your operations and your capacity to influence an industry.

Understanding these metrics and their relationships is critical for navigating the growth phase of your business. It's tempting to chase higher revenue or rapid expansion, but without profitability and thoughtful scaling, these pursuits can lead to instability. Many startups fall into the trap of prioritizing revenue or size at the expense of profit, only to discover that unsustainable growth can be as dangerous as stagnation.

This chapter explores how to strike the right balance among these three metrics. You'll learn what they represent, why profit remains the ultimate measure of success, and how focusing too heavily on one can jeopardize the others. We'll also look at how some of the world's most successful companies have managed this balance, using their strategies as inspiration for your business. By mastering the interplay of revenue, profit, and size, you'll be equipped to build a business that thrives in the long term.

Understanding the Metrics: Revenue, Profit, and Size Defined

In business, metrics are more than just numbers—they're the pulse of your company, offering insights into its health, sustainability, and potential for growth. Among the most critical metrics are revenue, profit, and size. Each serves a unique purpose, and understanding their roles is essential for making informed decisions and steering your business in the right direction.

Revenue: The Top Line

Revenue, often referred to as the "top line," represents the total income your business generates from sales. It's the starting point for understanding your financial performance and reflects your ability to attract customers and drive transactions. High revenue is a sign of market demand and customer interest, but it's not the full story.

For instance, in its early days, Amazon focused on driving revenue by reinvesting profits into growth. This strategy allowed Amazon to capture market share and establish itself as a dominant force in e-commerce. However, high revenue without profitability can be risky, as it may mask underlying inefficiencies or high costs.

Profit: The Bottom Line

Profit is the money left over after all expenses—such as production costs, salaries, and taxes—are deducted from revenue. Often called the "bottom line," profit is the ultimate indicator of a business's financial health. It shows whether your operations are sustainable and capable of creating long-term value.

Profitability is what allows a business to expand, invest in new opportunities, and weather economic challenges. Companies like Apple exemplify the power of profitability. While Apple generates substantial revenue, its focus on efficiency and premium pricing ensures industry-leading profit margins, enabling consistent reinvestment and innovation.

Size: The Scope of Your Business

Size refers to the scale of your operations, often measured by market share, number of employees, physical presence, or geographic reach. While size can be an indicator of influence and market power, it's not inherently tied to profitability or success.

Take Uber, for example. The company achieved rapid growth and global recognition, making it one of the most recognizable brands in its industry. However, its pursuit of scale has often come at the expense of profitability. This demonstrates the importance of balancing size with financial sustainability.

The Interplay Between the Metrics

While each metric provides valuable insights on its own, their true significance emerges when considered together. High revenue is meaningless if it doesn't lead to profit, and scaling too quickly can strain resources and lead to inefficiencies. A business that aligns revenue, profit, and size effectively is positioned for sustainable success.

For startups and small businesses, the challenge lies in prioritizing the right metric at the right time. Early on, revenue growth may take precedence as you establish market presence, but profit should always remain a focal point. Size can follow as your operations become scalable and efficient.

Conclusion

Revenue, profit, and size are the foundation of your business's financial story, each contributing to a different aspect of success. By understanding their individual roles and how they interact, you can make smarter decisions and set realistic goals for growth. These metrics aren't just numbers—they're tools for building a business that thrives in the long term.

Profit is the Ultimate Measure of Success:

Profit is the goal, not income

In the world of business, income often gets the spotlight. A surge in sales or a large revenue figure may look impressive on paper, but these numbers don't always tell the full story. What truly determines the sustainability and success of a business is not how much money it brings in, but how much it keeps—the profit. Profit, not income, is the ultimate measure of a business's ability to survive, grow, and thrive.

Why Profit Matters More Than Income

Income, or revenue, is the total amount a business earns from selling its products or services. While it's an important metric for gauging demand and market presence, it doesn't account for the costs of doing business. Without careful management, high revenue can coexist with low or even negative profits, leaving a company vulnerable to financial instability.

Profit, on the other hand, reflects the efficiency of your operations and your ability to create value beyond expenses. It's what allows you to reinvest in your business, pay dividends to shareholders, or save for future opportunities. Without profit, a business can't sustain itself over time, regardless of how impressive its revenue might seem.

Lessons from the Business World

Consider Costco, a company renowned for its low-margin pricing strategy. While it might appear that Costco earns its profit primarily from product sales, the real profit driver lies in its membership fees. This clever approach ensures consistent, high-margin revenue streams, demonstrating the importance of understanding where true profitability originates.

Similarly, in its early days, Amazon prioritized revenue growth at the expense of immediate profit. While this strategy helped the company capture market share, Amazon eventually shifted its focus to profitability by streamlining operations and introducing high-margin services like AWS (Amazon Web Services). This balance between revenue and profit solidified its long-term success.

Avoiding the Revenue Trap

Many businesses fall into the trap of chasing income at all costs, only to realize that high sales volumes don't necessarily translate into financial health. For instance, companies offering steep discounts to boost sales might achieve impressive revenue numbers but struggle to cover operational costs. This scenario is a stark reminder that revenue is only one piece of the puzzle.

Profit-oriented decision-making involves looking beyond short-term gains and considering long-term sustainability. It's about asking tough questions: Are your pricing strategies aligned with your costs? Are you reinvesting profits effectively? Are you avoiding unnecessary expenses that erode your margins?

Balancing Profit with Growth

While profit is the goal, it doesn't mean growth should be neglected. Strategic growth often requires short-term sacrifices in profitability, such as investing in new markets or products. The key is finding a balance—ensuring that growth initiatives are planned, calculated, and ultimately lead to stronger profitability in the future.

Apple exemplifies this balance by combining innovation with a focus on premium pricing and cost management. The result is a business that not only grows but does so with industry-leading profit margins.

Conclusion

Profit is more than just a number—it's the lifeblood of your business. It allows you to weather challenges, seize opportunities, and achieve long-term success. While income may be the starting point, profit is the ultimate destination. By keeping your focus on profitability and making decisions that prioritize sustainable growth, you can build a business that thrives in any market condition.

The Interplay: How Revenue, Profit, and Size Impact Each Other

Revenue, profit, and size are often viewed as separate metrics, but in reality, they are deeply interconnected. Each one influences the others in significant ways, and understanding their interplay is essential for building a successful and sustainable business. Balancing these metrics isn't about choosing one over the other; it's about leveraging their relationship to achieve long-term growth and stability.

Revenue Drives Opportunity but Isn't Enough Alone

Revenue is the starting point for every business—it reflects your ability to sell products or services and attract customers. High revenue can create opportunities for scaling and innovation by providing the funds needed to expand operations, develop new offerings, or enter new markets. However, without profitability, revenue alone can become a liability. If costs consistently outpace revenue, the business becomes unsustainable, no matter how large the income.

Consider Tesla, which for years prioritized revenue growth and market share over immediate profitability. While this allowed the company to establish itself as a leader in electric vehicles, the pressure to achieve consistent profitability eventually became critical. This highlights how revenue can be a stepping stone but must work in harmony with profit to ensure success.

Profit Ensures Stability but Can Limit Growth

Profit is the financial health indicator of a business—it shows how effectively you're converting revenue into sustainable earnings. High profit margins allow a business to reinvest in itself, weather market downturns, and maintain flexibility. However, an excessive focus on maximizing profit can sometimes stifle growth opportunities. Businesses that hesitate to invest in expansion, technology, or innovation to protect profits risk being outpaced by competitors.

For example, traditional retailers like Sears focused on short-term profitability but failed to adapt to changing consumer behavior and e-commerce trends. Meanwhile, companies like Amazon took calculated risks, reinvesting profits to grow their infrastructure and market reach, resulting in long-term dominance.

Size Amplifies Influence but Increases Complexity

Size, measured by market share, workforce, or geographic reach, often reflects a business's influence and capability to impact its industry. A larger size can lead to economies of scale, greater brand recognition, and increased bargaining power with suppliers. However, scaling too quickly without sufficient revenue or profit can strain resources and lead to operational inefficiencies.

Uber's rapid expansion into global markets demonstrated how focusing on size can lead to challenges. While the company achieved immense market penetration, its profitability suffered as operational costs skyrocketed. This underscores the importance of aligning size with sustainable revenue and profit strategies.

Finding the Right Balance

The interplay between revenue, profit, and size is a balancing act. Focusing too heavily on one metric at the expense of others can lead to problems. For instance, prioritizing revenue growth without managing costs can erode profitability. Similarly, scaling too quickly can outpace revenue generation, while an overemphasis on profit may hinder the investments needed for growth.

To find the right balance, businesses should:

1. Use revenue as a measure of demand and opportunity.

2. Prioritize profit to ensure financial health and sustainability.

3. Scale strategically, using size as a tool to amplify strengths without overextending resources.

Conclusion

Revenue, profit, and size are not competing goals but complementary metrics that together define a business's success. Understanding their interplay helps entrepreneurs make smarter decisions, whether they're managing costs, planning for growth, or pursuing market dominance. By carefully balancing these elements, you can create a business that thrives financially, operationally, and competitively.

Lessons from Giants: How Big Brands Prioritize Metrics

Successful companies don't grow by accident—they achieve greatness by understanding and prioritizing the metrics that matter most: revenue, profit, and size. By studying how industry giants have balanced these metrics, entrepreneurs can gain valuable insights into building sustainable businesses that thrive in competitive markets.

Amazon: Revenue as a Growth Engine

Amazon's early years were defined by relentless focus on revenue growth, even at the expense of profitability. The company prioritized capturing market share and dominating the e-commerce space, reinvesting all earnings into infrastructure, logistics, and new markets. Amazon's founder, Jeff Bezos, famously stated that the company wasn't chasing short-term profits but rather building a platform for long-term dominance.

Over time, Amazon shifted its focus, balancing revenue growth with profit through high-margin services like Amazon Web Services (AWS) and subscription models like Amazon Prime. The lesson here is clear: in the early stages, focusing on revenue can help establish market presence, but transitioning to profitability is essential for sustained success.

Apple: Profitability as the Core Metric

While many companies prioritize revenue or scale, Apple has consistently focused on profitability. By creating premium products with high margins, the company generates significant profits despite selling fewer units than some competitors. Apple's ability to maintain tight control over its supply chain, coupled with innovative pricing strategies, has cemented its position as one of the world's most profitable companies.

Apple's approach demonstrates the importance of aligning your business model with profitability from the outset. The company's success underscores that higher revenue doesn't always equate to higher profits; instead, the focus should be on value creation and efficiency.

Costco: Balancing Size and Profit with a Unique Model

Costco's business model is a masterclass in balancing size and profit. While the company operates on razor-thin margins for its products, it generates substantial profits through its membership fees. This model allows Costco to offer low prices, attracting large volumes of customers and creating significant scale, while maintaining steady profitability.

Costco's approach highlights the importance of understanding where your profit truly comes from. By identifying and leveraging a secondary revenue stream, businesses can balance competitive pricing, customer acquisition, and profit generation effectively.

Tesla: Scale as a Gateway to Profitability

Tesla's journey offers a powerful example of prioritizing size as a stepping stone to profitability. Early in its history, Tesla focused on scaling production and building its market share in the electric vehicle (EV) industry. This approach required significant upfront investment, leading to years of financial losses. However, once Tesla achieved economies of scale, it began to realize consistent profits, becoming a leader in the EV market.

The lesson from Tesla is that scaling strategically, even at a temporary cost to profitability, can position a business for long-term success. The key is ensuring that growth is backed by a clear path to financial sustainability.

Lessons for Entrepreneurs

The strategies employed by these giants demonstrate that no single metric should dominate decision-making. Instead, entrepreneurs must understand the unique needs of their business and prioritize metrics accordingly:

1. In the early stages, revenue growth may be the primary focus to establish market presence.

2. Profitability must follow to ensure the business is financially sustainable.

3. Scaling should be approached carefully, ensuring that size amplifies strengths rather than exposing weaknesses.

Conclusion

Big brands succeed because they understand the interplay of revenue, profit, and size and prioritize these metrics at the right time.

Whether you're launching a new venture or scaling an existing one, learning from these examples can help you make smarter decisions and build a business that grows steadily and sustainably. Focus on aligning your goals with your metrics, and your business can achieve its own version of greatness.

CHAPTER 20: BEYOND ADS AND PROMOTIONS: SMART, EFFECTIVE, STRATEGIC MARKETING

Marketing is often misunderstood as just flashy advertisements or social media campaigns. In reality, marketing is a multifaceted strategy that goes far beyond promotions. It's about understanding your audience, communicating your value, and building long-term relationships that drive success. Done correctly, marketing isn't an expense—it's an investment in your business's growth.

Effective marketing begins with clarity—knowing what your business stands for and who it serves. This clarity shapes every decision, from crafting messages to selecting the right channels. It's not just about shouting louder than your competitors; it's about resonating with the right audience in a way that makes them trust and choose you.

This chapter explores the essence of smart and strategic marketing. You'll learn when and why marketing matters most, uncover strategies tailored to your business's goals, and dive into how to evaluate and choose the right channels for maximum impact. Whether you're a startup working with a tight budget or an established business looking to expand, these insights will help you craft marketing efforts that deliver real results.

Smart marketing is about balance—between creativity and data, between broad reach and targeted efforts. It's a continuous process of refining and adapting to meet the evolving needs of your audience and market. Let's move beyond the noise of ads and promotions to uncover the strategies that truly drive growth and make your business unforgettable.

The Marketing When and Why

Marketing is not just a one-time event; it's a strategic and ongoing effort that needs to be deployed at the right times and for the right reasons. For many entrepreneurs, the question isn't just how to market but when to start and why it's essential. Timing and purpose are everything in marketing, as they dictate the effectiveness of your efforts and the return on your investment.

When to Start Marketing

The short answer? Sooner than you think. Marketing begins even before you officially launch your business. Building anticipation, testing ideas, and creating awareness are crucial steps that set the stage for your success. For example, Apple's iconic product launches begin with months of strategic teasers and promotions, ensuring that demand is sky-high before the first product hits the shelves.

For startups, marketing should begin as early as the validation phase —or even sooner. When you're brainstorming your business name, logo, domain, social media handles, and brand colors, you're already engaging in marketing. As mentioned earlier, marketing is everywhere—it's woven into every aspect of how your business presents itself.

Establishing a simple social media presence, creating a landing page, or building an email list can be powerful tools to gauge interest and attract early adopters. These initial steps don't require a large budget; instead, they rely on creativity and consistency to generate awareness and build trust. Waiting until everything is perfect risks losing valuable momentum, as early marketing efforts are key to establishing your presence and connecting with your audience before your official launch.

Why Marketing Matters

Marketing is how you connect your product or service with your target audience. Without it, even the best ideas can remain undiscovered. A great example is Tesla. The company doesn't spend heavily on traditional advertising but relies on its innovative marketing strategies, like live product unveilings and word-of-mouth buzz, to engage its audience. This approach works because Tesla understands its market and leverages its unique strengths to create excitement.

For small businesses, marketing is equally critical. It's how you communicate your value proposition, differentiate yourself from competitors, and build a loyal customer base. Whether it's through storytelling, testimonials, or targeted campaigns, effective marketing helps your audience see why your business is worth their time and money.

Aligning Marketing with Your Business Goals

Marketing should never be random; it must align with your business's stage and objectives. For instance:

Pre-Launch: Focus on generating awareness and building anticipation. Create buzz through teasers, pre-orders, or exclusive offers.

Launch Phase: Highlight your unique value and drive traffic to your business. This is the time for promotions, events, or grand openings.

Growth Stage: Shift towards retaining customers and attracting new segments. Use loyalty programs, upselling, and consistent branding to scale sustainably.

Mature Phase: Maintain engagement while exploring new opportunities. Rebranding, entering new markets, or launching additional products may require renewed marketing focus.

The key is to ensure that your marketing strategy evolves as your business grows. What works during the launch phase may not be as effective during the scaling phase, and that's okay. The important thing is to keep your audience at the center of your efforts.

Conclusion

The "when" and "why" of marketing aren't just theoretical—they're deeply tied to the success of your business. Starting early, understanding its purpose, and aligning it with your goals will ensure that your marketing isn't just an expense but a driver of growth. Whether you're attracting your first customer or scaling to new heights, marketing will always be your bridge to your audience and the foundation of your success.

Evaluating Marketing Channels: What Works for You?

The sheer variety of marketing channels available today can be both exciting and overwhelming. From traditional methods like outdoor billboards and newspaper ads to digital platforms and experiential marketing, each channel presents unique opportunities to connect with your audience. However, not all channels are right for every business. To maximize your resources and impact, you need to evaluate which ones align with your audience, goals, and budget.

Start with Your Audience

The first step in choosing the right channels is understanding where your audience spends their time. Different channels cater to different demographics and preferences. For example:

Social Media: Platforms like Instagram, TikTok, or Facebook are great for reaching younger, tech-savvy audiences.

Outdoor Advertising: Billboards, bus ads, or car wraps work well for businesses looking to target a wide, local audience in urban or high-traffic areas.

Print Media: Newspapers and magazines are still effective for reaching specific niches, like local communities or industry professionals.

Event Marketing: Posters, banners, and flyers are excellent for promoting local events, launches, or trade shows.

Digital Marketing: Email campaigns, PPC ads, and affiliate programs provide measurable and targeted ways to connect with specific customer segments.

For instance, Coca-Cola uses a mix of channels—everything from billboards and TV ads to social media campaigns and event sponsorships—to maintain its visibility and connection with audiences worldwide.

Explore the Full Range of Channels

Here's a breakdown of some additional marketing channels and their potential benefits:

Outdoor Billboards and Bus Ads: These are ideal for high-visibility campaigns in metropolitan areas. They work well for branding and creating widespread awareness.

Car Wrapping and Truck Ads: A mobile billboard that reaches diverse audiences, particularly in local markets, without requiring a stationary presence.

Shopping Cart Ads: Effective for targeting grocery shoppers, this method works well for food and household product brands.

TV and Radio: Traditional media still has a strong reach, particularly for campaigns targeting broad demographics. Super Bowl ads, for example, remain one of the most coveted spots for brands aiming to make a splash.

Direct Mail and Flyers: Tangible and personal, direct mail campaigns or distributing flyers can work well for local businesses, particularly when combined with discounts or coupons.

Event Posters and Banners: Perfect for building brand visibility at trade shows, festivals, or community events.

Magazines and Newspapers: These work for targeted, niche audiences who prefer in-depth content or are loyal to specific publications.

Affiliate Marketing: By partnering with affiliates who promote your product for a commission, you can tap into established audiences without upfront advertising costs.

Coupons and Discounts: Distributed via email, print, or social media, they can incentivize first-time buyers or reward loyal customers.

Measure the Effectiveness

Choosing the right channel is only the beginning. Regularly evaluate the performance of each channel using measurable metrics:

Outdoor and Print Ads: Monitor foot traffic or direct inquiries linked to campaigns in specific locations.

Digital Channels: Use analytics tools to track clicks, conversions, and engagement.

Event Marketing: Gather leads and measure attendance or post-event inquiries.

Affiliate Marketing: Track sales or referrals generated by affiliates.

For example, Amazon monitors the performance of its affiliate network meticulously, using data to determine which partnerships drive the most sales and adjusting its strategies accordingly.

The Balance Between Traditional and Modern Channels

A successful marketing strategy often combines traditional and modern channels. For instance:

1. A local coffee shop might use car wraps, posters, and event sponsorships to create local buzz, while simultaneously leveraging Instagram to showcase its ambiance and products.

2. A tech startup might prioritize digital channels like PPC and social media ads but still include magazine features or industry-specific trade shows to build credibility.

Costco, for example, doesn't rely heavily on TV or radio ads but uses its in-store environment, coupons, and word-of-mouth to drive customer loyalty.

Conclusion

With so many marketing channels available, the key is to focus on what works for your business and audience. There's no need to be everywhere at once—success comes from strategically selecting channels that align with your goals, audience preferences, and budget. Whether you're leveraging outdoor billboards, online ads, or affiliate partnerships, the right mix of channels will ensure your message resonates and delivers results.

The Best Marketing Strategy for Your Business

The ultimate marketing strategy is rooted in your product or service itself. When your offering is so compelling, valuable, and impactful that customers willingly become your advocates, you've unlocked the most powerful and cost-effective form of marketing. In this approach, your product or service does the heavy lifting—it inspires people to share their experiences, recommend it to others, and build trust around your brand without you needing to invest heavily in traditional marketing efforts.

Your Product as the Hero

At the core of this strategy is the idea that a truly exceptional product or service becomes its own best advertisement. When customers are genuinely delighted by what you offer, they naturally want to share their experiences. They might post about it on social media, tell their friends, or recommend it to their colleagues and companies, because of quality, good deal, packaging, slogan, logo, interesting look, etc. This word-of-mouth marketing is not only organic but also incredibly persuasive because it comes from a trusted source.

Consider Tesla's success. Tesla doesn't rely heavily on traditional advertising; instead, its cars speak for themselves. Owners rave about the performance, design, and technology, creating a loyal fanbase that willingly promotes the brand. Similarly, creating something remarkable will encourage your customers to do your marketing for you.

The Power of Authentic Advocacy

When customers advocate for your product or service, the impact is profound. Unlike paid advertising, which can sometimes feel impersonal or forced, recommendations from real users carry authenticity and trust. Imagine someone sharing on their social media: "This coffee shop has the best espresso I've ever had, and their membership program offers free refills—don't miss it!" That kind of genuine endorsement is priceless and far more effective than a paid ad.

For example, companies like Airbnb rely heavily on user-generated content. Guests often share their unique stays online, showcasing the platform's value to their networks. This type of organic promotion builds credibility and drives new users to explore the service without the need for traditional marketing.

Focus on Value and Experience

To activate this strategy, your product or service must deliver extraordinary value. It's not enough to be good; it needs to be remarkable. Think about the pricing, quality, customer service, and overall experience you're providing. Are you exceeding expectations? Are you solving problems in a way no one else does? When your customers feel they've found the best deal or an unbeatable solution, they become your most enthusiastic promoters.

Take Costco as an example. The retailer's famously low-priced hotdog combo has become a symbol of value, drawing customers who then share their experience with friends. It's a simple offering that creates buzz and loyalty, demonstrating that even small gestures can have a big impact.

Effortless and Cost-Effective Marketing

The beauty of this strategy lies in its efficiency. You don't need to spend heavily on ads or promotional campaigns because your customers do the broadcasting for you. Their word-of-mouth referrals are more persuasive than any advertisement because they come with a personal endorsement. It saves you money, energy, and time while amplifying your reach in a way that feels natural and trustworthy.

Conclusion

The best marketing strategy for your business is to create a product or service so outstanding that your customers become your marketers. By focusing on delivering exceptional value and experience, you empower your audience to spread the word on your behalf. This approach not only saves resources but also builds trust and credibility, laying the foundation for sustainable growth driven by authentic customer advocacy. When people believe in what you're offering, they'll tell the world—and that's the best kind of marketing there is.

CHAPTER 21: SMART GROWTH: STRATEGIES FOR SUSTAINABLE SUCCESS

Growth is the lifeblood of any business, but not all growth is created equal. Scaling a business without a thoughtful strategy can lead to wasted resources, strained operations, and missed opportunities. Smart growth, on the other hand, focuses on building a business that is not only larger but also stronger, more efficient, and more resilient.

At its core, smart growth is about balance—between retaining the customers you already have and attracting new ones, between driving revenue and managing costs, and between sticking to what works and exploring new opportunities. Each aspect contributes to a sustainable foundation that allows your business to thrive, even in competitive or challenging markets.

This chapter dives into the key strategies for achieving sustainable success through smart growth. You'll learn the importance of keeping your existing customers happy while reaching out to new ones, discover how to weigh the benefits of growing revenue against controlling costs, and explore ways to diversify your income streams. By focusing on these critical elements, you can ensure your growth efforts lead to long-term profitability and stability, not just short-term wins.

Customer Retention: The Foundation of

Sustainable Growth

While attracting new customers is essential for growth, retaining the customers you already have is the bedrock of sustainable success. Loyal customers are not just repeat buyers; they become brand advocates, spreading positive word-of-mouth and driving consistent revenue. Studies show that retaining customers is far more cost-effective than acquiring new ones. In fact, increasing customer retention by just 5% can boost profits by 25% to 95%, underscoring its significance.

Why Retention Matters

Customer retention is critical because it provides stability and predictability to your business. Acquiring a new customer often requires significant investment in marketing, sales efforts, and incentives, whereas retaining an existing customer builds on an already-established relationship. These loyal customers:

1. Spend more over time, often increasing their average purchase value.

2. Are more forgiving of minor mistakes, as they trust your brand.

3. Act as ambassadors, referring others to your business at no cost to you.

For example, Amazon's success hinges on its Prime membership program, which encourages loyalty through benefits like free shipping and exclusive deals. By focusing on retaining Prime members, Amazon ensures a steady stream of revenue and builds long-term customer relationships.

Strategies for Retaining Customers

1. **Deliver Consistent Quality:** Consistency builds trust. Ensure that your products or services meet or exceed expectations every time. A reliable experience is what turns first-time buyers into repeat customers.

2. **Engage Regularly:** Stay connected with your customers through personalized emails, loyalty programs, or exclusive offers. For example, Starbucks' rewards app encourages repeat visits by offering free drinks and discounts.

3. **Listen and Adapt:** Regularly seek feedback to understand what customers love and where you can improve. Addressing their concerns quickly shows that you value their opinions and are committed to meeting their needs.

4. **Go Beyond Transactions:** Build relationships with your customers. This can mean offering educational content, hosting events, or simply providing excellent customer service. Brands like Sephora excel by creating a community through tutorials, beauty advice, and user engagement.

Retention vs. Acquisition: Finding the Balance

While retention is the foundation, it's important to balance it with efforts to attract new customers. However, without a strong focus on retention, you risk spending resources on acquiring customers who may not stay. A loyal customer base provides the stability needed to expand sustainably, giving you the confidence to invest in growth initiatives without jeopardizing your core business.

Conclusion

Customer retention is not just a metric; it's a strategy for building a resilient and profitable business. By focusing on delivering value, building relationships, and engaging consistently, you can turn one-time buyers into lifelong customers. This loyalty doesn't just stabilize your revenue—it creates a foundation from which your business can grow smarter, stronger, and more sustainably.

Winning New Customers: Strategies for

Expanding Your Base

Attracting new customers is a crucial part of growing your business. While retaining existing customers provides stability, acquiring new ones ensures that your business continues to evolve, reach new markets, and scale. Winning new customers is not just about casting a wide net—it's about targeting the right audience with the right strategies, ensuring that your marketing efforts yield lasting relationships rather than one-time transactions.

Understand Your Ideal Customer

The first step in winning new customers is knowing who you're trying to reach. A well-defined customer profile allows you to tailor your marketing efforts effectively. This means understanding:

Demographics: Age, gender, income, and location.

Behavior: How they shop, what influences their decisions, and where they spend their time online or offline.

Needs and Pain Points: What problems they face and how your product or service solves them.

For example, Airbnb successfully expanded its customer base by identifying travelers seeking unique and affordable accommodations. They targeted these individuals through tailored online campaigns and user-generated content that showcased real guest experiences.

Leverage Multiple Channels

Reaching new customers requires a multi-channel approach. Different customers spend time in different places, so diversifying your marketing efforts increases your chances of connecting with them:

Social Media: Platforms like Instagram, TikTok, and LinkedIn allow businesses to target specific demographics with engaging content.

Search Engine Marketing (SEM): Google Ads and SEO strategies help attract customers actively searching for solutions.

Traditional Advertising: Billboards, flyers, or event sponsorships can reach local or broader audiences.

Partnerships and Referrals: Collaborate with complementary businesses or incentivize existing customers to refer friends.

For instance, Tesla uses a referral program that rewards customers who bring in new buyers, turning satisfied customers into active promoters of the brand.

Offer Incentives

Incentives can be a powerful motivator for attracting new customers. Discounts, free trials, or bundled offers give potential buyers a reason to choose your product or service. Consider examples like:

1. Spotify offering a free trial period for its premium service, encouraging users to experience its benefits before committing.

2. Costco's free one-day guest passes, allowing non-members to explore the store's value and consider joining.

Make sure your incentives align with your business goals and target audience. Over-discounting can attract price-sensitive customers who may not stick around, so balance generosity with long-term retention strategies.

Build Trust and Credibility

New customers are more likely to engage with businesses they trust. Establish credibility by:

1. Showcasing testimonials and reviews from satisfied customers.

2. Highlighting any awards, certifications, or media features that lend authority to your brand.

3. Being transparent about your policies, pricing, and values.

Brands like Patagonia leverage their commitment to sustainability to build trust and attract environmentally-conscious customers.

Focus on the Customer Experience

Winning a customer is not just about the first purchase—it's about creating a memorable experience that keeps them coming back. Ensure your onboarding process is smooth, your communication is clear, and your service is impeccable. A delighted first-time customer is more likely to recommend your business and return for future purchases.

Conclusion

Expanding your customer base is an essential part of business growth, but it requires more than just flashy ads or enticing offers. By understanding your ideal customer, leveraging diverse channels, and building trust through value-driven strategies, you can attract new customers who will become long-term supporters of your business. Winning new customers isn't just about numbers—it's about creating connections that drive sustained success.

Both old and new customers play crucial roles in the success of a business

In the journey to grow a successful business, balancing efforts between retaining existing customers and acquiring new ones is key. Both old and new customers bring unique value, and focusing solely on one group can limit your growth potential. While loyal customers provide stability and recurring revenue, new customers infuse your business with fresh energy, opportunities, and market insights.

The Value of Old Customers

Existing customers are often the foundation of your business. They've already experienced your product or service, making them more likely to trust and return for future purchases. Loyal customers:

Provide Consistent Revenue: Repeat buyers contribute to predictable cash flow and reduce reliance on constant acquisition efforts.

Act as Brand Advocates: Satisfied customers recommend your business to others, driving organic growth.

Cost Less to Retain: Research shows that retaining a customer costs significantly less than acquiring a new one.

Apple exemplifies the power of customer loyalty. Its ecosystem approach—integrating devices like iPhones, iPads, and Macs— encourages customers to stay within the brand, leading to repeat purchases and long-term relationships.

The Value of New Customers

While retaining customers is vital, new customers are equally important for growth and innovation. They:

Expand Market Reach: New customers help you enter untapped markets and broaden your brand's audience.

Offer Fresh Perspectives: Interacting with new customers can provide insights into evolving trends and preferences, helping you adapt your offerings.

Drive Revenue Growth: Acquiring new customers is crucial for scaling your business and offsetting natural customer attrition.

Consider Netflix, which consistently attracts new users by expanding its library with fresh, diverse content. By targeting different demographics and regions, Netflix ensures it remains a global leader in entertainment.

Striking the Right Balance

Both old and new customers are essential, but their importance can shift depending on your business's stage:

Startups and Early Stages: Focus more on acquiring new customers to establish a presence and build a customer base.

Growth and Maturity: Balance retention efforts with acquisition to maintain stability while scaling.

Established Businesses: Prioritize retention, leveraging loyal customers as your core revenue source while strategically attracting new buyers.

Starbucks exemplifies this balance. The company invests heavily in loyalty programs like Starbucks Rewards to retain customers while launching innovative campaigns to attract new ones, such as introducing seasonal drinks or expanding into global markets.

Conclusion

Old and new customers are two sides of the same coin—both are indispensable for a thriving business. Retaining loyal customers ensures stability and profitability, while acquiring new customers drives growth and innovation. By appreciating the unique roles each group plays and tailoring your strategies accordingly, you can build a business that not only grows but sustains its success over the long term.

Revenue Growth vs. Cost Control: The

Better Path to Profitability

Profitability is the ultimate goal of any business, but the path to achieving it often sparks a critical debate: should you focus on growing revenue or controlling costs? Both strategies have their merits, and the right approach depends on your business's stage, industry, and specific circumstances. Striking the right balance between the two is often the key to sustainable success.

The Case for Revenue Growth

Revenue growth is the most direct way to increase profitability. By expanding your market, increasing sales, or introducing new products and services, you can drive higher earnings and reinvest in your business for further growth.

For instance, Amazon prioritizes revenue growth by continually diversifying its offerings—adding AWS, Prime memberships, and third-party marketplace services. This focus on creating multiple income streams has propelled Amazon to become one of the most valuable companies in the world.

Advantages of focusing on revenue growth include:

Market Expansion: Reaching more customers can solidify your market position.

Economies of Scale: Higher sales volumes can reduce per-unit costs, increasing profitability over time.

Reinvestment Opportunities: Additional revenue can fund innovation, marketing, or infrastructure development.

However, pursuing revenue growth without considering costs can lead to inefficiencies and diminishing returns.

The Case for Cost Control

On the other hand, controlling costs is an often-underrated but powerful lever for boosting profitability. By streamlining operations, negotiating better supplier contracts, or optimizing workflows, businesses can improve their profit margins without needing to increase sales.

Costco is a prime example of a business that excels at cost control. By focusing on efficient supply chain management and maintaining low operational expenses, Costco offers customers unbeatable value while sustaining healthy profit margins, even with razor-thin product markups.

Advantages of cost control include:

Increased Margins: Lower costs translate directly into higher profitability.

Risk Mitigation: Controlled expenses reduce financial strain during economic downturns.

Sustainability: Efficient operations create a stable foundation for long-term growth.

However, excessive cost-cutting can harm product quality, employee morale, and customer satisfaction, which may negatively impact revenue.

The Interplay Between Revenue and Costs

The best path to profitability often lies in balancing revenue growth and cost control. A combined approach ensures that while your business expands, it remains efficient and financially sound. For example:

Tesla initially focused on growing revenue by scaling production and capturing market share in the electric vehicle industry. Over time, it worked to control costs through vertical integration and technological advancements, ultimately achieving sustained profitability.

McDonald's balances revenue growth with cost control by offering affordable menu items (cost control) while using value-driven promotions like meal deals to increase sales volume (revenue growth).

Which Path Should You Choose?

Your business's priorities should dictate your focus:

Startups and Early Stages: Revenue growth often takes precedence to establish market presence and attract investors.

Scaling Phase: A dual focus on revenue and cost control is essential to grow efficiently.

Mature Businesses: Cost control becomes more critical for maintaining profitability and weathering market fluctuations.

Conclusion

Revenue growth and cost control are not mutually exclusive; they are complementary strategies that, when balanced, lead to profitability. By understanding the strengths and limitations of each approach and aligning them with your business's stage and goals, you can chart a path to sustainable success. The key is to grow smartly, ensuring every dollar earned or saved contributes to a stronger, more resilient business.

Unlocking New Revenue Streams:

Diversify to Thrive

Relying on a single revenue stream can make your business vulnerable to market fluctuations, changing consumer behavior, or unforeseen disruptions. Diversifying your income sources not only protects your business from these risks but also creates opportunities for growth and innovation. Unlocking new revenue streams is a strategy that enables your business to thrive, even in the face of uncertainty.

Why Diversification Matters

A diversified revenue model provides stability and resilience. If one stream underperforms, others can compensate, ensuring a consistent flow of income. This strategy has been a hallmark of success for many global businesses:

Amazon started as an online bookstore but quickly expanded into electronics, cloud computing (AWS), subscription services (Prime), and advertising. Each new revenue stream contributed to Amazon's growth and reduced dependency on any single category.

Disney generates revenue from theme parks, streaming services (Disney+), merchandise, and box office releases. This diversification allows the company to leverage its brand across multiple markets and revenue channels.

For startups, diversification may seem ambitious, but it's a crucial long-term goal that begins with identifying complementary opportunities.

How to Identify New Revenue Streams

1. **Analyze Your Existing Business:** Look at your core products or services. Are there natural extensions or upsells you can offer? For example, a coffee shop could sell branded merchandise like mugs or launch a subscription service for specialty coffee deliveries.

2. **Leverage Your Expertise:** Use your team's skills or knowledge to create new offerings. For instance, a moving company could add packing services or offer storage solutions.

3. **Explore New Markets:** Consider how your existing offerings could serve different audiences. Tesla, for example, leveraged its electric vehicle technology to venture into battery storage solutions for homes and businesses.

4. **Adopt Technology:** Digital products and services often provide scalable and high-margin revenue opportunities. If your business operates in physical spaces, could you offer

virtual consultations, online courses, or subscription-based digital products?

Examples of Revenue Stream Innovation

1. **Costco:** Known for its low product margins, Costco generates significant profits from its membership fees, which create a steady, predictable income source.

2. **Apple:** Beyond selling devices, Apple earns substantial revenue from its App Store, Apple Music, and iCloud services, making its ecosystem sticky and highly profitable.

3. **McDonald's:** While its menu items drive volume, McDonald's generates considerable income from real estate, leasing properties to franchisees.

Balancing Innovation and Core Business

While diversification is important, it shouldn't distract from your core offering. Striking the right balance is essential:

1. Avoid overextending resources by testing new ideas on a small scale first.

2. Ensure new revenue streams align with your brand and add value to your customers.

3. Monitor performance and cut initiatives that don't deliver meaningful results.

Netflix provides a valuable lesson here. Initially focused on DVD rentals, the company pivoted to streaming services and later ventured into original content production. Each new stream reinforced its core value of delivering entertainment, creating a cohesive and thriving business model.

Conclusion

Unlocking new revenue streams is a powerful way to diversify your business, mitigate risks, and create opportunities for sustainable growth. By leveraging your strengths, analyzing market trends, and aligning new initiatives with your core values, you can ensure your business remains adaptable and resilient. Diversification isn't just about survival—it's about positioning your business to thrive in an ever-changing marketplace

CHAPTER 22: DOMINATING YOUR MARKET: COMPETING

In the dynamic world of business, competition is inevitable. To thrive, you must not only participate but dominate your market with strategies that strengthen your position, protect your unique offerings, and propel your business ahead of others. True competition isn't about merely surviving—it's about setting your business apart in a way that attracts customers, builds loyalty, and ensures long-term growth.

Dominating your market requires a multi-faceted approach. You need the strength of a robust product or service, the foresight to protect your intellectual property, the creativity to stay innovative, and the strategic mindset to form alliances that amplify your reach. These strategies don't just shield you from competitors—they actively create opportunities to outpace and outperform them.

This chapter will guide you through the key elements of smart competition, including building strength in your core offerings, safeguarding your business against imitators, staying ahead through innovation, and leveraging partnerships to create an unbeatable position in your market. By embracing these principles, you can transform competition from a challenge into a catalyst for success

Being Strong: The Ultimate Competitive

Strategy

In business, strength is the foundation of success. The strongest companies dominate their markets not through luck or gimmicks but by consistently delivering exceptional value, building trust, and standing out from the competition. Strength doesn't just mean having a great product or service—it encompasses operational efficiency, customer loyalty, brand recognition, and the ability to adapt to challenges.

Building Strength Through Quality

The first step to being strong is excelling in what you offer. A superior product or service creates a lasting impression, encourages repeat business, and attracts word-of-mouth referrals. Customers are more likely to choose a brand that consistently meets or exceeds their expectations.

Take **Apple**, for example. Its strength lies in creating innovative, high-quality products that seamlessly integrate into a broader ecosystem. This approach not only attracts new customers but also retains existing ones, reinforcing its dominance in the tech market. By prioritizing quality and user experience, Apple maintains a strong competitive edge.

Resilience: Adapting to Market Changes

A strong business is also resilient. Market trends, economic downturns, and shifts in consumer behavior are inevitable, but companies that adapt quickly turn challenges into opportunities. **Netflix** is a prime example. Originally a DVD rental service, it pivoted to streaming just as the market began to shift, leaving competitors scrambling to catch up. Its ability to foresee and respond to change solidified its position as an industry leader.

Resilience also comes from building a diversified revenue base and a robust operational structure. When one part of your business faces pressure, other areas can support stability and growth.

Investing in Your Team

Your team is one of your greatest sources of strength. Skilled, motivated, and loyal employees drive innovation and ensure seamless operations. Strong companies prioritize hiring talented individuals, offering competitive benefits, and fostering a positive culture. Companies like **Google** thrive because they empower their employees with the resources and freedom to innovate, making them a leader in technology and creativity.

Customer Loyalty as Strength

Strength also comes from customer trust and loyalty. A loyal customer base not only provides stable revenue but also acts as a shield against competitors. **Costco** exemplifies this by focusing on value for its members, maintaining consistent quality, and reinforcing trust through its membership model. Its loyal customers ensure steady foot traffic and long-term profitability.

The Power of Consistency

Consistency in delivery, messaging, and customer service builds a reputation that competitors struggle to match. When customers know what to expect, they return, and they spread the word. **McDonald's** has mastered this strategy. No matter where you are in the world, you know what a Big Mac will taste like. This consistency has made McDonald's a global icon.

Conclusion

Being strong in business is not about overpowering competitors through sheer force; it's about building a foundation of quality, resilience, and trust that makes your business a leader in its field. By focusing on delivering exceptional value, investing in your team, adapting to change, and earning customer loyalty, you can position your business to not only compete but dominate. Strength doesn't just win battles—it defines the leaders of the market.

Protecting Your Business: Intellectual Property and Market Positioning

In the competitive world of business, safeguarding what sets you apart is crucial. Your unique ideas, products, services, and brand identity are the lifeblood of your enterprise. Without proper protection, competitors can copy or dilute your offerings, undermining your market position and profitability. Protecting your business isn't just a defensive measure—it's a proactive strategy to ensure long-term success and maintain a competitive edge.

The Importance of Intellectual Property (IP)

Intellectual Property (IP) protection is vital for preserving your unique innovations and ideas. Whether it's a product design, software, brand name, or marketing concept, IP laws provide legal safeguards that prevent others from exploiting your creations.

Trademarks: Protect your brand identity, including names, logos, and slogans. For example, Nike's swoosh logo and "Just Do It" tagline are instantly recognizable and legally shielded.

Patents: Safeguard inventions, ensuring that competitors can't replicate your innovations. Tesla, for instance, holds numerous patents on its electric vehicle technologies, giving it a competitive advantage.

Copyrights: Secure your creative works, such as books, music, and software. Disney's extensive library of characters and films is heavily protected under copyright law.

Trade Secrets: Safeguard confidential processes or recipes, like Coca-Cola's secret formula, which remains one of the most famous trade secrets in the world.

Registering your IP not only protects your creations but also adds value to your business. Investors and partners view strong IP portfolios as a sign of innovation and security.

Market Positioning as Protection

Market positioning is about carving out a distinct space for your brand in the minds of customers. A well-defined position not only attracts your target audience but also makes it difficult for competitors to mimic your success.

Differentiate Your Brand: Highlight what makes your business unique. Apple's focus on design and user experience sets it apart from other tech companies, creating a strong market position.

Build Trust and Loyalty: Consistency and reliability foster customer loyalty, which acts as a protective barrier. Brands like Patagonia build trust by aligning their business practices with their values, such as sustainability.

Create Emotional Connections: Emotional branding creates a bond that's hard for competitors to break. Nike doesn't just sell shoes—it inspires customers with a "can-do" spirit through its marketing and product designs.

Positioning your business effectively ensures that even if competitors try to replicate your offerings, customers will recognize and prefer your brand.

Defending Against Copycats

Competitors copying your ideas or products is inevitable in a competitive market, but you can take steps to minimize the impact:

Monitor the Market: Keep an eye on competitors to spot potential infringements or imitations early.

Enforce Your Rights: Don't hesitate to take legal action when someone violates your IP rights. For example, Lego has successfully defended its brick design against copycats, preserving its market dominance.

Continue Innovating: Staying ahead through constant innovation makes it harder for competitors to catch up. Amazon continuously adds features and services to its platform, keeping competitors at bay.

Balancing Protection with Accessibility

While protecting your business is essential, avoid becoming overly restrictive. Being too guarded can stifle collaboration and opportunities for growth. Tesla, for instance, made some of its patents open source to encourage the development of electric vehicles, strengthening its leadership in the industry.

Conclusion

Protecting your business through intellectual property and market positioning is not just about defending against competitors—it's about securing your long-term growth and value. By safeguarding your unique assets and carving out a distinct identity in the marketplace, you ensure that your business remains resilient, innovative, and preferred by customers. In a world of fierce competition, strong protection is the foundation of enduring success.

Compete with Innovation: Staying Ahead of Trends

In a fast-paced business landscape, innovation is not just a competitive advantage—it's a necessity. Companies that consistently innovate and adapt to emerging trends position themselves as market leaders, while those that resist change risk obsolescence. To stay ahead, businesses must foster a culture of innovation, embrace new technologies, and anticipate customer needs before the competition does.

The Role of Innovation in Competitive Advantage

Innovation allows businesses to create unique value, differentiate themselves, and capture new markets. It's about more than introducing new products—it involves improving processes, enhancing customer experiences, and rethinking business models.

Apple's Ecosystem: Apple doesn't just sell individual devices; it innovated by creating an integrated ecosystem of products and services, making it hard for competitors to match the seamless experience.

Netflix's Streaming Model: By shifting from DVD rentals to streaming, Netflix disrupted the entertainment industry and set a new standard for content consumption.

Tesla's EV Leadership: Tesla's advancements in battery technology, autonomous driving, and sustainable energy have redefined the automotive industry, leaving competitors scrambling to catch up.

Innovation like this doesn't just attract customers—it redefines entire industries, setting the innovators far ahead of the pack.

Embrace Emerging Trends

Identifying and leveraging trends early can provide a significant competitive edge. Staying ahead of trends requires vigilance and the willingness to take calculated risks:

Monitor Industry Developments: Stay informed about technological advancements, market shifts, and changing consumer behavior. Platforms like Gartner or McKinsey's insights are valuable resources.

Experiment and Iterate: Test small-scale innovations before rolling them out broadly. For instance, Starbucks pilots new menu items in select locations to gauge customer interest before a nationwide launch.

Think Beyond Your Industry: Cross-industry trends often spark groundbreaking ideas. Airbnb took inspiration from the sharing economy to revolutionize the hospitality sector.

Fostering a Culture of Innovation

A company's ability to innovate is directly tied to its culture. Encouraging creativity, collaboration, and experimentation among employees can drive groundbreaking ideas:

Encourage Employee Input: Employees on the front lines often have the best insights into customer pain points and potential solutions. Google's "20% time" policy, which allows employees to work on passion projects, has led to innovations like Gmail.

Reward Risk-Taking: Celebrate efforts to innovate, even if they fail. This creates an environment where employees feel safe experimenting without fear of repercussions.

Invest in R&D: Dedicate resources to research and development to stay at the forefront of your industry. Pharmaceutical companies, for example, rely heavily on R&D to discover and launch new drugs.

Adaptability: The Key to Staying Relevant

Innovation isn't a one-time event—it's a continuous process. Businesses that adapt quickly to changing circumstances are better positioned to outlast competitors:

Kodak's Lesson: Despite inventing the digital camera, Kodak failed to adapt to the shift from film to digital photography, leading to its downfall.

Amazon's Evolution: Amazon began as an online bookstore but continuously adapted, introducing new categories, Prime services, AWS, and more, keeping it ahead of competitors in multiple industries.

Conclusion

Competing with innovation means staying proactive, embracing change, and consistently seeking new ways to create value. By fostering a culture that encourages creativity, keeping a close eye on emerging trends, and adapting quickly to market demands, businesses can secure their place at the forefront of their industry. In the race for market dominance, innovation isn't just a strategy—it's a mindset that ensures long-term success.

Strategic Alliances: Partnering to Strengthen Your Market Position

In today's interconnected business world, going it alone isn't always the best strategy. Strategic alliances—partnerships between businesses to achieve mutual goals—can be a powerful way to strengthen your market position, reach new customers, and share resources. By collaborating with the right partners, you can leverage their strengths to complement your own, creating a synergy that drives growth and innovation.

The Power of Collaboration

Strategic alliances allow businesses to pool their resources, expertise, and networks to achieve what might be difficult individually. This collaboration can take many forms, such as joint ventures, co-branding, or supply chain partnerships.

For example:

Starbucks and PepsiCo: Starbucks partnered with PepsiCo to distribute its bottled coffee drinks globally. This alliance allowed Starbucks to tap into PepsiCo's vast distribution network, significantly expanding its reach.

Spotify and Uber: Spotify integrated its music platform into Uber rides, enhancing the customer experience for both companies and strengthening their market appeal.

Such alliances demonstrate that two businesses working together can achieve far more than they could alone.

Choosing the Right Partner

Not all partnerships are created equal. Selecting the right partner is critical to the success of a strategic alliance. Look for businesses that:

Complement Your Strengths: Find partners whose capabilities fill gaps in your own. For instance, a small food producer might partner with a logistics company to improve distribution.

Share Your Values: Aligning on core values ensures a smoother collaboration and prevents conflicts.

Have a Compatible Audience: Partnerships are most effective when both companies target similar or overlapping customer bases.

Take the collaboration between **Apple and Hermès**, which produced high-end Apple Watch bands. This partnership combined Apple's technology with Hermès' luxury branding, appealing to a niche market of affluent, fashion-conscious consumers.

Benefits of Strategic Alliances

1. **Access to New Markets:** Partnerships can open doors to audiences or regions you wouldn't have been able to reach on your own.

2. **Cost and Risk Sharing:** By sharing the costs and risks of new initiatives, both partners can test ideas without overextending resources.

3. **Enhanced Credibility:** Aligning with an established brand can boost your reputation and increase customer trust.

4. **Innovation Opportunities:** Collaborative efforts often spark new ideas, leading to innovative products or services.

For example, **McDonald's** partnered with Coca-Cola decades ago, and the two brands have worked together ever since, offering value-driven meal deals and joint promotions that benefit both companies.

Navigating Challenges

While alliances can be beneficial, they also come with potential challenges:

Conflicting Goals: Misaligned objectives can create tension. Clear communication and shared goals are essential.

Resource Imbalances: If one partner brings significantly more to the table, the alliance may feel inequitable.

Loss of Control: Collaborations require compromise, which may mean relinquishing some control over certain aspects of your business.

Amazon's partnership with third-party sellers on its marketplace highlights the need for careful management. While the alliance benefits Amazon by expanding its product offerings, it also requires strict oversight to maintain quality and customer trust.

Leveraging Alliances for Market Domination

The most successful alliances are those that create value for both partners and their customers. By focusing on complementary strengths, shared values, and long-term objectives, businesses can turn partnerships into powerful tools for growth and innovation.

Conclusion

Strategic alliances are more than just collaborations—they are opportunities to multiply your business's strengths, minimize risks, and expand your reach. In a competitive market, partnering wisely can set you apart, offering advantages that help you dominate your industry. The key lies in finding the right partner, aligning on shared goals, and fostering a relationship built on mutual trust and respect. Together, you can achieve what neither could accomplish alone.

CHAPTER 23: GROWING YOUR WORKFORCE, GROWING YOUR BUSINESS: TEAM SCALE

Scaling a business isn't just about increasing production or expanding your market; it's also about growing the team that supports it. As your business evolves, the demands on your workforce will change, requiring new roles, additional skills, and a larger team to meet those needs. Neglecting to scale your team effectively can result in missed opportunities, overworked staff, and a loss of momentum.

Team scaling, however, is not without its challenges. It requires balancing growth with culture, ensuring that the people you bring on board align with your company's values and mission. It also demands strategic decisions about whether to hire new talent, promote from within, or invest in training for existing employees.

This chapter will explore the intricacies of scaling your workforce as your business grows. From understanding why team growth is as critical as business expansion, to addressing the challenges of scaling effectively, and deciding between hiring and promoting, you'll gain insights into how to build a workforce that grows in step with your business. After all, a strong team isn't just a support system—it's the engine that drives your company forward.

Scaling Your Team Alongside Your

Business

As your business grows, the team that supports it must expand and evolve to meet increasing demands. A well-scaled team is not just about adding more people—it's about ensuring that the structure, skills, and culture of your workforce align with your business's growth trajectory. Scaling your team alongside your business is critical for sustaining momentum, maintaining operational efficiency, and driving innovation.

Why Team Growth is Essential

When a business expands, so do its challenges. More customers mean more inquiries, higher production levels require more hands-on-deck, and new markets demand specialized skills. Without a team that grows in step with your business, you risk bottlenecks, burnout, and a decline in service quality.

Consider **Amazon's rapid expansion**: The company grew from a small team managing an online bookstore to a global workforce handling logistics, cloud computing, and streaming services. Each stage of its growth required strategic team scaling to ensure operational efficiency and customer satisfaction.

The Importance of Structure

Scaling your team requires more than just hiring—it involves reevaluating and restructuring roles and responsibilities. As businesses grow, certain functions become more complex, necessitating the creation of new positions or departments.

For instance:

1. A startup founder might initially handle all customer service, but as the company grows, this role could expand into a dedicated customer support team.

2. A logistics company expanding into new regions might need regional managers to oversee operations, ensuring that the scale doesn't compromise service quality.

Establishing clear structures and hierarchies prevents confusion, streamlines decision-making, and fosters accountability as your business scales.

Balancing Growth and Culture

As you scale your team, maintaining your company culture becomes a vital challenge. Adding new members brings fresh perspectives but also risks diluting the values and identity that made your business successful in the first place.

Google exemplifies this balance by embedding its culture into the onboarding process and maintaining open communication channels, even as the company grew to employ tens of thousands globally. Clear articulation of your values and a focus on hiring individuals who align with your mission can help preserve your company's ethos during rapid expansion.

Scaling at the Right Pace

Scaling too quickly can lead to inefficiencies, while scaling too slowly risks overburdening your existing team. A measured approach ensures that your growth is sustainable:

1. Assess your current workload and project future needs.

2. Identify gaps in skills or capacity that could hinder growth.

3. Prioritize roles that directly impact your business's ability to meet its growth objectives.

For example, **Slack** initially focused on building a small but highly skilled team to perfect its product before scaling its workforce to support broader adoption. This staged growth allowed the company to maintain its quality and efficiency.

Conclusion

Scaling your team alongside your business is a strategic process that requires foresight, planning, and adaptability. By aligning team growth with business objectives, maintaining a strong company culture, and scaling at the right pace, you can build a workforce that not only supports your expansion but propels it forward. A well-scaled team isn't just a resource—it's a competitive advantage that ensures your business thrives in a dynamic market.

Risks and Challenges of Scaling:

Preparing Your Team for Growth

Scaling a business is often seen as a milestone of success, but growth comes with its own set of challenges, especially when expanding your team. Without careful preparation, scaling can expose your business to risks that undermine its efficiency, culture, and profitability. Preparing your team for this evolution is not just a managerial task—it's a strategic necessity.

One of the primary risks of scaling without preparation is operational strain. When a team is unprepared for the increased workload that accompanies growth, cracks begin to show. Deadlines are missed, quality diminishes, and customer satisfaction suffers. For example, many e-commerce startups experience fulfillment delays during peak demand periods if they expand sales without bolstering their logistics teams. Growth amplifies every weakness in your operation, making it essential to shore up your team beforehand.

Another challenge lies in preserving your company culture. Rapid hiring often means bringing in employees who may not fully align with your organization's values or mission. The early-stage camaraderie and shared vision that defined your team can become diluted. This shift is common in companies like tech startups that grow rapidly, only to find that their cultural identity becomes fragmented, alienating both old and new team members. To scale successfully, you must ensure that your culture evolves without losing its essence.

Financial risks are another key consideration. Expanding a team requires investment—not just in salaries but also in training, equipment, and infrastructure. Overestimating your needs can lead to overstaffing and wasted resources, while underestimating can leave your business ill-equipped to handle opportunities. Companies like Amazon mitigate such risks by scaling methodically, hiring temporary staff during seasonal peaks to test their capacity needs before making permanent changes.

Leadership gaps present yet another hurdle. As teams grow, the need for experienced managers to oversee new departments or expanded operations becomes apparent. Without sufficient leadership, even the best teams can falter. Organizations like Starbucks invest heavily in leadership development programs to ensure their team grows alongside their footprint.

To prepare your team for growth, it's vital to plan deliberately. Define the roles and responsibilities that will be critical at each stage of your expansion. Invest in leadership development to cultivate internal talent ready to step into larger roles. Adopt scalable systems and processes that support communication and project management across a growing team, ensuring no one feels left behind or overwhelmed.

At the same time, nurture your company culture. Make your values a central part of your hiring and onboarding processes, embedding them in the DNA of every new team member. Growth shouldn't mean losing what made your business unique—it should mean amplifying it.

Scaling your team is not just about adding numbers—it's about adding the right people in the right way. By understanding the risks, addressing challenges head-on, and preparing thoughtfully, you can turn team growth into a powerful engine for your business's long-term success.

Hiring vs. Promoting: Building the Right

Team for the Future

As your business scales, one of the most crucial decisions you'll face is whether to hire new talent or promote from within. Both approaches have their merits and challenges, and the right choice often depends on your company's specific needs, culture, and growth trajectory. Balancing these two strategies is key to building a team that supports your long-term vision while maintaining stability and morale.

The Case for Promoting from Within

Promoting employees from within your organization can boost morale, foster loyalty, and strengthen your company culture. When team members see opportunities for advancement, they're more likely to remain committed and motivated. This approach also reduces onboarding time, as internal candidates are already familiar with your processes, values, and goals.

For example, companies like **Starbucks** have long championed promoting baristas into managerial roles. This practice not only rewards loyalty but ensures leaders have a deep understanding of the company's culture and operations. Similarly, **Walmart** frequently promotes associates into higher-level positions, cultivating a pipeline of experienced talent.

However, internal promotions can sometimes create gaps in other areas of your organization. Promoting one employee may leave their previous role vacant, requiring additional hiring or reshuffling. It's also important to ensure that promotions are based on merit and readiness, not just tenure.

The Benefits of Hiring New Talent

Hiring externally can bring fresh perspectives, new skills, and specialized expertise to your team. As your business grows, you may need skills that your current employees don't possess. External hires can help bridge these gaps and bring innovative ideas to the table.

For instance, when **Apple** was growing its design team, it hired external experts like Jony Ive, whose vision and creativity played a pivotal role in shaping the company's iconic products. Similarly, startups often recruit seasoned professionals from larger companies to guide their scaling processes with industry experience.

However, hiring externally can be time-consuming and expensive. New hires need time to acclimate to your company's culture and processes, and there's always the risk that they may not align with your team dynamics. Careful screening and onboarding are critical to ensuring a successful fit.

Striking the Right Balance

The most effective approach often combines both strategies. Promote from within to retain institutional knowledge and reward loyalty, while hiring externally to bring in fresh skills and perspectives. This balance allows you to strengthen your team from the inside while ensuring you're prepared for new challenges.

Consider adopting these practices:

1. Use internal promotions for roles that require a deep understanding of your company's culture and operations.

2. Hire externally for specialized or technical roles where new skills and perspectives are essential.

3. Provide training and mentorship to prepare current employees for future promotions, building a pipeline of ready talent.

Conclusion

The decision to hire or promote is not an either/or choice—it's a dynamic strategy that evolves with your business needs. By understanding the strengths and limitations of each approach, you can build a team that not only supports your immediate goals but positions your company for sustainable success. The right mix of internal growth and external expertise ensures your team remains adaptable, innovative, and prepared for the future.

CHAPTER 24: TECH ADVANTAGE: HOW TO LEVERAGE TECHNOLOGY FOR SCALING

Scaling a business without leveraging technology is like trying to climb a mountain without gear—possible but unnecessarily difficult. Technology enables businesses to streamline operations, reach broader audiences, and deliver better products or services at scale. The right tech choices can transform how efficiently you operate and how effectively you compete.

Start by evaluating your current processes and identifying bottlenecks. Could automation simplify repetitive tasks? Could cloud computing reduce IT infrastructure costs? Tools like customer relationship management (CRM) systems, enterprise resource planning (ERP) software, or even simple inventory management platforms can optimize day-to-day operations. For example, platforms like **Salesforce** or **HubSpot** enable businesses to manage customer relationships and sales pipelines seamlessly.

Customer experience is another area where technology makes a massive impact. Businesses like **Amazon** thrive on their ability to use data to recommend products, personalize experiences, and speed up transactions. Tools like AI chatbots, data analytics platforms, or user-friendly mobile apps can help even small businesses replicate similar personalized experiences, building loyalty and engagement.

Technology is also pivotal for expanding your reach. Online marketplaces like **eBay**, advertising platforms like **Google Ads**, and social media giants like **Instagram** enable businesses to access global audiences without massive marketing budgets. Emerging technologies like augmented reality (AR) and virtual reality (VR) allow companies to offer immersive experiences, creating new ways to engage customers, such as virtual try-ons or interactive product demonstrations.

However, technology investments should be approached strategically. Not every business needs proprietary software or the latest AI model. Start by adopting proven tools that align with your immediate needs, keeping an eye on how they can scale as your business grows. Remember, the goal of leveraging technology isn't just to make operations faster or easier—it's to build a foundation for sustainable growth and innovation.

CHAPTER 25: RISK-FREE SCALING

Scaling a business is an exciting but challenging process that requires careful navigation to avoid pitfalls. Risk-free scaling doesn't mean the absence of risks—it means minimizing and managing them so they don't derail your growth. The key is to scale strategically, ensuring your business maintains stability, quality, and financial health throughout the expansion process.

One of the most common mistakes businesses make during scaling is growing too quickly without adequate preparation. Rapid expansion can strain resources, disrupt cash flow, and dilute company culture. To scale safely, start by evaluating your existing operations. Identify bottlenecks, assess team capacity, and ensure that processes are scalable. For example, upgrading your technology infrastructure or streamlining workflows can prepare your business for higher volumes without overwhelming your team.

Financial planning is critical during this phase. Scaling often requires significant investment in areas like hiring, equipment, marketing, or inventory. Ensure your cash flow can support these expenditures without jeopardizing day-to-day operations. Explore funding options carefully, whether it's reinvesting profits, securing loans, or bringing in investors, and always keep a buffer for unexpected expenses.

Maintaining quality during growth is another vital aspect of risk-free scaling. Expanding into new markets, launching new products, or increasing production can sometimes compromise the standards that set your business apart. Regularly review and adjust processes to ensure your offerings remain consistent and customers stay satisfied.

Finally, don't forget the importance of adaptability. Even with the best planning, challenges and surprises are inevitable during scaling. By remaining flexible and open to change, you can pivot quickly and keep your business on track.

Risk-free scaling is not about avoiding growth—it's about growing smartly, sustainably, and strategically. With thoughtful preparation and constant vigilance, you can expand your business without unnecessary risks, setting the stage for long-term success.

STEP 5: MULTIPLY - EXPONENTIAL GROWTH

Step 5, Multiply, is about taking your business to the next level through exponential growth. It's not just about increasing sales or expanding reach—it's about creating a scalable system that multiplies your impact, revenue, and influence. This phase is where you replicate the success of your proven business model and extend it strategically across new markets, product lines, or regions.

Exponential growth doesn't happen by chance. It requires careful planning, strong systems, and the ability to manage complexity while staying true to your core values. Whether you're franchising, expanding into new territories, or leveraging mergers and acquisitions, the focus should always be on sustainable and strategic scaling.

This phase also demands an eye for opportunity and a willingness to adapt. Markets evolve, and competition intensifies as you grow. By staying agile and leveraging your strengths, you can navigate these challenges and turn them into opportunities for growth. The goal isn't just to grow—it's to multiply smartly and sustainably while minimizing risks and preserving the quality that defines your brand.

In this step, you'll explore strategies for achieving exponential growth, secure the resources needed for multiplication, and build the team and systems required to sustain it. With the right approach, this phase will position your business to dominate your industry and achieve lasting success.

Multiplication is the next level of growth—a leap from building a strong foundation to replicating your success on a larger scale. At this stage, your focus shifts from managing one thriving business to creating multiple streams of income, influence, and opportunity. Multiplying your business is not just about expanding; it's about scaling smartly and strategically while maintaining the quality and values that made your original venture successful.

There are several paths to multiplication, each with its own opportunities and challenges. Franchising allows you to leverage the investment and energy of others while expanding your brand. Corporate expansion keeps full control in your hands but demands more resources and direct involvement. Mergers and acquisitions provide a way to accelerate growth by joining forces with existing entities, while national and global strategies open new markets and audiences.

The key to effective multiplication lies in choosing the right strategy based on your goals, resources, and market conditions. It's also about creating systems and processes that ensure consistency, efficiency, and scalability. As you move into this phase, remember that multiplying a business is not merely about numbers—it's about replicating your success in ways that are sustainable and impactful. This chapter will explore the paths to multiplication, helping you decide which approach aligns with your vision for exponential growth.

Franchising vs. Corporate Expansion: Pros

and Cons

When it comes to multiplying your business, two of the most popular strategies are franchising and corporate expansion. Both offer distinct paths to scaling, but each comes with its own set of opportunities and challenges. Understanding the pros and cons of each approach is crucial to making an informed decision that aligns with your business goals, resources, and vision.

Franchising: Spreading Success Through Others

Franchising involves allowing independent operators (franchisees) to run their own version of your business under your brand. This model lets you scale quickly by leveraging the capital, effort, and local knowledge of franchisees.

Pros of Franchising

1. **Faster Growth**: Franchising allows you to expand rapidly without investing heavily in new locations or operations.

2. **Shared Financial Burden**: Franchisees bear the cost of opening and running new outlets, reducing your financial risk.

3. **Local Expertise**: Franchisees often have strong knowledge of their markets, helping the brand succeed in diverse locations.

4. **Scalable Model**: Once systems and training are in place, replication becomes relatively straightforward.

Cons of Franchising

1. **Control Challenges**: Maintaining consistent quality and customer experience across franchises can be difficult.

2. **Brand Risk**: Poorly managed franchises can damage your reputation, even if they are independently owned.

3. **Shared Profits**: While you collect franchise fees and royalties, a significant portion of profits remains with the franchisee.

4. **Complex Setup**: Establishing a successful franchise system requires detailed manuals, training programs, and legal compliance.

Example: **McDonald's** is a quintessential franchising success story, with over 90% of its locations operated by franchisees. This model has allowed the brand to scale globally while minimizing financial and operational risk. However, it also requires rigorous systems to ensure every burger, no matter where it's made, meets McDonald's standards.

Corporate Expansion: Building an Empire from Within

Corporate expansion involves opening and managing new locations yourself, maintaining full control over operations, employees, and profits. This model suits businesses that prioritize consistency and long-term control.

Pros of Corporate Expansion

1. **Complete Control**: You dictate every aspect of operations, ensuring quality and brand consistency.

2. **Higher Profit Potential**: Unlike franchising, all profits flow back into your business.

3. **Unified Culture**: Employees and managers remain directly aligned with your vision and goals.

4. **Flexibility**: Changes to products, services, or branding can be implemented uniformly and swiftly.

Cons of Corporate Expansion

1. **Capital Intensive**: Opening and running new locations require significant investment in infrastructure, staff, and marketing.

2. **Slower Growth**: Without franchisees sharing the financial burden, expansion can take longer.

3. **Increased Risk**: All operational and financial risks rest solely on your shoulders.

4. **Management Complexity**: Overseeing multiple locations can strain your resources and leadership team.

Example: **Starbucks** is a leading example of corporate expansion. By owning and operating the majority of its stores, Starbucks maintains strict control over quality, branding, and customer experience. However, this approach requires substantial investment and operational expertise.

Choosing the Right Path

The choice between franchising and corporate expansion depends on your business model, financial resources, and long-term vision. If rapid growth with minimal upfront investment appeals to you, franchising may be the better option. However, if maintaining full control and maximizing profit are your priorities, corporate expansion might be more suitable.

In some cases, businesses blend the two strategies. **Domino's**, for example, franchises most of its stores but also operates corporate-owned locations to retain control over key markets and set a standard for franchisees.

Conclusion

Both franchising and corporate expansion offer viable routes to multiplying your business. The right choice depends on your goals, risk tolerance, and ability to manage the complexities of each model. By carefully evaluating the pros and cons, you can choose a path that not only accelerates your growth but ensures your business thrives in the long term.

Mergers and Acquisitions: Joining Forces

for Growth

Mergers and acquisitions (M&A) are powerful strategies for multiplying your business by combining resources, expertise, and market share. These methods allow businesses to grow rapidly, access new markets, and achieve economies of scale that would take years to develop organically. However, M&A also come with their own set of challenges, making it crucial to approach these strategies with a clear plan and careful consideration.

Understanding Mergers and Acquisitions

1. **Mergers**: A merger occurs when two companies combine to form a single entity. This typically happens between businesses of similar size or complementary strengths, allowing them to pool resources and eliminate redundancies.

2. **Acquisitions**: In an acquisition, one company purchases another, either to absorb it completely or to operate it as a subsidiary. Acquisitions often involve a larger company acquiring a smaller one to access its products, customers, or expertise.

Both strategies aim to create a stronger, more competitive business by leveraging the assets and capabilities of multiple organizations.

Advantages of M&A

1. **Accelerated Growth**: M&A can provide instant access to new markets, customers, and revenue streams. For example, **Facebook's acquisition of Instagram** allowed it to

dominate social media in the photo-sharing space without building a competing platform from scratch.

2. **Cost Savings**: By merging operations or eliminating redundancies, M&A can significantly reduce costs. For instance, **Delta Air Lines** merged with **Northwest Airlines** to streamline operations and expand its market share while cutting overhead.

3. **Diversification**: Acquiring companies in different industries or regions can spread risk and reduce dependence on a single market. **Disney's acquisition of Marvel, Lucasfilm, and Pixar** diversified its content offerings and helped it become a leader in the entertainment industry.

4. **Access to Talent and Technology**: Acquisitions often bring in specialized talent and advanced technology, boosting innovation. **Google**, for example, acquired **DeepMind** to enhance its artificial intelligence capabilities.

Challenges of M&A

While M&A can unlock significant opportunities, they also come with risks that must be managed effectively.

1. **Cultural Integration**: Merging two companies often means blending different corporate cultures, which can lead to conflicts and reduced employee morale. A well-known example is the **Daimler-Benz and Chrysler merger**, which ultimately failed due to cultural clashes.

2. **Financial Risks**: Acquisitions can be expensive, and if the acquired company doesn't perform as expected, it can burden the parent company. **AOL's acquisition of Time Warner** is a cautionary tale of overestimating synergies.

3. **Operational Complexity**: Combining systems, processes, and teams can create logistical challenges that disrupt day-to-day operations.

4. **Regulatory and Legal Issues**: Depending on the size and scope of the merger or acquisition, antitrust laws or other regulatory hurdles may arise.

Keys to Successful M&A

1. **Strategic Fit**: Ensure the target company aligns with your business goals and complements your strengths.

2. **Thorough Due Diligence**: Conduct detailed assessments of the target company's finances, operations, and culture to identify potential risks.

3. **Clear Integration Plans**: Develop a step-by-step roadmap for merging operations, aligning teams, and achieving synergies.

4. **Transparent Communication**: Keep stakeholders informed to minimize resistance and build trust during the transition.

Conclusion

Mergers and acquisitions are transformative tools for multiplying your business and gaining a competitive edge. When executed strategically, they can unlock opportunities that organic growth simply can't match. However, the stakes are high, and the risks are real. By carefully evaluating potential partners, addressing challenges head-on, and planning meticulously, you can harness the power of M&A to propel your business to new heights.

Expanding Your Reach: National and

Global Growth Strategies

Expanding your business beyond its initial market—whether nationally or globally—is a bold step that can unlock massive growth opportunities. However, reaching new territories involves more than just opening a new location or shipping products abroad. It requires strategic planning, cultural awareness, and operational readiness to navigate the complexities of broader markets successfully.

National Expansion: Capturing a Wider Domestic Audience

Expanding nationally is often the first step for businesses looking to grow beyond their local reach. This strategy allows you to tap into untapped markets within your country while leveraging your existing infrastructure and brand recognition.

1. **Assess Market Potential**: Start by analyzing regions with demand for your products or services. For instance, **Starbucks** initially expanded by targeting urban areas where its coffee culture resonated, gradually moving into suburban and rural markets.

2. **Adapt to Regional Differences**: Even within the same country, consumer preferences, regulations, and competition can vary. **Costco**, for example, tailors its inventory to reflect regional needs, offering unique products that resonate with local customers.

3. **Build Scalable Operations**: Ensure your systems—logistics, supply chain, and staffing—can support multi-location management without compromising quality or efficiency.

Global Expansion: Entering International Markets

Going global offers access to entirely new customer bases and revenue streams, but it also comes with unique challenges such as language barriers, cultural differences, and regulatory hurdles. To succeed internationally, a tailored approach is essential.

1. **Research and Prepare**: Before entering a new country, conduct in-depth market research. **McDonald's**, for instance,

adapts its menu in every country, offering items that cater to local tastes, like the McAloo Tikki Burger in India or Teriyaki Burgers in Japan.

2. **Choose the Right Entry Strategy**: Businesses can expand internationally through various models, including direct investment, partnerships, or franchising. **IKEA** often establishes its own stores to maintain brand control, while **KFC** relies on local franchisees who understand the market better.

3. **Understand Legal and Regulatory Requirements**: Each country has its own rules regarding business operations, taxes, and labor laws. A failure to comply can lead to legal and financial consequences. For example, **Uber** faced regulatory pushback in several countries because it didn't fully adapt to local laws.

4. **Cultural Sensitivity**: Understanding and respecting local customs and traditions are critical. A lack of cultural awareness can alienate potential customers, as seen with brands that fail to translate marketing materials appropriately or offer products that don't align with local values.

Leveraging Technology for Expansion

Technology plays a crucial role in scaling nationally and globally. E-commerce platforms like **Amazon** and **Shopify** allow businesses to reach customers worldwide without needing physical stores. Digital marketing tools such as Google Ads and Facebook provide targeted advertising to specific demographics, ensuring your message resonates with the right audience.

Logistics and supply chain technology also simplify expansion. Companies like **FedEx** and **DHL** specialize in international shipping, enabling businesses to deliver products seamlessly across borders.

Mitigating Risks in Expansion

Expanding your reach requires significant investment and comes with risks like currency fluctuations, political instability, or cultural missteps. To mitigate these risks:

1. Conduct a risk assessment before entering new markets.

2. Start with a pilot program or limited launch to test the waters.

3. Partner with local experts or consultants to navigate unfamiliar territory.

Conclusion

National and global expansion are powerful strategies for multiplying your business, but they require careful planning, adaptability, and a deep understanding of new markets. Whether you're targeting neighboring states or overseas continents, success lies in research, preparation, and strategic execution. By leveraging the right tools and making informed decisions, you can extend your business's reach while staying true to your core values and vision.

CHAPTER 27: RISK-FREE MULTIPLICATION

Multiplying your business is a thrilling stage of growth, but it can also be fraught with risks. Scaling too quickly, neglecting foundational elements, or misjudging market conditions can lead to costly mistakes. Risk-free multiplication is about expanding strategically, ensuring that every move is deliberate, sustainable, and aligned with your long-term vision.

The first step in minimizing risks is understanding your capacity. Before multiplying, assess your current operations to ensure they can handle increased demands. For example, do you have the right systems, team, and processes in place to support additional locations, product lines, or services? Identifying and addressing these gaps upfront is critical to avoiding breakdowns during expansion.

Financial planning is equally essential. Multiplication requires significant investment, whether it's opening new outlets, hiring more staff, or marketing to new audiences. Over-leveraging your resources or relying too heavily on external funding can create vulnerabilities. Build a detailed budget, include contingency plans, and ensure you have enough cash flow to sustain growth.

Another crucial element is maintaining consistency. As your business grows, ensuring that quality, customer experience, and brand identity remain intact becomes increasingly challenging. Develop clear operational guidelines and invest in training programs to replicate your success across new ventures.

Finally, stay adaptable. Markets evolve, and unforeseen challenges are inevitable. Whether it's economic shifts, new competition, or changing customer preferences, a flexible approach allows you to pivot when necessary and keep your growth on track.

Risk-free multiplication doesn't mean avoiding risks entirely—it means identifying, minimizing, and managing them effectively. With careful planning, financial prudence, and a commitment to quality, you can expand your business confidently and sustainably, setting the stage for exponential success.

STEP 6: SUCCESS - THE REAL SUCCESS

S uccess isn't just about reaching a milestone; it's about creating a self-sustaining enterprise that thrives beyond your direct involvement. Step 6, "The Real Success," focuses on the ultimate goal of any entrepreneur: building a business that operates independently, creates lasting value, and supports everyone involved —customers, employees, and stakeholders alike.

In this stage, you shift your role from being the driving force behind every decision to becoming a visionary leader who enables the business to run smoothly without constant oversight. It's about transitioning from a founder-centric model to a system-driven enterprise where the team and processes are the true heroes.

To achieve this, you'll focus on two critical areas: redefining leadership and building systems that ensure scalability, consistency, and efficiency. You'll learn how to empower your team, delegate effectively, and trust the systems you've built to maintain quality and momentum. Success at this stage is no longer measured by how hard you work but by how well the business works without you.

The final element of this step is risk management. Even the most successful businesses face challenges, and complacency is the enemy of sustained success. Identifying potential risks, staying adaptable, and continuously improving will protect your achievements and set the stage for further growth and innovation.

This step is the culmination of your entrepreneurial journey—a transition from striving for success to living it. By mastering this phase, you'll ensure that your business not only survives but thrives, creating a legacy that endures for years to come.

It's Not About You Anymore: Leadership

Beyond the Founder

One of the most profound shifts in an entrepreneur's journey comes when the business evolves beyond the founder. In the early stages, your passion, vision, and tireless efforts are the driving forces behind every decision and achievement. But true success means building an enterprise that thrives independently—a business that isn't dependent on any one person, even you.

As a founder, it's natural to feel deeply connected to your business. It's your creation, a reflection of your ideas and hard work. However, for your business to grow and sustain itself, it needs to become less about you and more about the team, systems, and culture you've built. This transition is essential not only for the business's long-term health but also for your personal growth as a leader.

Transitioning from Founder-Led to Team-Led

Shifting from a founder-centric model to a team-led one involves empowering others to take ownership. This doesn't mean stepping away entirely but rather stepping back strategically. Delegating responsibilities, trusting your team to make decisions, and fostering a collaborative environment are critical to this evolution. For example, when **Howard Schultz** of Starbucks returned as CEO in 2008 after stepping away, his focus wasn't on micromanaging but on inspiring and realigning his team to the company's mission.

Building a Leadership Legacy

Great leaders don't just run a business—they build a legacy. A leadership legacy is about developing people who can carry your vision forward, even in your absence. This means investing in training, mentorship, and creating opportunities for your team to grow. Consider how **Bill Gates** transitioned Microsoft's leadership to **Steve Ballmer** and later to **Satya Nadella**, ensuring continuity and innovation beyond his tenure.

Letting Go for Greater Impact

It can be challenging to let go of control, especially when you've poured so much into your business. But letting go doesn't mean losing relevance—it means amplifying your impact. By stepping back from daily operations, you can focus on strategic decisions, innovation, and long-term growth. Your role evolves into that of a visionary leader, ensuring that the business adapts to change while staying true to its core values.

True leadership isn't about holding on to power; it's about empowering others. When your business no longer relies on you to function, that's when you've truly succeeded. It's a moment of liberation—not just for you, but for the organization you've built to thrive beyond your direct influence.

The Shift: From Person-Driven to System-Driven

A successful business starts with passion, energy, and vision—often embodied by a driven founder or key individual. But to scale and thrive in the long term, a business must transition from relying on individual effort to operating as a well-oiled machine driven by systems. This shift from person-driven to system-driven is a hallmark of sustainable success.

Why the Shift is Necessary

In the early stages of a business, much depends on you: your decisions, problem-solving, and hands-on involvement. While this approach works in the beginning, it becomes a bottleneck as the business grows. No matter how talented or hardworking an individual is, one person can only do so much.

Consider **Steve Jobs** at Apple. During its early days, Jobs was deeply involved in every aspect of the business, from product design to marketing. However, Apple's transformation into one of the world's most valuable companies was fueled by the systems, processes, and culture he helped establish, enabling the company to innovate and operate efficiently without constant input from its founder.

Building a System-Driven Business

Transitioning to a system-driven model requires more than just delegating tasks. It involves creating processes, tools, and frameworks that ensure consistency and scalability.

1. **Document Processes**: Every key operation—whether it's customer service, manufacturing, or marketing—should have a documented process. This ensures consistency, even as the team grows or changes.

2. **Leverage Technology**: Tools like CRM systems, inventory management software, and automation platforms can streamline operations and reduce reliance on manual oversight. For example, **Amazon**'s logistics systems allow it to fulfill millions of orders daily with remarkable precision.

3. **Establish KPIs and Monitoring**: Define key performance indicators (KPIs) to measure success and monitor progress. This keeps the team aligned and accountable while giving you a clear picture of the business's health.

4. **Foster a Culture of Accountability**: Systems work when people respect and follow them. Creating a culture of

accountability ensures that everyone takes ownership of their role in the process.

The Benefits of Being System-Driven

When a business is system-driven, it becomes less dependent on any one person and more focused on operational excellence. This shift provides several advantages:

Scalability: Systems allow the business to handle increased demand without sacrificing quality.

Consistency: Customers experience the same level of service and quality, no matter who's involved.

Time Freedom: As systems take over repetitive tasks, leaders can focus on strategic growth rather than day-to-day firefighting.

Resilience: A system-driven business can withstand changes in personnel, including the founder stepping back.

Conclusion

Moving from person-driven to system-driven is a transformative shift that enables businesses to achieve sustainable growth and long-term success. It's not about removing the human element but about empowering people with the tools, processes, and systems needed to excel. By embracing this approach, you ensure that your business can operate at its best—independently of any single individual, including yourself.

Empowering the Team: Why Collective

Success Matters

In any successful business, the whole is greater than the sum of its parts. No matter how talented or visionary a leader may be, no single person can achieve the scale, innovation, and resilience that a well-empowered team can deliver. Empowering your team isn't just a leadership skill—it's a strategic advantage that transforms your business into a dynamic, thriving ecosystem.

Why Empowering the Team is Critical

When you empower your team, you're not merely delegating tasks —you're cultivating ownership, accountability, and innovation. Empowered employees feel trusted and valued, which translates to higher morale, better performance, and stronger loyalty. This culture of empowerment allows businesses to adapt to challenges, seize opportunities, and consistently deliver excellence.

For example, **Google** has built its success on a foundation of empowerment. Through initiatives like "20% time," employees are encouraged to dedicate a portion of their work hours to passion projects. This freedom has led to breakthroughs like Gmail and Google Maps, innovations that might not have emerged in a top-down environment.

How to Empower Your Team

Empowering a team is a deliberate process that requires trust, resources, and support. Here are some key ways to foster empowerment:

1. **Clear Communication**: Set expectations and share the company's vision so that every team member understands how their role contributes to the bigger picture. **Zappos**, for example, ensures every employee aligns with its mission of delivering exceptional customer service, fostering a sense of purpose at every level.

2. **Provide Resources and Training**: Equip your team with the tools, knowledge, and opportunities they need to succeed. For instance, **Starbucks** offers its employees (referred to as partners) comprehensive training programs, helping them

deliver consistent service and empowering them to make decisions that enhance customer experiences.

3. **Encourage Decision-Making**: Give employees the authority to make decisions within their roles. This doesn't mean stepping away entirely but trusting your team to take initiative. **The Ritz-Carlton**, for instance, allows employees to spend up to $2,000 per guest to resolve issues without requiring management approval, empowering them to deliver exceptional service.

4. **Recognize and Reward Contributions**: Celebrate achievements, big and small. Recognition builds confidence and reinforces the behaviors that drive success. From formal awards to simple words of appreciation, acknowledgment fuels motivation and engagement.

The Benefits of Collective Success

An empowered team brings transformative benefits to your business:

Innovation: Empowered employees think creatively and bring fresh ideas to the table.

Adaptability: When challenges arise, a confident and autonomous team can respond quickly and effectively.

Scalability: As your business grows, an empowered team ensures operations run smoothly without constant oversight.

Sustainability: Building a culture of empowerment creates a business that thrives independently of any single individual.

Consider the legacy of **Apple under Tim Cook**. While Steve Jobs' brilliance was foundational, Cook's leadership empowered Apple's team to expand into new markets, innovate in product categories, and sustain its position as a global leader.

Conclusion

Empowering your team is the cornerstone of collective success. It's about creating an environment where individuals feel valued, trusted, and motivated to perform at their best. By investing in your people and fostering a culture of ownership and collaboration, you're not just building a business—you're building a powerhouse capable of achieving extraordinary things. When your team succeeds, your business flourishes, and the impact extends far beyond what you could achieve alone.

CHAPTER 29: BUILDING SYSTEMS THAT SUSTAIN SUCCESS

What Makes a Great System: Key

Components

A great system is the backbone of any successful business. It ensures consistency, scalability, and efficiency, allowing your operations to run smoothly and freeing you to focus on strategic growth. But not all systems are created equal. A truly great system is one that is robust, adaptable, and aligned with your business goals. Here are the key components that define such a system:

1. Simplicity and Clarity

Complex systems often lead to confusion and inefficiency. A great system is straightforward and easy to understand, ensuring that every team member knows how to use it effectively. Simplicity doesn't mean sacrificing functionality—it means eliminating unnecessary steps and focusing on what works. For example, **Toyota's Just-In-Time production system** is both simple and effective, ensuring parts are delivered precisely when needed, minimizing waste and maximizing efficiency.

2. Standardization and Consistency

A strong system provides clear guidelines that produce consistent results, regardless of who is operating it. Standardization is particularly crucial for businesses with multiple locations or teams. Take **McDonald's**, for instance: their systems ensure that a Big Mac tastes the same whether you're in New York, Tokyo, or Paris. This consistency builds trust and reliability, key factors in customer loyalty.

3. Scalability

As your business grows, your systems must grow with it. A great system is designed to handle increased demand without compromising performance. For example, **Amazon's logistics system** is highly scalable, allowing the company to process millions of orders daily while maintaining accuracy and speed. Scalability ensures that your success isn't limited by the capacity of your systems.

4. Automation and Technology Integration

Incorporating technology into your systems streamlines operations, reduces human error, and saves time. Automation tools like customer relationship management (CRM) software, inventory tracking systems, and project management platforms can transform how your business operates. **Netflix**, for instance, leverages sophisticated algorithms to automate content recommendations, enhancing the customer experience while driving engagement.

5. Flexibility and Adaptability

Markets evolve, customer preferences change, and unforeseen challenges arise. A great system isn't rigid—it adapts to new circumstances while maintaining core functionality. For example, during the COVID-19 pandemic, many restaurants adapted their systems to accommodate online orders and delivery services, ensuring continued operations despite restrictions.

6. Measurability and Monitoring

What gets measured gets managed. Effective systems include metrics and feedback loops to track performance and identify areas for improvement. This could involve setting key performance indicators (KPIs), implementing dashboards, or conducting regular reviews. **Tesla**, for example, uses real-time data from its manufacturing lines to identify inefficiencies and optimize production.

7. Alignment with Business Goals

Finally, a great system is aligned with your company's objectives and values. It's not about implementing the latest tools or trends— it's about creating processes that support your mission and help you achieve your vision. For instance, **Zappos' system for customer service** is built entirely around their goal of delivering exceptional customer experiences, empowering employees to go above and beyond for customers.

Conclusion

A great system is more than just a set of tools or processes—it's the foundation that supports and drives your business forward. By focusing on simplicity, consistency, scalability, and adaptability, you can build systems that not only meet your current needs but also position your business for long-term success. Whether you're a startup or a global enterprise, investing in strong systems is one of the smartest moves you can make to ensure your business thrives.

Measuring and Monitoring: Ensuring Systems Deliver Results

A system is only as effective as its outcomes. Measuring and monitoring your systems ensures they deliver the results your business needs, maintaining efficiency, quality, and growth. By tracking performance and making data-driven adjustments, you can transform your systems into powerful engines of success.

Why Measuring and Monitoring Matters

Systems are dynamic—they operate in real-world conditions that are always changing. Without consistent oversight, even the most well-designed systems can drift off course, leading to inefficiencies, errors, or missed opportunities. Monitoring ensures that systems continue to meet their objectives and adapt to new challenges.

For example, **Amazon** tracks every aspect of its logistics system, from package delivery times to warehouse efficiency. This constant measurement allows Amazon to maintain its industry-leading speed and reliability, making adjustments wherever performance lags.

Key Steps to Measuring and Monitoring

1. **Define Success Metrics**
   Start by identifying the key performance indicators (KPIs) that align with your goals. For instance, if you're monitoring a customer service system, metrics like average response time, resolution rate, and customer satisfaction scores might be critical.

2. **Establish Feedback Loops**
   Create processes for regularly collecting and analyzing data. Tools like dashboards or reports can provide insights at a glance, while more detailed reviews uncover deeper trends. Feedback loops ensure you stay informed about how systems are performing in real-time.

3. **Schedule Regular Audits**
   Periodically review your systems to ensure they remain relevant and effective. Audits help identify inefficiencies, redundancies, or areas where performance can be improved. For example, **Toyota's Kaizen philosophy** emphasizes continuous improvement through regular review and incremental changes.

4. **Benchmark Against Industry Standards**
   Compare your system's performance to industry norms or competitors. This can reveal whether your systems are leading the pack or lagging behind and help you set realistic improvement targets.

5. **Involve Your Team**
   Encourage employees to share their insights about system performance. Those working within the system often identify issues or opportunities that might not be visible from a higher level.

Real-World Example: Starbucks

Starbucks uses a robust system of monitoring to maintain its global standards. From tracking the speed of service to gathering customer feedback on new products, Starbucks ensures consistency across thousands of locations. This data-driven approach not only identifies areas for improvement but also uncovers opportunities to innovate, such as introducing mobile ordering to reduce wait times.

The Benefits of Active Monitoring

Improved Efficiency: Regular tracking identifies bottlenecks or waste, allowing for quicker fixes.

Enhanced Quality: Monitoring ensures that standards are consistently met, reinforcing customer trust.

Scalability: Measured systems reveal what works and can be replicated across new markets or locations.

Proactive Problem Solving: Early detection of issues prevents small problems from becoming major disruptions.

Conclusion

Measuring and monitoring systems isn't an optional task—it's a critical practice for ensuring they deliver on their promise. By defining success metrics, collecting and analyzing data, and making informed adjustments, you create a cycle of continuous improvement. This proactive approach keeps your business running smoothly, positions it to scale effectively, and ensures you remain competitive in an ever-changing market. Monitoring doesn't just protect your systems—it propels your business toward sustained success.

CHAPTER 30: RISK-FREE SUCCESS

Success is never guaranteed, but by mitigating risks, you can ensure that your achievements are sustainable and protected over the long term. Risk-free success doesn't mean eliminating all risks—that's impossible in the dynamic world of business. Instead, it means identifying potential threats, managing them effectively, and building resilience into your operations so that setbacks don't derail your progress.

Anticipating Risks

The first step to risk-free success is understanding what could go wrong. This includes financial risks, operational disruptions, market changes, or even reputational damage. Successful companies are proactive in identifying these risks, planning for contingencies, and responding swiftly when challenges arise. For example, **Netflix** pivoted from DVD rentals to streaming when market trends shifted, safeguarding its dominance in entertainment.

Building Resilience

Risk-free success also means building a resilient organization—one that can weather changes and adapt to unexpected events. This involves maintaining strong cash reserves, fostering a culture of innovation, and creating systems that ensure business continuity even in challenging times. Companies like **Apple** exemplify resilience, consistently innovating and adapting to changing consumer demands while maintaining a robust supply chain.

Balancing Caution with Opportunity

While managing risks, it's essential not to become overly cautious. Success often requires calculated risks and seizing opportunities when they arise. Risk-free doesn't mean risk-averse—it means taking informed actions while staying prepared for potential outcomes.

Sustaining Success

Sustaining success involves continuously evaluating your strategies, systems, and market position. It's about avoiding complacency and staying ahead of trends, competitors, and disruptions. Regularly refining your approach ensures that your business remains relevant and competitive.

Conclusion

Risk-free success is about balance—between ambition and caution, growth and stability, innovation and consistency. By anticipating challenges, building resilience, and staying adaptable, you can ensure that your success isn't fleeting but enduring. It's not just about reaching the top; it's about staying there while being prepared for whatever comes next.

TIME TO CHANGE THE WORLD

Congratulations! You've journeyed through the 6 Steps of the PRISMs Method, equipping yourself with the tools, strategies, and mindset to not only build a business but to create a legacy. Now, it's time to apply everything you've learned—not just to grow your own success, but to make an impact that resonates far beyond yourself.

Your Business Can Be a Force for Good

A successful business isn't just about profits; it's about purpose. Whether you're solving everyday problems, creating jobs, or inspiring others to pursue their dreams, your work can change lives. Think of companies like **Tesla**, which redefined the auto industry while championing sustainability, or **Patagonia**, which has turned its environmental mission into a business model that inspires millions. The world doesn't just need businesses; it needs visionaries who dare to think bigger.

Inspire Through Action

Your entrepreneurial journey is a story waiting to inspire others. Share your lessons, mentor aspiring entrepreneurs, and contribute to your community. When you lift others as you rise, you create a ripple effect of success. Just as you've been inspired by those who came before, your story could become the spark that ignites someone else's dream.

Stay Hungry, Stay Humble

No matter how much success you achieve, remember that the journey never truly ends. Markets evolve, technologies advance, and new challenges emerge. Stay curious, keep learning, and adapt with the times. The most successful entrepreneurs, like **Jeff Bezos**, **Oprah Winfrey**, and **Elon Musk**, never stop innovating, dreaming, and striving for more.

The World Awaits Your Contribution

The world is full of opportunities waiting for someone like you—someone with the courage to dream, the persistence to execute, and the resilience to overcome obstacles. Whether your business transforms an industry or simply makes a difference in your community, your efforts matter.

Make It Count

You've built the foundation. Now it's time to build your legacy. Take the risks, face the challenges, and embrace the rewards of making your vision a reality. The PRISMs Method isn't just a roadmap for startups; it's a philosophy for success, designed to help you thrive and leave your mark.

Now go out there and change the world—one bold step at a time.

Please Remember:

Dare to dream

Dare to act

Dare to move forward

Anything is possible

Help more people

COMMON STARTUP PITFALLS AND HOW TO AVOID THEM

S tarting a business is an exhilarating journey, but it's not without its challenges. Many entrepreneurs encounter pitfalls that can derail their success, often due to lack of experience or inadequate preparation. By understanding these common mistakes and learning how to avoid them, you can set yourself up for a smoother, more successful path.

1. Lack of Clear Focus

The Pitfall: Many startups try to do too much at once—offering too many products, targeting too many customer segments, or spreading resources too thin. This lack of focus can dilute your efforts and confuse your audience.

How to Avoid It: Start small and specific. Identify your core offering and your target customer. Perfect one thing before expanding. For example, **Airbnb** began by focusing solely on renting out air mattresses in shared spaces before scaling to entire homes and luxury properties.

2. Skipping Market Validation

The Pitfall: Investing time and money into a product or service without validating whether there's demand for it can lead to wasted resources and eventual failure.

How to Avoid It: Use simple, cost-effective methods to validate your idea. Create prototypes, conduct surveys, or test with a small audience. As **Dropbox** did, a demo video showcasing its concept was enough to gather early interest and refine its product before full-scale development.

3. Ignoring Cash Flow Management

The Pitfall: Many startups run out of money before they can become profitable, often due to underestimating costs or mismanaging cash flow.

How to Avoid It: Maintain a detailed budget and closely monitor your cash flow. Prioritize essential expenses and keep reserves for unexpected challenges. Remember, businesses like **Amazon** initially thrived by reinvesting profits strategically while carefully managing costs.

4. Overestimating Growth Speed

The Pitfall: Assuming quick profitability or rapid growth can lead to overhiring, overinvesting, or taking on unsustainable debt.

How to Avoid It: Plan for realistic growth and remain flexible. Scale your operations incrementally, ensuring your systems, team, and finances can handle increased demand. Even a giant like **Tesla** faced hurdles when scaling production too rapidly without addressing operational challenges.

5. Neglecting Marketing and Branding

The Pitfall: Believing that a great product or service will sell itself is a common mistake. Without effective marketing, even the best ideas can go unnoticed.

How to Avoid It: Invest in building a strong brand and marketing strategy from the start. Focus on telling your story and connecting with your audience through the right channels. **Nike's "Just Do It" campaign** is a prime example of branding that resonates deeply and drives loyalty.

6. Not Building the Right Team

The Pitfall: Trying to do everything yourself or hiring the wrong people can limit your business's potential.

How to Avoid It: Surround yourself with a team that complements your skills and shares your vision. As **Steve Jobs** famously said, "It doesn't make sense to hire smart people and tell them what to do; we hire smart people so they can tell us what to do."

7. Resistance to Change

The Pitfall: Sticking rigidly to your original plan, even when market conditions or feedback indicate the need for change, can lead to stagnation or failure.

How to Avoid It: Stay adaptable and open to pivots. When **Instagram** started, it was a location-based app called Burbn. By adapting to user feedback, it pivoted to become the photo-sharing platform we know today.

8. Underestimating Competition

The Pitfall: Ignoring competitors or failing to differentiate yourself can make it hard to stand out in a crowded market.

How to Avoid It: Conduct thorough competitive analysis and focus on what makes your business unique. Whether it's exceptional customer service like **Zappos** or product innovation like **Apple**, find your edge and capitalize on it.

Conclusion: Learn, Adapt, Thrive

Mistakes are inevitable in any entrepreneurial journey, but they don't have to define your story. By staying informed, proactive, and adaptable, you can navigate these common pitfalls and turn challenges into opportunities. Every setback is a lesson, and every obstacle is a stepping stone to greater success. Armed with this knowledge, you're ready to face the road ahead with confidence and resilience.

YOUR ENTREPRENEURIAL TOOLKIT

A s you embark on your entrepreneurial journey, having the right tools at your disposal can make the difference between success and struggle. While passion and vision are essential, the practical resources you use to plan, build, and grow your business are equally critical. Here's a toolkit to guide you through each step of the PRISMs method and beyond.

1. Strategic Planning Tools

Business Plan Templates: A clear business plan outlines your goals, strategies, and financial projections. Tools like **LivePlan** or **SBA's Business Plan Tool** can simplify this process.

SWOT Analysis Framework: Identify your business's strengths, weaknesses, opportunities, and threats to develop a resilient strategy.

Mind Mapping Software: Use tools like **MindMeister** or **Miro** to brainstorm ideas and connect them visually.

2. Financial Management Tools

Budgeting and Accounting Software: Platforms like **QuickBooks**, **Xero**, or **FreshBooks** help you manage cash flow, track expenses, and prepare for tax season.

Funding Platforms: If seeking funding, explore **Kickstarter**, **Indiegogo**, or **AngelList** for crowdfunding and investor connections.

Break-Even Calculator: Many online tools help calculate when your business will turn profitable.

3. Validation and Market Research Tools

Survey Platforms: Tools like **SurveyMonkey** or **Google Forms** help you gather customer insights.

Analytics Platforms: Use **Google Analytics** to track website traffic and understand audience behavior.

Prototyping Tools: Create mockups with tools like **Canva**, **Figma**, or **Adobe XD** to test your ideas before investing heavily.

4. Marketing and Branding Tools

Social Media Management: Platforms like **Hootsuite** or **Buffer** streamline your social media campaigns.

Email Marketing Services: Use **Mailchimp** or **Constant Contact** to build and engage your audience.

SEO and Content Tools: **SEMrush**, **Ahrefs**, or **Yoast SEO** help optimize your online presence and attract customers.

5. Operational Tools

Project Management Software: Platforms like **Trello**, **Asana**, or **Monday.com** keep your team aligned and organized.

CRM Systems: Customer Relationship Management tools like **Salesforce**, **HubSpot**, or **Zoho CRM** help manage customer interactions and sales pipelines.

Inventory Management Tools: For retail or e-commerce businesses, consider tools like **Shopify** or **Square** for streamlined inventory control.

6. Legal and Compliance Tools

Incorporation Services: Services like **LegalZoom** or **Incfile** simplify business registration and compliance.

Contract Templates: Platforms like **Rocket Lawyer** or **DocuSign** provide customizable legal agreements.

Tax Preparation Software: Use tools like **TurboTax Business** to navigate tax requirements.

7. Team Building and Collaboration Tools

Hiring Platforms: Use **LinkedIn**, **Indeed**, or **AngelList Talent** to find top talent for your team.

Communication Tools: Platforms like **Slack**, **Microsoft Teams**, or **Zoom** enable seamless communication across teams.

Employee Engagement Tools: Leverage tools like **BambooHR** or **15Five** to foster a positive workplace culture.

8. Personal Growth and Mindset

Books and Podcasts: Stay inspired and informed with resources like **"The Lean Startup" by Eric Ries** or podcasts like **"How I Built This" by Guy Raz**.

Time Management Tools: Apps like **Notion**, **Todoist**, or **Focus@Will** help you manage your time effectively.

Mentorship Networks: Join communities like **SCORE** or **Entrepreneur's Organization** to connect with experienced mentors.

How to Build Your Toolkit

Your entrepreneurial toolkit will evolve as your business grows. Start with the essentials that align with your current stage and gradually add more specialized tools as you scale. Remember, the best tools are those that save you time, increase efficiency, and support your unique business goals.

Conclusion: Your Toolkit, Your Success

Your entrepreneurial toolkit is more than just a collection of resources—it's a foundation for smarter decision-making, efficient operations, and sustainable growth. With the right tools, you're equipped to overcome challenges, seize opportunities, and turn your vision into reality. The journey ahead will demand creativity, adaptability, and resilience, but with these tools at your side, you're ready to face whatever comes your way.

ABOUT THE AUTHOR

Morning Lee is an entrepreneur, innovator, and strategist who has spent years navigating the world of startups and business ventures. With a wealth of experience across diverse industries—he has built a reputation for turning challenges into opportunities and failures into stepping stones for success.

From selling computer parts in college to founding and scaling successful businesses, Morning's journey is one of perseverance, adaptability, and an unwavering commitment to growth. Not all of his ventures succeeded—many taught him invaluable lessons about risk, resilience, and the art of building something sustainable. His successes, including shipping, moving, real estate companies, stand as proof of his ability to learn, adapt, thrive in a competitive world.

Morning is passionate about helping others achieve their entrepreneurial dreams. Drawing from his personal experiences, he developed the **6-Step PRISMs Method**—a framework designed to guide aspiring entrepreneurs toward Risk-Free startup success. His unique blend of motivational, conversational, and practical advice resonates with readers who are ready to take control of their futures.

Beyond business, Morning values innovation, collaboration, and the power of community. He believes in the transformative potential of entrepreneurship—not just as a path to financial freedom but as a way to impact lives, solve problems, and create lasting legacies.

Through his businesses, work, books, videos, mentorship, consulting, advising, Morning Lee is committed to empowering others to dream big, start smart, and build businesses that matter.

www.ingramcontent.com/pod-product-compliance
Lightning Source LLC
Chambersburg PA
CBHW061023220326
41597CB00019BB/3075